# BARRON'S

# PAINLESS

# Spanish

**Carlos B. Vega, Ph.D.**
**Revised by Dasha D. Davis, M.A.**

**Third Edition**

## Dedication

This book is dedicated to the Spanish teacher in particular, and to the teaching profession in general, the noblest and hardest of all human endeavors. We cannot imagine a world without teachers, as we cannot imagine a world without a sunrise or a tree without branches and leaves. Hail to the teacher, for he or she brings light to what otherwise would be a world of darkness.

Published by Barron's Educational Series, Inc.
750 Third Avenue
New York, NY 10017
**www.barronseduc.com**

ISBN: 978-1-4380-0772-4

Library of Congress Control Number: 2015958586

9 8 7 6 5 4 3 2

Barron's Educational Series, Inc. print books are available at special quantity discounts to use for sales promotions, employee premiums, or educational purposes. For more information or to purchase books, please call the Simon & Schuster special sales department at 866-506-1949.

Printed in Canada

# CONTENTS

Introduction     ix

Reference pages     xi

## Lección 1: La familia es nuestro sostén y reposo/The family is our support and comfort     1

Piénsalo bien/Think it through: Definite and Indefinite
Articles     6

Más es mejor/More is better     9

Habla popular/Everyday speech     13

Bien vale la pena/It's well worth it: Nombres y
apellidos (first and last names)     14

Dilo como yo/Say it like I do: The Spanish alphabet     17

Alma hispánica/Hispanic soul: Miguel de Cervantes     19

Pluma en mano/Pen in hand: Fiestas familiares/
Family parties     21

Así somos/This is who we are: The early history of Spain     23

Brain Ticklers—The Answers     24

## Lección 2: Deportes para todos los gustos/Sports for all tastes     27

Piénsalo bien/Think it through: The Spanish language
in America: the early years     31

Más es mejor/More is better     32

Habla popular/Everyday speech     33

Bien vale la pena/It's well worth it: Courtesy phrases     35

Dilo como yo/Say it like I do: Syllables     37

Alma hispánica/Hispanic soul: Lope de Vega     39

Pluma en mano/Pen in hand: La corrida de toros/
Bullfighting     40

Así somos/This is who we are: Hispanic countries,
capitals, and nationalities     42

Brain Ticklers—The Answers     44

## Lección 3: La casa es nuestro hogar y felicidad/The house is our home and happiness **45**

Piénsalo bien/Think it through: Colors, days of the
    week, months, date — 49
Más es mejor/More is better — 53
Habla popular/Everyday speech — 54
Bien vale la pena/It's well worth it: Cardinal
    numbers 100–1,000 — 55
Dilo como yo/Say it like I do: Pronunciation of
    the *d* and *t* — 57
Alma hispánica/Hispanic soul: Santa Teresa de Jesús — 59
Pluma en mano/Pen in hand: Nuestra casa de
    Villafranca del Bierzo/Our house in
    Villafranca del Bierzo — 61
Así somos/This is who we are: The early history
    of the Americas — 63
Brain Ticklers—The Answers — 64

## Lección 4: El buen comer es un arte/ Good eating is an art **65**

Piénsalo bien/Think it through: Interjections — 70
Más es mejor/More is better — 71
Habla popular/Everyday speech — 73
Bien vale la pena/It's well worth it: Ordinal numbers — 73
Dilo como yo/Say it like I do: Pronunciation of the *c*, *q* — 75
Alma hispánica/Hispanic soul: José Martí — 77
Pluma en mano/Pen in hand: El restaurante "Tío
    Pepe" de Nueva York/Tío Pepe restaurant in New York — 79
Así somos/This is who we are: Early education in
    the Americas — 80
Brain Ticklers—The Answers — 81

## Lección 5: Vestir bien nos ayuda a triunfar en la vida/ Dressing well helps us succeed in life **83**

Piénsalo bien/Think it through: The verb, Parts 1 and 2 — 87
Más es mejor/More is better: The human body — 95
Habla popular/Everyday speech — 97

Bien vale la pena/It's well worth it: Telling the weather 97
Dilo como yo/Say it like I do: Pronunciation of the
    *g*, *j* and double consonants *ch*, *ll*, and *rr* 102
Alma hispánica/Hispanic soul: Azorín 104
Pluma en mano/Pen in hand: La moda de hoy/
    Today's fashion 106
Así somos/This is who we are: The Hispanic
    heritage of the United States 107
Brain Ticklers—The Answers 109

## Lección 6: Estudiamos para mejorar nuestra condición humana/ We study to become better people 111

Piénsalo bien/Think it through: The verb, Part 3 116
Más es mejor/More is better 125
Habla popular/Everyday speech 126
Bien vale la pena/It's well worth it: Professions;
    Telling time 127
Dilo como yo/Say it like I do: Pronunciation of the
    *ñ* and the *b-v* 131
Alma hispánica/Hispanic soul: Juan Ramón Jiménez 134
Pluma en mano/Pen in hand: La universidad de
    Salamanca/The University of Salamanca 136
Así somos/This is who we are: Women in early America 138
Brain Ticklers—The Answers 139

## Lección 7: Sin economía no hay país/ The economy is vital to every country 141

Piénsalo bien/Think it through: The adjective 146
Más es mejor/More is better 151
Habla popular/Everyday speech 152
Bien vale la pena/It's well worth it: Your résumé
    (curriculum vitae) 155
Dilo como yo/Say it like I do: Pronunciation of the *h* 158
Alma hispánica/Hispanic soul: Rómulo Gallegos 159
Pluma en mano/Pen in hand: Mi primera carta en
    español/My first Spanish letter 161
Así somos/This is who we are: The treasures of Spain 164
Brain Ticklers—The Answers 168

## Lección 8: Cuatro ruedas para todo/ Four wheels for everything    171

Piénsalo bien/Think it through: The adverb            176
Más es mejor/More is better                          178
Habla popular/Everyday speech                        180
Bien vale la pena/It's well worth it: The job interview   181
Dilo como yo/Say it like I do: Pronunciation of
    the $x$, $y$, $z$                                184
Alma hispánica/Hispanic soul: Antonio Machado        185
Pluma en mano/Pen in hand: La contaminación
    ambiental/Air pollution                          187
Así somos/This is who we are: The treasures of Mexico    189
Brain Ticklers—The Answers                           191

## Lección 9: No hay mejor educación que el viajar/Traveling is the best education    193

Piénsalo bien/Think it through: About the Spanish
    language                                         198
Más es mejor/More is better                          199
Habla popular/Everyday speech                        200
Bien vale la pena/It's well worth it: Holidays       201
Dilo como yo/Say it like I do: Pronunciation of
    the vowels                                       202
Alma hispánica/Hispanic soul: Ricardo Palma          203
Pluma en mano/Pen in hand: Mis vacaciones pasadas/
    My last vacation                        ·        206
Así somos/This is who we are: The treasures of Peru  208
Brain Ticklers—The Answers                           210

## Lección 10: Con buen gobierno avanzan los pueblos/Nations advance with good government    211

Piénsalo bien/Think it through: The pronoun,
    Parts 1 and 2                                    215
Más es mejor/More is better                          223
Habla popular/Everyday speech                        225
Bien vale la pena/It's well worth it: The active and
    passive voices                                   226
Dilo como yo/Say it like I do: Diphthongs            227

Alma hispánica/Hispanic soul: Federico García Lorca 229

Pluma en mano/Pen in hand: El descubrimiento
de América/The Discovery of America 231

Así somos/This is who we are: Hello, I am a Hispanic! 234

Brain Ticklers—The Answers 236

## Lección 11: El arte es maravilloso/ Art is wonderful 239

Piénsalo bien/Think it through: The conjunction 246

Más es mejor/More is better 249

Habla popular/Everyday speech 251

Bien vale la pena/It's well worth it: The structure
of the basic Spanish sentence 252

Dilo como yo/Say it like I do: $b$ and $v$ 254

Alma hispánica/Hispanic soul: Benito Pérez Galdós 255

Pluma en mano/Pen in hand: Sobre la amistad/
About friendship 256

Así somos/This is who we are: The Burial of the
Count of Orgaz 259

Brain Ticklers—The Answers 260

## Lección 12: El amor nos une a todos/ Love binds us together 263

Piénsalo bien/Think it through: The preposition 268

Más es mejor/More is better 270

Habla popular/Everyday speech 273

Bien vale la pena/It's well worth it: Neuter article 274

Dilo como yo/Say it like I do: The synalepha or
linking of words 275

Alma hispánica/Hispanic soul: Ana María Matute 276

Pluma en mano/Pen in hand: La boda de mi
hermano/My brother's wedding 278

Así somos/This is who we are: The legend of
El Dorado/Eldorado 279

Brain Ticklers—The Answers 280

## Lección 13: La naturaleza es vida/ Nature is life 281

Piénsalo bien/Think it through: The verb, Part 4 286

Más es mejor/More is better 291

Habla popular/Everyday speech     292

Bien vale la pena/It's well worth it: Augmentatives
and diminutives     293

Dilo como yo/Say it like I do: Footnote to Spanish
pronunciation     295

Alma hispánica/Hispanic soul: José Hernández     296

Pluma en mano/Pen in hand: El Boquerón/The Boquerón     298

Así somos/This is who we are: The City of Buenos Aires     300

Brain Ticklers—The Answers     302

# Appendix A

Spanish online reference sources     303

# Appendix B

Spanish model verb conjugation     304

# Appendix C

Irregular gerunds and/or past participles     309

# Appendix D

Spanish word order exercise     310

# Appendix E

Matching exercise     312

# Appendix F

Vocabulary exercise     313

# Appendix G

Dividing words into syllables     314

# Index     315

# INTRODUCTION

¿Qué hace un pez?—What does this Spanish pun mean? Read this book and find the answer buried within its pages. In addition to learning Spanish jokes/puns, other reasons to learn Spanish include travel, career, and business opportunities; better communication with more people; helping others; and understanding English better through the process of "learning a language."

With *400 million Spanish speakers worldwide in 31 different countries and **37 million in the United States speaking Spanish in the home, learning Spanish is a wise and practical mission. To aid you in this, we provide language instruction within a real context. Not only will you be learning real Spanish, but we will also expose you to the real Hispanic world: culture, history, and writing. All these factors contribute to a broader understanding and appreciation of life in the Hispanic culture. In other words, you will be submerged in real, authentic Spanish in all of its wonderful aspects. Let us say this—if a person wants to learn English, the best way is to learn not just the meanings of words, but how words are used in real-life conversations and situations. For example I can learn such common words as "life," "people," "year," "place" by reading Jefferson or Lincoln or a tabloid. The words are the same, but the contexts in which they are used differ greatly. One context has vigor, punch, and meaning; it teaches not only the language but the soul of a people. To learn a language is to also learn about the people who speak it and what they represent.

With this comprehensive guide to learning *Painless Spanish*, it is also important to note that the best and most effective way to learn a language is by immersing oneself in the target language, preferably in a country of origin. Few beginning learners have this luxury or opportunity; therefore, you must speak it and hear it as often as you can within your current situation. Listen to Spanish radio or watch Spanish movies to help with pronunciation, accent, and rhythm. As you become accustomed to the sound of the language and learn more vocabulary, you will want to learn the basic "why" and "how" of Spanish grammar. This book provides a wide array of grammar explanations and opportunities for you to practice the new concepts, including online quizzes and activities that represent the material within the lessons.

This book has a total of 13 lessons. In each one you will learn an important aspect of the Spanish language and of the Hispanic culture and history. Each of the 13 lessons is divided into 9 main parts or sections, with titles given in both Spanish and English, as follows: **Part 1.** The lesson opens with a main theme, which serves as the basis for most of the lessons; **Part 2.** Piénsalo bien/Think it through. Basic grammar; **Part 3.** Más es mejor/More is better. Additional vocabulary; **Part 4.** Habla popular/Everyday speech. Common idioms, expressions, and sayings; **Part 5.** Bien vale la pena/It's well worth it. General information of interest; **Part 6.** Dilo como yo/Say it like I do. Basic pronunciation of Spanish sounds; **Part 7.** Alma hispánica/Hispanic soul. Reading of classic Hispanic authors; **Part 8.** Pluma en mano/Pen in hand. Composition practice; and **Part 9.** Así somos/This is who we are. Cultural aspects of the Hispanic world. Bilingual titles, as shown above, are also provided within the texts of every lesson.

This book has been designed to fit various teaching and learning methods. Although it is meant primarily to be used at the introductory level for middle-school students, it can also be useful for the intermediate or even the advanced levels, for review purposes, and for self-teaching. Each of the 13 lessons could be covered in one week for a total of 13 weeks, or roughly an academic semester. However, some lessons may take a bit longer because of the complexity of the grammar, such as lessons 5, 6, and 10; thus, a longer time frame may be more realistic. Throughout each lesson you will find numerous attention grabbers and brain ticklers that have the titles: ¡Ojo! (Watch out!), ¿Te acuerdas? (Do you remember?), ¿Cuánto sabes? (How much do you know?), and ¿Sabías que? (Did you know?).

We congratulate you on your decision to learn Spanish. No doubt it will broaden your perspective of the world, and increase your ability to communicate with those you weren't able to communicate with before.

¡Adelante y manos a la obra!

---

*https://www.ethnologue.com/statistics/size*
**http://www.pewresearch.org/fact-tank/2013/09/05/what-is-the-future-of-spanish-in-the-united-states/*

# REFERENCE PAGES

## Cardinal numbers 1–1000

Counting in Spanish is easy. You may have some difficulty counting from 16 to 19, but not the rest. Let's see first 1 to 10:

| | |
|---|---|
| uno | one |
| dos | two |
| tres | three |
| cuatro | four |
| cinco | five |
| seis | six |
| siete | seven |
| ocho | eight |
| nueve | nine |
| diez | ten |

No big deal, right? However, you need to watch out for *cinco, siete,* and *nueve* as you count further. Why? Because the spelling is somewhat different, as you will see later.

11 to 15:

| | |
|---|---|
| once | eleven |
| doce | twelve |
| trece | thirteen |
| catorce | fourteen |
| quince | fifteen |

Now 16 to 19 (¡*cuidado!*):

| | |
|---|---|
| dieciséis | sixteen |
| diecisiete | seventeen |
| dieciocho | eighteen |
| diecinueve | nineteen |

Literally, what you are saying is: ten plus six, ten plus seven, etc.

20 to 29:

| | |
|---|---|
| veinte | twenty |
| veintiuno | twenty-one |
| veintidós | twenty-two |
| veintitrés | twenty-three |
| veinticuatro | twenty-four |
| veinticinco | twenty-five |

| | |
|---|---|
| veintiséis | twenty-six |
| veintisiete | twenty-seven |
| veintiocho | twenty-eight |
| veintinueve | twenty-nine |

30 to 99:

| | |
|---|---|
| treinta | thirty |
| cuarenta | forty |
| cincuenta | fifty |
| sesenta | sixty |
| setenta | seventy |
| ochenta | eighty |
| noventa | ninety |

*Note:* When saying thirty-one, forty-four, fifty-seven, sixty-three, ninety-nine, etc., you must say it in three words: *treinta y uno, cuarenta y cuatro, cincuenta y siete, sesenta y tres, noventa y nueve.* Also, remember what we said about *cinco, siete, nueve.* Look at the spelling of *cincuenta, setenta, noventa,* and you will see the difference, especially in the last two (not *sie, nue.*)

100 to 130:

| | |
|---|---|
| cien | one hundred |
| ciento uno | one hundred one |
| ciento dos | one hundred two |
| ciento tres | one hundred three |
| ciento diecinueve | one hundred nineteen |
| ciento veintiuno | one hundred twenty-one |

*Follow same pattern, using *ciento* and the number until *ciento treinta* (one hundred thirty).

Starting with 131, add the "y" between the tens and ones:

| | |
|---|---|
| ciento treinta y uno | one hundred thirty-one |
| ciento treinta y dos | one hundred thirty-two |
| ciento cuarenta y uno | one hundred forty-one |
| ciento cincuenta y uno | one hundred fifty-one |

200 to 1000:

| | |
|---|---|
| doscientos | two hundred |
| doscientos uno | two hundred one |
| doscientos diez | two hundred ten |

| | |
|---|---|
| doscientos dieciséis | two hundred sixteen |
| doscientos treinta y uno | two hundred thirty-one |
| | |
| trescientos | three hundred |
| cuatrocientos | four hundred |
| quinientos | five hundred |
| seiscientos | six hundred |
| setecientos | seven hundred |
| ochocientos | eight hundred |
| novecientos | nine hundred |
| | |
| mil | thousand |
| dos mil dieciséis | two thousand sixteen |

## Spanish Alphabet

The Spanish alphabet has a total of 27 letters or symbols: 5 vowels and 22 consonants. The name of the letter (when spelling) is different than the pronunciation of the letter in a word.

Pronunciation of letters (in spelling):

| | | |
|---|---|---|
| a (ah) | j (hoe-tah) | r (eh-ray) |
| b (bay) | k (kaw) | rr (er-ray) |
| c (say) | l (e-lay) | s (essay) |
| d (day) | m (em-ay) | t (tay) |
| e (ay) | n (en-ay) | u (oo) |
| f (eh-fay) | ñ (en-yay) | v (oo-vay) |
| g (hay) | o (oh) | x (eh-keys) |
| h (ah-chay) | p (pay) | y (ye) |
| i (ee) | q (coo) | z (zay-tah) |

### PRONUNCIATION
Vowel sounds:

a (ah) *padre* – pah-dray
e (ay) *madre* – mah-dray
i (ee) *primo* – pree-moh
o (oh) *niño* – nee-nyoh
u (oo) *abuelo* – ah-boo-ay-loh
(when said quickly, sounds like *ah-bway-loh*)

| Rule: | Example: |
|---|---|
| ñ – n with *tilde*, sounds like onion or canyon | *niño* – nee-nyoh (boy) |
| c – before an *e* or an *i* sounds like *s*, before any other letter sounds like *c* in cat | *cero* – say-roh (zero)<br><br>*cuñado* – coo-nyah-doh (brother-in-law) |
| g – before an *e* or an *i* sounds like *h*, before any other letter sounds like *g* in girl | *Jorge* – hor-hay (George)<br><br>*tengo* – tayn-goh (I have) |
| h – silent | *hotel* – oh-tale (hotel) |
| j – sounds like *h* | *hijo* – ee-hoh (son) |
| ll – sounds like *y* | *ella* – ay-yah (she) |
| rr – rolled *r* | *burrito* – boo-ree-toh |
| y – sounds like *i* (ee) | *y* – ee (and, plus) |

## ACCENTS

Accents are placed on top of vowels to indicate that a syllable is given extra stress when pronounced. Accents are used when the normal accent rule is broken or to indicate different meanings for words that are spelled the same.

One-syllable words with accents are not pronounced differently – *tú* (you), *él* (he), *sí* (yes).

## Multiple syllables require STRESS when pronounced

For example: tíos (aunts and uncles or just uncles) – pronounced TEE-ohs, with the stress going on the syllable that has the accent/capital letters. This is different than if it was pronounced with the stress on the last syllable, like tee-OHS. It is so significant that it would be pronouncing the word wrong.

Try it!
nación – (nation) – nah-see-OHN
policía – (police) – poh-lee-SEE-ah
Ramírez – (last name) – Rah-MEER-ayz
María – (first name) – Mah-REE-ah

## NO ACCENTS

When a word has no written accent, there is an "implied" accent when pronounced, according to the following rule – if a word ends with a vowel, n, or s – the stress goes on the next to the last syllable, usually the next to last vowel.

1. padre (father) – implied stress goes on next to last syllable (or next to last vowel) PAH-dray
2. hermano (brother) – implied stress goes on next to last syllable (or next to last vowel) air-MAH-noh

If a word ends in ANYTHING other than a vowel, n, or s – stress goes on last syllable (or last vowel).

- ciudad (city) – see-oo-DAHD
- tener (to have) – tay-NAYR

# La familia es nuestro sostén y reposo

# The family is our support and comfort

¡Hola! Me llamo Carlos. *Yo tengo doce años y soy alto y rubio. Mi familia es grande.* Yo tengo a mi *padre, madre,* y un *hermano* y una *hermana.* Mi madre *tiene* un hermano. *Se llama* Martín. Martín es mi *tío.* La *esposa* de Martín es mi *tía. Ellos* tienen dos *hijos,* Roberto y Fernando. Roberto y Fernando *son* mis *primos.* Ellos son *simpáticos.* Tengo *un abuelo,* Mario y *una abuela,* Juanita.

## Vocabulario básico

| | |
|---|---|
| ¡Hola! | hello! |
| Me llamo | I call myself/my name is |
| Yo tengo doce* años | I have twelve years |
| | (I am twelve years old) |
| soy | I am |
| alto | tall |
| rubio | blonde |
| Mi familia* es grande | my family is big |
| padre | father |
| madre | mother |
| hermano(s) | brother(s) |
| hermana(s) | sister(s) |
| tiene | has |
| Se llama | He calls himself/His name is |
| tío | uncle |
| esposa | wife |
| tiá | aunt |
| Ellos tienen | they have |
| hijo(s) | son (sons or children) |
| son | are |
| primo(s) | cousin(s) |
| simpáticos | nice |
| abuelo | grandpa (grandfather) |
| abuela | grandma (grandmother) |

*For numbers, see reference page at beginning of book.
*Familia is a cognate, which is a Spanish word that looks and means the same as the English word.

### NOUN GENDER & DEFINITE ARTICLES

Spanish nouns can either be feminine, masculine, singular, or plural. If the noun refers to a person, such as *padre*, then it will take on the gender (feminine or masculine) of the person to whom it refers. Since *padre* means father, then the word *padre* is a masculine noun. Likewise, *madre* refers to a woman, so it is a feminine noun. All nouns have genders even if they don't refer to a person. You may have noticed that many nouns that end with the letter <u>o</u> are generally masculine; nouns that end with the letter <u>a</u> are generally feminine. Another way to tell the gender of a Spanish noun is by learning the definite article (meaning *the*) that goes with it, included in the vocabulary list. *El* (singular) and *los* (plural) are used in front of masculine nouns; *la* (singular) and *las* (plural) are used in front of feminine nouns.

## BRAIN TICKLERS
### Set # 1

#### *Ejercicios* (Exercises)

A. Fill in the blanks with the correct Spanish or English word:

1. Mi hermana es (is) la _____ de (of) mis padres.

2. Mis tíos son los _____ de mis primos.

3. The Spanish word, *familia*, is an example of a(an) _____, which means that it looks and means the same as the English word.

4. *El, los, la,* and *las* are called <u>definite articles</u> and they mean _____ in English.

5. *El* and *los* are used in front of _____ nouns; *La* and *las* are used in front of _____ nouns.

B. Give the Spanish for the following words (include the definite article for each noun):

1. the mother _____

2. the brothers _____

3. My name is _____

4. the cousins _____

5. the son _____

(Answers are on page 24.)

## ¡OJO!—WATCH OUT!

In Spanish, when exclamation and question marks are used, there is the regular one at the end, like in English, but there is ALSO an upside-down exclamation or question mark at the beginning of the sentence. Notice the upside-down marks in the next section. When typing, use *insert symbol* for these, plus accented letters and the ñ with the tilde accent above it. If using often, create a shortcut key stroke.

# PIÉNSALO BIEN
# THINK IT THROUGH

## The article. El artículo

There are four articles in Spanish with their usual plural forms:

Definite articles:

So called because they determine the extension of the noun they precede.

*Ayer compré el libro que querías* ./ Yesterday I bought the book you wanted—meaning that both you and the other person know what the book is.

### DEFINITE ARTICLES:

| singular | plural |
|---|---|
| masculine: *el* | *los* |
| feminine: *la* | *las* |

These four articles in Spanish equal one single article: *the*, with no reference whatsoever to gender or number:

| | |
|---|---|
| *el libro* | the book |
| *la casa* | the house |
| *los libros* | the books |
| *las casas* | the houses |

Indefinite articles:

It is not the same to say *el libro* (the book) as *un libro* (a book). When we say *el libro*, we are referring to a particular book, but when we say *un libro*, we make no reference to a particular book, but to any book.

*Ayer compré un libro para entretenerme* ./ Yesterday I bought a book to entertain myself.

### INDEFINITE ARTICLES:

| singular | plural |
|---|---|
| masculine: *un* | *unos* |
| feminine: *una* | *unas* |

These four articles in Spanish equal either *a*, *an*, or *some* in the plural:

| | |
|---|---|
| *un libro* | a book |
| *una casa* | a house |
| *unos libros* | some books |
| *unas casas* | some houses |

**Important:** Combined with the prepositions *a* or *de*, the masculine singular definite article *el* fuses together with both: *a + el > al, de + el > del*, but NOT with the masculine singular pronoun *él*. This happens all the time, no exceptions. Examples:

| | |
|---|---|
| *Fui al cine.* | I went to the movies. |
| *el motor del carro* | the engine of the car |

### ¡OJO!—WATCH OUT!

With feminine nouns beginning with a stressed *a* or *ha*, the masculine article is used, as in: *el agua* (the water), *el hambre* (hunger), to avoid cacophony (combination of discordant sounds).

## BRAIN TICKLERS
### Set # 2

### *Ejercicios*

A. Give the definite article for the following:

1. _____ hermanos
2. _____ familias
3. _____ abuelo
4. _____ esposa
5. _____ madre

B. Give the indefinite article for the following:

1. _____ primos     4. _____ hijo

2. _____ padres     5. _____ madre

3. _____ tías

C. Fill in the blanks with the definite or indefinite article.

1. _____ herramientas (tools) que te presté ayer son muy caras. (definite)

2. En esa librería venden _____ libros muy raros. (indefinite)

3. _____ edificio que está en la esquina no me gusta. (definite)

4. Mis padres salen siempre con _____ tíos de mi amiga. (definite)

5. Cuando pueda me voy a comprar _____ zapatos negros. (indefinite)

## ¿Cuánto sabes?* Try to answer these questions by yourself:

D. Complete the dialogue between Marta and Carlos.

Marta: Hola, me _____ Marta. ¿Cómo te _____?
Carlos: Me _____ Carlos.
Marta: ¿_____ estás?
Carlos: Muy _____. ¿Y tú?
Marta: _____.

E. 1. How would you say in Spanish: How old are you?

2. How would you answer the above question?

*It means *How much do you know?* Learn it well as we will be using it throughout this book. See page 10 for additional vocabulary for this section.

(Answers are on page 24.)

¿**Sabías que?** Spanish uses both an informal and formal "you." Informal is for talking to friends, children, and pets. The formal "you" is used with strangers or to show respect to someone you know that is older. Tú (you, singular) and Vosotros (you all, plural) are informal; Usted (you, singular) and Ustedes (you all, plural) are formal.

# MÁS ES MEJOR
# MORE IS BETTER

In this section we are including additional vocabulary relating to the main theme of the lesson.

## Family

| | |
|---|---|
| los abuelos | grandparents |
| el cuñado(a) | brother-in-law, sister-in-law |
| los cuñados | brothers- and sisters-in-law |
| el hombre | man |
| la mujer | woman |
| el esposo | husband/spouse |
| la esposa | wife/spouse |
| el niño | boy/child |
| la niña | girl |
| el bebé | baby |
| el chico | boy |
| la chica | girl |
| el amigo | friend (boy) |
| la amiga | friend (girl) |
| el (la) estudiante | student |
| hija(s) | daughter(s) |
| padres | parents |

*Notice the difference in many of the above words is masculine or feminine (gender), and the article changes based on gender (el, la, los, las).*

---

Definite Articles—*el* is used before singular, masculine nouns; *la* before singular, feminine nouns. *Los,* plural, masculine; *las,* plural feminine. All mean "*the.*"

Also, feminine nouns usually end with *a,* and masculine nouns with *o* (there are exceptions).

## Adjectives

| | |
|---|---|
| bueno(a) | good |
| inteligente | intelligent |
| mal/malo(a) | bad |
| bajo(a) | short |
| artístico(a) | artistic |
| bonito(a) | pretty |
| guapo(a) | good-looking |
| joven | young |
| viejo(a) | old |
| pequeño(a) | small |

## Common greetings and introductions

| | |
|---|---|
| Hola. ¿Cómo estás? | Hi, How are you? |
| ¿Qué tal? | How's it going? |
| ¿Qué pasa? | What's going on/happening? |
| Bien/Mal | Good/Bad |
| ¿Y tú? | And you? |
| ¡Hasta luego! | See you later! |
| Hasta mañana | See you tomorrow |
| Adiós | (Good)bye |
| Buenos días | Good morning |
| Buenas tardes | Good afternoon |
| Buenas noches | Good evening |
| regular (cognate) | regular. OK |
| más o menos | more or less |
| muy | very |
| ¿Cómo te llamas? | What is your name? (informal) |
| (*ll* sounds like a *y*) | |
| ¿Cómo se llama? | What is your name? (formal) |
| Se llama … | His/her name is …/Your name is … |
| encantado/a | It's a pleasure to meet you |
| mucho gusto | much pleasure (to meet you) |
| perdón | Excuse me. |
| ¿Cuántos años tienes? | How old are you? (How many years do you have?, literally) In Spanish, talking about how old someone is uses the verb "*tener*" – to have. *Tienes* means (do) you have. |
| Yo tengo …. años. | I am … years old (I have …. years, literally.) *Yo tengo* means I have. |

## Adjective—noun agreement and order

Not only do nouns have a gender, but adjectives have to "agree in gender (masculine or feminine) and number (singular or plural)" with the noun they describe. To make an adjective agree with a feminine noun, add *a*; for masculine, add *o*. To make it plural, add *s* for those ending in a vowel, and *es* to all others. Some change endings for gender, some do not. If the adjective ends with an *o* or an *a (only)*, then it has to agree with the gender of the noun – *chica simpática* (nice girl) or *chicos simpáticos* (nice boys). Adjectives like *inteligente* don't change based on gender, because they don't end with an *o* or an *a*, but do change for singular or plural. *Chica inteligente* and *chico inteligente* are both correct. Also, generally adjectives will go AFTER the nouns in Spanish, whereas in English they are put in front of the nouns (nice girl, but Spanish looks like girl nice).

Examples of adjectives agreeing in gender (masculine/feminine) and number (singular/plural):

*hijo alto* (tall son) – *hija alta* (tall daughter) – *hijos altos* (tall sons) – *hijas altas* (tall daughters) – *hermano joven* (young brother) – *hermana joven* (young sister) – *hermanos jovenes* (young brothers or young brothers and sisters)

## Making nouns plural

To make a noun plural, just add <u>s</u> if it ends with a vowel and <u>es</u> if it ends with a consonant. When there is more than one person in a group and there is at least one male, the plural noun used to describe the group always takes the plural masculine form. The plural of *padre* is *padres*, and can mean fathers (plural) or it can also mean mothers and fathers (parents). *Hermano y hermana* (brother and sister) change to *hermanos* (brothers and sisters). *Abuelo y abuela* (grandfather and grandmother) change to *abuelos* (grandparents). In other words, in the plural, the masculine form takes precedence if there are both males and females in the group. However, keep in mind that the plural form can mean also fathers, brothers, and grandfathers (all males). If only females are described, then the plural is in the feminine – *hermanas, madres, abuelas*.

## Vowel

| | |
|---|---|
| mesa | mesas |
| hombre | hombres |
| niño | niños |

## Consonant

| | |
|---|---|
| árbol | árboles |
| mujer | mujeres |
| papel | papeles |

If the noun ends in -*z*, you change it to *c* and then add -*es*, as in:

| | |
|---|---|
| lápiz | lápices |
| nariz | narices |
| pez | peces |

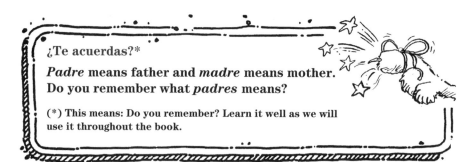

¿Te acuerdas?*

*Padre* means father and *madre* means mother.
Do you remember what *padres* means?

(*) This means: Do you remember? Learn it well as we will
use it throughout the book.

# HABLA POPULAR
# EVERYDAY SPEECH

## Idioms, common expressions, and sayings

An idiom is a peculiar or characteristic way a language has to express something, and it is essential to learn the idiom. For example, as English uses the verb *to be* when referring to the weather (it is cold, it is windy), Spanish uses *hacer*, which means *to do/make*, as in *hace frío, hace viento*. Obviously, such idioms could not be translated literally for they would be meaningless.

Common expressions cannot be translated literally either, for they are made up of words that lose their individual meaning to mean something else. Look at these English idiomatic expressions:

> dressed to kill
> cute as a button

How would you convey the same meaning in Spanish? Only by understanding what is being said in the whole phrase, and not by the meaning of the individual words. Thus, we would say:

> elegantemente vestido
> tan bonita como una flor

Sayings express a long-established truth, such as a proverb or adage. Usually, there is something similar in Spanish. Here are two examples of common sayings:

| | |
|---|---|
| De tal palo tal astilla. | Like father like son. |
| El amor es ciego. | Love is blind. |

---

### ¿Sabías que?

How much do you think Christopher Columbus's trip cost Spain? It cost 1,167,542 *maravedís*, or approximately $151,780 in today's U.S. dollars.

# BIEN VALE LA PENA
# IT'S WELL WORTH IT

## Nombres y apellidos (first and last names)

Usually, Spanish people have two first names and two last names; one is the father's and the other is the mother's (maiden name). No middle initial is used in Spanish as is customary in the United States. What distinguishes two persons with the same first and last names is the mother's last or maiden name. For example:

Rodrigo González Suárez. González is the father's last name, and Suárez is the mother's last or maiden name. In other words, contrary to what is customary in the United States, the mother's last name is always present in all Spanish full names.

Many Spanish first names are taken from the names of saints, such as Pablo, Juan, Pedro, José, and the same for women: María, Guadalupe, Asunción, Teresa. And many last names end in "ez," as in Fernández, Rodríguez, Hernández. The *ez* stands for *son or daughter of* (Fernando, Rodrigo, Hernando), just like Williamson, Peterson, Robertson, in which the *son* stands for the same (William, Peter, Robert).

Spanish, like English, also uses nicknames, which are called *apodos*, like Pepe for José, Enolé for Manolo, Rafi for Rafael, Lelito for Consuelo (Consuelito), Cachita for Caridad, and even others that are totally made up, like Coqui for María.

Many English common first names have equivalents in Spanish. Here are a few:

| English | Spanish | English | Spanish |
|---------|---------|---------|---------|
| Charles | Carlos | Anthony | Antonio |
| Elizabeth | Isabel | Louis | Luis |
| Emily | Emilia | Philip | Felipe |
| Robert | Roberto | Christine | Cristina |
| Mary | María | Anne | Ana |
| Peter | Pedro | Pauline | Paulina |

| English | Spanish | English | Spanish |
|---------|---------|---------|---------|
| Paul | Pablo | Regine | Regina |
| Margaret | Margarita | John | Juan |
| Susan | Susana | Ralph | Rafael |

## BRAIN TICKLERS
### Set # 3

*Ejercicios*

A. Answer these questions in English:

1. If you were living in a Hispanic country, how would you write your full name?

2. Do you use an apodo? What is it?

3. The Spanish last name Martínez means _____.

4. Do you know the Spanish equivalent for Martha?

B. Answer the following questions based on the previous lessons.

1. Where do Spanish adjectives go in relation to a noun?

2. Adjectives have to agree with their nouns in what ways?

3. How do you make a noun plural if it ends with a vowel? If it ends with a consonant?

4. Marta is talking to her friend, Carlos. Which Spanish pronoun for "you" would be used (tú, usted, vosotros, or ustedes)? If Marta were talking to her teacher? If Marta were talking to more than one teacher?

5. If you were living in a Hispanic country, how would you say your name?

C. What are the Spanish equivalents to the following numbers (see reference pages at beginning of book):

1. 10 _____       5. 100 _____
2. 14 _____       6. 154 _____
3. 20 _____       7. 500 _____
4. 25 _____

(Answers are on pages 24–25.)

### ¡OJO!—WATCH OUT!

Spanish, like English, uses titles for people. Some of the most common are:

| Spanish | Abbv. | English | Abbv. |
|---------|-------|---------|-------|
| Señor | Sr. | Mister/Sir | Mr. |
| Señora | Sra. | Madam | Mrs. |
| Señorita | Srta. | — | Miss |
| — | Sa. | | Ms. |
| Don | D. | — | — |
| Doña | Dña. | — | — |

## Explanations

*Señorita* refers mainly to an unmarried woman, but also to a young woman.

*Sa.*, similar to *Ms.* in English, makes no reference to a woman's marital status.

*Don* was originally an honorary title, but it now applies to a man of status, and also to an older man.

*Doña* is the same as above but applied to a woman.

When referring to a Don or Doña, always use the title before the person's first name, as in Don Miguel, Doña Consuelo. Sr. and Sra. are used before last names, as in Sr. García, Sra. Suárez.

In a Hispanic country, a married woman takes the husband's last name but always keeps her maiden name, as in: Consuelo Vega de Suárez; Suárez is the husband's last name, and Vega her maiden name. However, today, many married women leave out the *de* (which literally means *of*) and say their name: Consuelo Vega Suárez. Professional titles are also used in Spanish, as in *Dr.* Ramírez (a physician) and *Lic.* Escobar (a lawyer). Feminine forms are *Dra.* and *Licda.* Since Spanish names always have masculine and feminine forms, it is easier to identify the gender of a person's profession; for example, *abogado - a, maestro - a, enfermero - a.* When this is not possible, the article identifies it, as in *el bombero* (fireman), *la bombero* (firewoman.) In some cases, when the noun ends in *a,* as in *policía* (police), the only way to refer to a policewoman is by saying *la mujer policía,* or *el oficial de policía* (police officer) or *la oficial de policía* (also police officer, but a woman). In other words, some nouns can change their gender by the ending, "*o-a,*" or by the article, *el, la,* while others can't.

# DILO COMO YO
# SAY IT LIKE I DO

## The Spanish alphabet/El alfabeto español

The Spanish alphabet has a total of 27 letters: 5 vowels and 22 consonants. The name of the letter (when spelling) is different than the pronunciation of the letter in a word. See reference pages at beginning of the book for pronunciations.

| | | |
|---|---|---|
| a | j | r |
| b | k | rr |
| c | l | s |
| d | m | t |
| e | n | u |
| f | ñ | v |
| g | o | x |
| h | p | y |
| i | q | z |

## Explanations

There is no *w* in the Spanish alphabet, but it is used in all foreign proper names, as in Washington. The same applies to the *k*, which is used almost exclusively in words taken from other languages, such as *kilómetro, kilogramo*.

There is some debate as to whether "rr" forms a separate letter. The "rr" sounds like a "rolled r," like a motorboat with the tongue (not the lips) fluttering in the mouth. Try it and say *burrito* with a rolled r. It takes practice! In 1994, the Spanish Royal Academy eliminated the "ch" and the "ll" from the alphabet and changed the pronunciation of "y" from "I griega" to "ye," as well as the "b" (be) and "v" (ve).

Refer to reference pages at the beginning of the book for pronunciation and accent rules.

### ¡OJO!—WATCH OUT!

How many words in English end in the suffix *-tion*? Thousands. Well, in Spanish, that suffix is *ción*, changing the *t* to *c* and adding an accent mark on the *ó*. All of the other letters in both English and Spanish are the same. Also, in Spanish, all such words are feminine. Here are a few of these:

| Inglés | Español |
| --- | --- |
| constitution | constitución |
| revolution | revolución |
| creation | creación |
| information | información |
| nation | nación |

There are, however, a few exceptions, but generally the words are the same.

### ¿Te acuerdas?

Do you remember what sound the double *l* (*ll*) makes? Or the *g* when it is before an *e* or an *i* ?

## BRAIN TICKLERS
### Set # 4

1. How does an accent affect the pronunciation of a word?

2. If a word does not have an accent the stress is implied. For the word, *amigo*, where would the stress be placed when saying the word?

3. What sound in English does two "l"s (*ll*) make in a word? _____

4. What sound in English does a *j* make?

_____

5. The word **años** (years) has a tilde on the **n**. What sound in English does the **ñ** make? _____

(Answers are on page 25.)

# ALMA HISPÁNICA
# HISPANIC SOUL

You are about to read various passages from some of the finest Hispanic writers of all time. What is truly important for you is to focus on the reading itself and not so much on the meaning of the words. As you come upon each word, take your time and try to pronounce it correctly and don't rush through it—read at a normal pace.

## Miguel de Cervantes

Cervantes (1547–1616) was a seventeenth-century Spanish novelist, dramatist, and poet. He is considered Spain's best writer and one of the world's leading literary figures. Although he wrote many important works, none compares to *Don Quijote de la Mancha*, hailed as the greatest novel ever written in Spanish. It was published in two parts, in 1605 and 1615, and has been translated into all world languages.

Don Quijote was an old man obsessed with the idea of becoming a knight-errant and undoing all wrongs. He read so many books on chivalry that his brain was affected and one day he set out to follow his quest. At the end of a long journey, he recovered his sanity and returned home, where he died peacefully.

The following passage describes Don Quijote's departure from his town:

Y así, sin dar parte a persona alguna de su intención y sin que nadie le viese, una mañana, antes del día, que era uno de los calurosos del mes de julio, se armó de todas sus armas, subió sobre Rocinante ... y por la puerta falsa de su corral salió al campo, con grandísimo contento y alborozo de ver con cuanta facilidad había dado principio a su buen deseo.

**Translation:** So, without telling anyone of his intention, and without anyone seeing him, one morning before dawn (which was one of the hottest of the month of July), he put on all of his armor, got on Rocinante (name of his horse) ... and by the gate of the yard left toward the country with the greatest happiness and satisfaction at seeing how easy the beginning of his great purpose/adventure was.

# PLUMA EN MANO
# PEN IN HAND

## Fiestas familiares/Family parties

Las fiestas familiares son muy alegres y divertidas. En mi casa, cada año celebramos los cumpleaños, los aniversarios, los bautizos, las graduaciones, el Día de Acción de Gracias, las Navidades, el Año Nuevo, el Día de los Reyes Magos y las bodas (weddings), cuando las hay. En esas fechas (On those dates), se reúne toda la familia y cantamos, bailamos y comemos hasta reventar.

## Vocabulary

las fiestas – parties
alegres – happy
divertidas – fun
casa – house
cada año celebramos – each year we celebrate
los cumpleaños – birthdays
los bautizos – baptisms
el Día de Acción de Gracias – Thanksgiving
las Navidades – Christmases
el Año Nuevo – the New Year
el Día de los Reyes Magos – Three Kings Day
se reúne – gets together
cantamos – we sing
bailamos – we dance
comemos – we eat

## BRAIN TICKLERS
### Set # 5

*After reading the above carefully,
do the following:*

1. *Aniversarios* and *graduaciones* are cognates, which means they look and mean the same in both languages. What do you think they mean?

2. In which celebrations, mentioned in the Fiestas Familiares passage, do you participate?

3. Do all cultures celebrate all these occasions?

4. What do the following verbs have in common: *celebramos*, *cantamos*, *bailamos*, and *comemos*? How does this connect to their meanings in English?

(Answers are on page 25.)

# ASÍ SOMOS
# THIS IS WHO WE ARE

## The early history of Spain

Just like its language, Spain is a very old country, dating back to antiquity. There are, however, three main periods of Spanish history: Roman, Visigoth, and Arab or Muslim. All three civilizations invaded Spain and settled there, leaving an indelible mark on its culture. The Romans dominated Spain for almost 600 years, the Visigoths for 200, and the Arabs (or Moors, as they are called in Spain) for almost 800 years. Do the math and you will see that all three were in Spain for a combined period of 1,600 years. The Romans gave Spain its language, Latin, from which Spanish is derived. The Visigoths initiated the reconquest from the Arabs and proclaimed Catholicism as Spain's religion; the Arabs transmitted their great knowledge in the arts and sciences. A visit to any city in Spain, but especially Toledo, would reveal many traces of the rich and lasting legacies of the three civilizations. A leading figure in Spain's reconquest was Rodrigo Díaz de Vivar, known to history as *El Cid* (the Lord).

Finally, in the fifteenth century, Spain established its own cultural and political identity and became a united nation through the marriage of two outstanding monarchs: Queen Isabella of Castile, and King Ferdinand of Aragon, known as the *Reyes Católicos* (Catholic Monarchs). They both reigned with equal powers, and with their wisdom and vision made Spain the most powerful and influential country in all of Europe as well as half the world.

# BRAIN TICKLERS — THE ANSWERS

## Set # 1, page 4

**A.**
1. hija
2. padres
3. cognate
4. the
5. masculine, feminine

**B.**
1. la madre
2. los hermanos
3. me llamo
4. los primos
5. el hijo

## Set # 2, page 7

**A.**
1. los
2. las
3. el
4. la
5. la

**C.**
1. Las
2. unos
3. El
4. los
5. unos

**E.**
1. Cuántos años tienes?
2. Tengo … años.

**B.**
1. unos
2. unos
3. unas
4. un
5. una

**D.**
llamo, llamas
llamo
Cómo
bien/mal
Regular, Bien, Mal

## Set # 3, page 15

**A.**
1. Answers will vary.
2. Answers will vary.
3. Son of Martín
4. Marta

**B.**
1. after
2. gender, number
3. add "s"; add "es"
4. tú, usted, ustedes
5. Answers will vary. (First name(s), then middle, father's last name, mother's maiden name)

**C.**

1. diez
2. catorce
3. veinte
4. veinticinco
5. cien
6. ciento cincuenta y cuatro
7. quinientos

## Set # 4, page 19

1. puts stress on that syllable
2. on the "i" like ah-MEE-goh
3. y like "yellow"
4. h like "helicopter"
5. ny like "onion" or "canyon"

## Set # 5, page 22

1. anniversaries and graduations
2. answers will vary
3. No.
4. All end in "mos"; this ending is the *we* form of the verb.

# Deportes para todos los gustos

# Sports for all tastes

*Cada* región *tiene* su *deporte* favorito: en *Estados Unidos* es *el béisbol, el baloncesto*, y el *fútbol americano*; en *Europa* y en la América *hispánica* es el *fútbol* o soccer, en el *Caribe se juega* más al béisbol o a la *pelota. Otros* deportes *son* el golf, el tenis, el voleibol, el boxeo, *la natación*, el hockey *sobre hielo*, y en *España* y *en algunos países* hispánicos *la corrida de toros*.

*Jugar* a un deporte requiere *el equipo necesario*. En el béisbol *es* la pelota, *el guante*, el bate, *la máscara*, o en el tenis *la raqueta* y la pelota.

## Vocabulario básico

| | |
|---|---|
| cada | each |
| tiene | has |
| deporte(s) | sport(s) |
| Estados Unidos | United States |
| el béisbol | baseball |
| el baloncesto (also básquetbol) | basketball |
| fútbol americano | American football |
| Europa | Europe |
| hispánica | Spanish |
| fútbol | soccer |
| Caribe | Caribbean |
| se juega | is played |
| más | more or most |
| pelota | ball/baseball |
| otros | other |
| son | are |
| la natación | swimming |
| sobre hielo | on ice |
| España | Spain |
| en algunos países | in some countries |
| la corrida de toros | bullfights |
| jugar | playing |
| el equipo necesario | the necessary equipment |
| es | is |
| el guante | glove |
| la máscara | mask |
| o | or |
| la raqueta | racquet |

---

### ¿Sabías que?

Around 1524, the northeastern coastline of North America, stretching from New Jersey to Rhode Island, was named *Land of Esteban Gómez* (according to the Ribero map). Gómez was a Portuguese explorer in the service of Spain. On his voyage, he had seen Cape Cod, Massachusetts Bay, and the mouths of the Connecticut, Delaware, and Hudson rivers. He called the Hudson *Río San Antón*.

---

## BRAIN TICKLERS
### Set # 6

### Ejercicios

Answer the following questions about sports based on the previous page:

1. _____ es el deporte favorito en los Estados Unidos.

2. En los Estados Unidos, fútbol es _____ (English word).

3. ¿Qué deporte es el más popular en los países hispánicos? (use vocabulary list for comprehension)

4. List the sports terms that are similar in Spanish and in English (cognates).

(Answers are on page 44.)

### ¡OJO!—WATCH OUT!

Nationalities, languages, days, and months are not capitalized in Spanish.

# PIÉNSALO BIEN
# THINK IT THROUGH

## The Spanish language in America: the early years

Spanish was the first European language spoken in America, 100 years before English. Christopher Columbus spoke it and wrote it well, and it was his favorite language. The first native American to speak Spanish was an Arawak Indian who accompanied Columbus to Spain, where he was baptized Diego Colón, Columbus's son and heir. The first North American native to speak it was Francisco de Chicora, of the expedition of Lucas Vázquez de Ayllón to the land of Chicora. He learned Spanish in Spain, where he went with Ayllón.

Right after the discovery of America, Spanish became the leading language of Europe, just as English is today. It expanded quickly throughout the Americas, as Spain established its presence in the Caribbean, Mexico, and Peru. In 1513, Juan Ponce de León brought it to North America through Florida, followed by Álvar Núñez Cabeza de Vaca, Hernando de Soto, Francisco de Coronado, and others. Latin was also used at the time but mainly in writing. Nahuatl, Quechua, and Maya were the main languages of the indigenous peoples of Hispanic America, the Aztecs, Incas, and Mayas, in that order. The Spanish missionaries learned the languages well and wrote many important books about them. The missionaries were also instrumental in extending the teaching of Spanish throughout the continent. One of those missionaries in North America was the venerable Friar Junípero Serra.

¿Sabías que? **Friar Junípero Serra is credited with having founded California through the many missions he established in the region. In today's U.S. Capitol's Rotunda, there is a statue of Father Serra in honor of his many accomplishments.**

## BRAIN TICKLERS
### Set # 7

*¿Cuánto sabes?*

1. Do you know the name of the woman who helped finance Columbus's voyage?
2. Do you know the names of the three ships Columbus used in his famous voyage?
3. Do you know the country from which Columbus left?

(Answers are on page 44.)

# MÁS ES MEJOR
# MORE IS BETTER

## Nouns

| | |
|---|---|
| el uniforme | uniform |
| la anotación/puntuación | score |
| el campeonato | championship |
| el partido | match, game |
| el juego | play, game |
| el gol | goal |
| el fanático | fan |
| el ciclismo | cycling |
| el campeón/la campeona | champion |
| el árbitro | umpire |
| el entrenador/la entrenadora | coach |
| la cancha | court |
| la pista | track |
| la piscina | pool |
| la pesca | fishing |
| la bicicleta | bicycle |
| el punto | point |
| el campo de deportes | playing field |

| la carrera | race |
| la lucha libre | wrestling |
| el levantamiento de pesas | weight lifting |
| el casco | helmet |
| los bolos | bowling |
| el empate | a tie |

## Verbs

| nadar | to swim |
| correr | to run |
| saltar | to jump |
| coger | to catch |
| anotar | to score |
| ganar | to win |
| perder | to lose |
| tirar | to throw |
| cazar | to hunt |
| pescar | to fish |
| bucear | to swim underwater |
| practicar | to practice |

# HABLA POPULAR
# EVERYDAY SPEECH

Here are more common Spanish verb idioms/expressions:

| estar más muerto que vivo | to be more dead than alive |
| ser un MacPato | to be very wealthy |
| tragárselas todas | to be naïve |
| bañarse como un gato | to take a quick bath |
| pensar con la cabeza, no con los pies | to think with your head, not your feet |
| verse en un aprieto | to find oneself in a tight spot |
| tratar con guantes de seda | to treat someone gently/ with kid gloves |
| ser un hacha | to be very skillful |
| volver a las andadas | to behave as usual |

## Verbs

| | |
|---|---|
| ser/estar | to be |
| tener | to have |
| llamarse | literally, to call oneself (reflexive verb) When you say *me llamo* in Spanish, you're saying *my name is* (or I am called). What is your name in Spanish can be asked in two ways: *¿Cómo te llamas?* and *¿Cuál es tu nombre?* For the first you respond: *me llamo* and for the second *mi nombre es.* Usually, however, for the first you should give both your first and last names, while for the second only the first one. |
| nacer | to be born |
| querer | to love/want |

## Conjugation of the above verbs in the present tense

| | |
|---|---|
| ser | soy, eres, es, somos, sois, son |
| estar | estoy, estás, está, estamos, estáis, están |
| tener | tengo, tienes, tiene, tenemos, tenéis, tienen |
| llamarse | me llamo, te llamas, se llama, nos llamamos, os llamáis, se llaman |
| nacer | naces, nace, nacemos, nacéis, nacen (The first person, *I* is never conjugated in this verb.) |
| querer | quiero, quieres, quiere, queremos, queréis, quieren |

# BIEN VALE LA PENA
# IT'S WELL WORTH IT

## Courtesy phrases. Frases de cortesía

Some common Spanish courtesy phrases:

| | |
|---|---|
| ¡Hola! | Hello! |
| ¡Gracias! | Thank you! |
| ¡Muchas gracias! | Many thanks! |
| ¡De nada!/¡No hay de qué!/ ¡No es nada! | You're welcome! |
| ¡Por favor! | Please! |
| ¡Con gusto!/¡Encantado!/a! | With pleasure! |
| ¡Gusto en conocerlo! | Nice to meet you! |
| ¡Con mucho gusto! | With much pleasure! |
| ¡El gusto es mío! | The pleasure is mine! |
| ¡Perdón! | Excuse me!/Pardon me! |
| ¡Con permiso! | Excuse me! |
| ¡Bienvenido!/a! | Welcome! |
| ¡Adiós! | Goodbye! |
| ¡Hasta luego!/¡Hasta la vista! | See you later! |
| ¡Nos vemos! | See you! |
| ¡Que esté bien! | Be well! |
| ¡Cuidese! | Take care! |
| ¡Muy agradecido!/a! | I am very grateful! |
| ¡Que pase un buen día! | Have a nice day! |
| ¡Encantado/a de verle! | Nice to see you! |
| ¡Lo siento! | Sorry! |
| ¡Cuánto lo siento! | I am very/so sorry! |
| ¡La culpa es mía! | It is my fault! |
| Saludos a | Regards to |
| ¡Felicidades!/¡Enhorabuena! | Congratulations! |
| ¡Buen viaje! | Have a nice trip! |
| ¡Qué pena!/¡Qué lástima! | What a shame/pity! |
| ¡Me encanta! | I love it! |
| ¡Que le aproveche! | Enjoy your meal! |
| ¡Es usted muy amable! | You're very kind! |
| ¡Por supuesto!/¡No faltaba más! | Of course! |
| ¡Buenos días! | Good morning! |
| ¡Buenas tardes! | Good afternoon! |

| | |
|---|---|
| ¡Buenas noches! | Good evening!/Good night! |
| ¡Mis mejores deseos! | My best wishes! |
| ¡Salud! | Cheers!/To your health! |

# BRAIN TICKLERS
### *Set # 8*

**Ejercicio**

Completa los espacios en blanco con la frase de cortesía según se da en paréntesis:

1. (Many thanks!) ¡_____ por el regalo!
2. ¡Hasta luego y (nice to meet you!) _____!
3. ¿Te compraste un carro nuevo? (Congratulations!) ¡_____!
4. (You're welcome!) ¡_____! Lo hice con mucho gusto.
5. Tengo mucho sueño. (Good night!) ¡_____!

¿Te acuerdas?
Hispanics generally have two last names; the first is the _____ and the second is the _____. The abbreviation of Señor is _____, of Señora _____, and of Señorita _____.

(Answers are on page 44.)

# DILO COMO YO
# SAY IT LIKE I DO

## The syllable. La sílaba

Here we will deal with dividing words into syllables.

Generally, a syllable in Spanish is formed by a consonant and a vowel, although a vowel by itself can also form a syllable, as in: *igual> i-gual, acero> a-ce-ro*. A consonant by itself can't form a syllable in Spanish. When a consonant is between two vowels, it forms a syllable with the second vowel, as in: *rebanada> re-ba-na-da, mecánico> me-cá-ni-co*.

Here is step one:

In Spanish, the consonants *ch, ll, rr*, are double consonants and can't be separated. They must form a syllable with a vowel, as in: *noche> no-che, pollo> po-llo, carro> ca-rro*. Never separate these double consonants in Spanish.

Step two:

There are also combinations or groups of consonants that can't be separated in Spanish. These are

| consonant groups | examples | consonant groups | examples |
|---|---|---|---|
| bl | pueblo> pue-blo | fr | africano> a-fri-ca-no |
| br | cabra> ca-bra | gl | regla> re-gla |
| cl | aclamar> a-cla-mar | gr | lograba> lo-gra-ba |
| cr | recreo> re-cre-o | pl | plaza> pla-za |
| dr | padre> pa-dre | pr | apretar> a-pre-tar |
| fl | flaco> fla-co | tr | retroceso> re-tro-ce-so |

Step three:

When there are two consonants in a row, one after the other, the first consonant forms a syllable with the preceding vowel, and the second with the following vowel, as in: *observar> ob-ser-var, inmovilidad> in-mo-vi-li-dad*. The same occurs if both consonants happen to be the same, as in: *ennoblecer> en-no-ble-cer*.

When there are three consonants in a row, the first two form a syllable with the preceding vowel, and the third with the following vowel, as in: *perspectiva> pers-pec-tiva, obstinado> obs-ti-na-do*.

When there is a group of three or more consonants, and the last two are *bl, br, cl, cr, dr, fl, fr, gl, gr, pl, pr, tr*, they form a syllable with the following vowel, and the others with the preceding vowel, as in *temblor> tem-blor, infracción> in-frac-ción*.

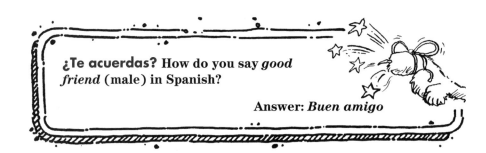

¿**Te acuerdas?** How do you say *good friend* (male) in Spanish?

Answer: *Buen amigo*

### ¡OJO!—WATCH OUT!

How many adjectives in English end with the suffix *-able*? Thousands. Well, listen carefully: not only is that suffix the same in Spanish, but in many cases the entire word is as well:

| Español | Inglés |
|---|---|
| formidable | formidable |
| admirable | admirable |
| indispensable | indispensable |
| comparable | comparable |
| inseparable | inseparable |

# ALMA HISPÁNICA
# HISPANIC SOUL

## Lope de Vega

Lope de Vega (1562–1635) was a Spanish dramatist and creator of Spain's National Theatre. He was a contemporary of Cervantes, who admired him greatly. He wrote many plays and stands today as Spain's greatest playwright. The following passage is from one of his best-known historical plays, *Peribáñez y el comendador de Ocaña*. It is written in verse. You should have no problem making out most of the words, but, again, focus on the reading and on your pronunciation.

Bartolo (one of the characters) speaks:

Nunca en el abril lluvioso
halles hierba en verde prado,
mas que si fuera en agosto.
Siempre te venza el contrario
cuando estuvieses celoso,
y por los bosques bramando
halles secos los arroyos.

### Translation:*

Never in rainy April
you find green meadow grass,
more than if it were in August.
The opposite always defeats you
when you were jealous,
and through the roaring forests
you find dry streams.

*translated with help of Google Translate

# PLUMA EN MANO
# PEN IN HAND

## *La corrida de toros/Bullfighting*

Se dice que más que un deporte la corrida de toros es un arte, y quizá la gente en parte tenga razón (they are right). Es un arte por el espectáculo en sí, por la vestimenta (attire) o traje de luces del torero y por su donaire (gracefulness). También puede considerarse un deporte por haber dos contrincantes parejos (even): el torero o matador y el toro. Cualquiera de los dos tiene las de ganar o perder (win or lose), aunque al torero lo ayudan grandemente los banderilleros\*, a pie (on foot), o a caballo que poco a poco van debilitando (weakening) al animal, que le van mermando (reducing) la vida. El torero tiene habilidad, experiencia, quizá más agilidad, pero mucha menos fuerza (strength) que el toro que con sólo un roce (rubbing/brush) lo puede tumbar al suelo (knock him to the ground) y con sus cuernos (horns) o peso mandarlo al otro mundo (send him to the other/next world), con capa y todo (with cape and all).

A pesar de ser un arte o deporte muy polémico (controversial), principalmente entre los anglosajones (Anglo Saxons), sigue ocupando un lugar de primerísimo orden en los pueblos hispánicos y con majetuosas plazas de toros (bullrings).

\**banderilleros*: men on horseback or foot carrying barbered darts (called *banderillas*) that are stuck into the bull's neck.

# BRAIN TICKLERS
*Set # 9*

The Pluma en Mano (Pen in Hand) discusses the tradition of bullfighting that leads back to prehistoric times. Even though bullfighting is a controversial pastime because the bull is killed, it continues to have an important place in Spanish towns and bullrings.

*Read the previous passage carefully, and then answer the following:*

1. What do you think of the tradition of bullfighting? Why do some people like this tradition (sport) and why do you think some dislike this tradition?

(Answers are on page 44.)

---

### ¿Sabías que?

Sugarcane was introduced in America by Christopher Columbus, who brought it on his second voyage from the Canary Islands. It had been brought to Spain by the Moors who had cultivated it in North Africa. Hernán Cortés was its first grower, and his method was so successful that it has been the only one used since then. Also, the avocado, originally from South America, was brought to Mexico by Cortés. George Washington tasted it for the first time while in Barbados.

# ASÍ SOMOS
# THIS IS WHO WE ARE

Hispanic countries, capitals, and
nationalities. All names are given
in Spanish.

| Country | Capital | Nationality |
| --- | --- | --- |
| Argentina | Buenos Aires | argentinos |
| Bolivia | La Paz | bolivianos |
| Chile | Santiago | chilenos |
| Colombia | Bogotá | colombianos |
| Costa Rica | San José | costarricenses |
| Cuba | La Habana | cubanos |
| Ecuador | Quito | ecuatorianos |
| El Salvador | San Salvador | salvadoreños |
| España | Madrid | españoles |
| Guatemala | Guatemala | guatemaltecos |
| Honduras | Tegucigalpa | hondureños |
| México | Ciudad México | mexicanos |
| Nicaragua | Managua | nicaragüenses |
| Panamá | Panamá | panameños |
| Paraguay | La Asunción | paraguayos |
| Perú | Lima | peruanos |
| Puerto Rico | San Juan | puertorriqueños/ portorriqueños |
| República Dominicana | Santo Domingo | dominicanos |
| Uruguay | Montevideo | uruguayos |
| Venezuela | Caracas | venezolanos |

**Notes:**

- Names of countries and capitals are capitalized. Nationalities are not.
- To make the names of nationalities feminine, change the *o* to *a*, except *costarricense* and *nicaragüense*, which are the same for both. In the case of *español*, to make it feminine, add *a> española.*
- Some names of countries use the article *el>* El Ecuador, El Paraguay, El Perú, El Uruguay (with or without capital E), except La República Dominicana.
- Most of the countries are spelled the same in Spanish and English, with the exception of La República Dominicana (Dominican Republic), and España (Spain) and, of course, in English, without the written accent mark in the case of México, Panamá, Perú. As for the capitals, they are also spelled the same in both languages, with the exception of La Habana (Havana), and Ciudad México (Mexico City) and, of course, in English, without the written accent marks in the case of Bogotá, San José, Ciudad México, Panamá, La Asunción. Notice also the use of the *ñ* in salvadoreños, españoles, hondureños, panameños, puertorriqueños/portorriqueños, and the use of *ü* in nicaragüenses.
- In Hispanic America, the largest city in every country is also the capital.

# BRAIN TICKLERS—THE ANSWERS

## Set # 6, page 30

1. Béisbol
2. soccer
3. fútbol
4. Answers may vary, but might include básquetbol, béisbol, fútbol americano, raqueta, máscara, equipo.

## Set # 7, page 32

1. Queen Isabella
2. Niña, Pinta, Santa María
3. Spain

## Set # 8, page 36

1. Muchas gracias
2. gusto en conocerlo/la (as well)
3. Felicidades/Enhorabuena
4. De nada/No hay de qué, No es nada
5. Buenas noches

**¿Te acuerdas?**
1. Father's last name; mother's maiden name; Sr. ; Sra. ; Srta.

## Set # 9, page 41

1. Answers will vary.

# La casa es nuestro hogar y felicidad

# The house is our home and happiness

Mi *casa* es muy *hermosa*. En *ella vive* toda mi familia, un *perro* y un *gato*. *También* tenemos un *canario* que se llama "Coco". *En total*, la casa tiene tres *habitaciones*, una *cocina amplia*, *comedor* y dos *baños*. Todas las habitaciones, o cuartos, están en el *segundo piso* y *lo demás* en el *primero*. La casa, *por fuera*, está *pintada* de *blanco* con su *puerta principal roja*. A mí, *lo que más me gusta* es *el jardín*, todo él *lleno de hermosas plantas y flores* y una *fuente* en el *centro* con un *chorro de agua imponente*.

## Vocabulario básico

| | |
|---|---|
| casa | house |
| hermosa | pretty |
| ella | it |
| vive | lives |
| perro | dog |
| gato | cat |
| también | also |
| canario | canary |
| en total | in all |
| habitaciones | rooms |
| cocina amplia | large kitchen |
| comedor | dining room |
| baños | bathrooms |
| segundo | second |
| piso | floor/stories |
| lo demás | the rest |
| primero | first |
| por fuera | on the outside |
| está pintado | is painted |
| blanco | white |
| puerta principal roja | red front door |
| lo que más me gusta | what I like best |
| el jardín | garden |
| lleno de | full of |
| hermosas plantas y flores | beautiful plants and flowers |
| fuente | fountain |
| centro | center |
| chorro de agua | stream of water |
| imponente | grand |

**¡OJO!—WATCH OUT!**

*Biblioteca* in English is *library*. The word in Spanish for *bookstore* is *librería*, often confused with *library*. Avoid making this mistake.

# BRAIN TICKLERS
## *Set # 10*

### *Ejercicios*

A. Basado en el pasaje, dinos (tell us) si cada una de estas afirmaciones es *verdadera* (true) o *falsa* (false):

1. La casa tiene tres habitaciones y dos baños.　　　　V　F

2. La casa está pintada roja.　　V　F

3. Lo que más me gusta es la cocina.　　　　V　F

4. Hay una fuente en el jardín.　　V　F

B. Traduce la palabra o las palabras entre paréntesis.

1. Mi habitación está en el (<u>second floor</u>).

2. En el jardín de mi casa hay muchas (<u>plants and flowers</u>).

3. La casa está pintada (<u>white</u>).

(Answers are on page 64.)

48

# PIÉNSALO BIEN
# THINK IT THROUGH

## Colors. Colores

**Note:** Colors can either be nouns or adjectives. As a noun, they need the article, which is always masculine, *el*, for example, *me gusta más el rojo* (I like the red one better). As an adjective, they must agree in gender and number with the noun. For adjectives that end with a vowel, add an -*s* to agree with a plural noun. For adjectives that end with a consonant, add -*es*. Here are the basic colors:

| | | |
|---|---|---|
| blanco | white | |
| negro | black | |
| gris | gray | (same for masculine and feminine) |
| rojo | red | |
| azul | blue | (same for masculine and feminine) |
| verde | green | (same for masculine and feminine) |
| marrón/carmelita | brown | (always *marrón/carmelita* for both masculine and feminine. For the plural of *marrón*, add –*es*, and take out the accent mark, as you are adding another syllable. For brown, you could also use *café* for the masculine and feminine.) |
| rosado | pink | |
| plateado | silver | (always *plata* for both masculine and feminine. You could use *plateado/ plateada*.) |
| dorado | gold | |

| | | |
|---|---|---|
| amarillo | yellow | |
| morado | purple | |
| violeta | violet | (same for masculine and feminine) |
| cobre | copper | (same for masculine and feminine) |
| mostaza | mustard | (same for masculine and feminine) |
| crema | cream | (same for masculine and feminine) |
| anaranjado | orange | |

Some of the words commonly used with colors are:

| | |
|---|---|
| claro | light (not clear) |
| obscuro | dark |
| llamativo | bright |
| apagado | dull |
| opaco | opaque |
| desteñido | faded |
| semi+color | semi+color |

## Days of the week. Months of the year

### Días de la semana (Days of the week)

In Spanish, the week starts on a Monday. Days of the week are usually not capitalized. All seven days are masculine.

| | |
|---|---|
| lunes | Monday |
| martes | Tuesday |
| miércoles | Wednesday |
| jueves | Thursday |
| viernes | Friday |
| sábado | Saturday |
| domingo | Sunday |

### Meses del año (Months of the year)

The months are not capitalized either.

| | |
|---|---|
| enero | January |
| febrero | February |
| marzo | March |
| abril | April (notice the *b* in Spanish, not *p*) |
| mayo | May |
| junio | June |
| julio | July |
| agosto | August (notice there is no *u* in Spanish) |

| | |
|---|---|
| septiembre | September (you can write it with a *p*, or without it> setiembre) |
| octubre | October (notice there is no *u* in English) |
| noviembre | November (notice the *ie* in Spanish) |
| diciembre | December (notice *di* in Spanish, not *de*) |

## ¡OJO!—WATCH OUT!

**The date in Spanish.** In Spanish, you start with the day of the month, followed by the month, and then the year, as in:

*4 de enero de 2011* (January 4, 2011)

The abbreviated form would be:

*4–1–11*

A mistake here can be very costly, so be careful!
Day of the month + month + year. That's the way it is done in Spanish. If you want to add the day of the week, you can do it this way:

Day of the week + day of the month + month + year>
(*el*) *lunes, 4 de enero de 2011.*

Notice the use of *de* in Spanish before the month. Contrary to English, Spanish uses cardinal numbers for the date, as in

| | |
|---|---|
| *hoy es nueve* | today is the 9th |

unless it is the first of the month, in which case in most of Hispanic America they would use the ordinal number, as in

*Hoy es el primero (1o.) de marzo.*
Today is the 1st of March.

Often, the article *el* is included, as in

*Hoy es el 17 de agosto.*    Today is the 17th of August.

But if the day of the week is mentioned, the article is omitted before the number, as in

*Se fueron a Europa el martes 4 de abril.*
(They went to Europe Tuesday, April 4th.)

There are several ways of asking the date in Spanish:

| | |
|---|---|
| *¿Qué día es hoy?* | What day is today? |
| *¿A cómo estamos?* | What's the date? |
| *¿Qué fecha es hoy?* | What's today's date? |

## BRAIN TICKLERS
### Set # 11

**Ejercicios**

A. Contesta estas preguntas:

1. ¿De qué color es la camisa/blusa (shirt/blouse) hoy?

2. ¿Y de qué color son los zapatos (shoes) hoy?

3. Las manzanas (apples) por fuera (outside) pueden ser _____ o _____ de color.

4. El color del sol (sun) es _____.

5. Los árboles (trees) en el verano (summer) son siempre de color _____.

\*Remember to add -s or -es to the color when describing plural nouns.

B. Match the definition in column A with the word in column B:

| Column A | Column B |
|---|---|
| 1. Es el color de la luna (moon). | a. amarillo |
| 2. Es el color de la noche. | b. blanco |
| 3. Son los colores de las franjas (stripes) en la bandera (flag) de los Estados Unidos. | c. negro |
| | d. rojo y blanco |
| 4. Es el color del acero (steel). | e. gris |
| 5. Es el color de la banana. | |

C. Write five sentences in Spanish using each one of the following colors. Use *es* for is or *son* for are.

1. verde
2. marrón
3. plata
4. amarillo
5. violeta

(Answers are on page 64.)

# MÁS ES MEJOR
# MORE IS BETTER

Here are other words you should learn. They all relate to the house.

## Nouns

| | |
|---|---|
| el techo | roof/ceiling |
| la pared | wall |
| el pasillo | hallway |
| el sótano | basement |
| el ático | attic |
| el cuarto de estar | family room |
| la calefacción | heat |
| el aire acondicionado | air conditioning |
| la lámpara | lamp |
| la luz | light |
| la silla | chair |
| la mesa | table |
| la bañadera | bathtub |
| el lavabo | washbasin |
| el inodoro | toilet |
| la puerta | door |
| la ventana | window |
| la lámpara | lamp |
| el sofá | sofa |
| el cuadro | picture |
| la sala | living room |
| el dormitorio/cuarto | bedroom |

## Verbs

| | |
|---|---|
| vivir | to live |
| subir | to go up |
| bajar | to go down |
| limpiar | to clean |
| cocinar | to cook |
| barrer | to sweep |
| bañarse | to bathe/take a bath |

| | |
|---|---|
| ducharse | to shower/take a shower |
| descansar | to rest/relax |
| sentarse | to sit down |

### ¿Sabías que?

The first trader in North America was a Hispanic by the name of Rodríguez. He traded pots and pans after the purchase of Manhattan Island from the Dutch.

# HABLA POPULAR
# EVERYDAY SPEECH

More common idioms, expressions, and sayings:

| | |
|---|---|
| a la derecha/izquierda | to the right/left |
| al lado de | next to/beside |
| como siempre | as usual |
| echar de menos | to miss |
| echar la casa por la ventana | to spare no expense/ all the way |
| mientras tanto | meanwhile |
| ir de paseo | to go out for a walk/ stroll, or simply to go out to have a good time |
| ¡De película! | awesome!/wonderful! |
| Al que madruga Dios le ayuda. | The early bird catches the worm. |
| Por mejor lo haría Dios. | Everything happens for the best. |

### ¡OJO!—WATCH OUT!

Here is a Spanish word almost everybody knows: *siesta*.
Literally it means *to take a nap*, and in a way that's what
it is; however, it is also a time put aside to be with the
family, to have lunch together, to go over what everybody
has done and plans to do for the rest of the day. A *siesta* is
always taken in the midafternoon, when most businesses
close for two or three hours. It is also a time to relax and to
digest the biggest meal of the day, which everyone savors
with a glass or two of wine. If you would have such a feast
at lunchtime, you would need a *siesta* too, whether taken
at home or at work; in other words, you would not be able
to function, walking around like a zombie for the rest of
the day!

# BIEN VALE LA PENA
# IT'S WELL WORTH IT

## Cardinal numbers 100–1,000

You may think that this is another big hurdle you have to jump,
but it is not. The key word here is *cientos*, which literally means
*hundreds*. Then, if you know how to count from 1 to 10, you are
in good shape. Why? Well, let's count from 100 to 1,000 and you
will find out:

| | |
|---|---|
| cien/ciento* | one hundred |
| doscientos | two hundred |
| trescientos | three hundred |
| cuatrocientos | four hundred |
| quinientos | five hundred |
| seiscientos | six hundred |
| setecientos | seven hundred |
| ochocientos | eight hundred |
| novecientos | nine hundred |

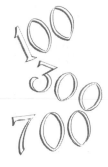

This is what you have to notice:

1. Notice the spellings of 500> *quinientos* (not cincocientos), 700> *setecientos* (not sietecientos), 900> *novecientos* (not nuevecientos). Here you have to watch out!

2. *Ciento* and *uno* are variable and may change in gender and number, as in
   *doscientos libros* (two hundred books, *libros* being masculine/plural), and
   *doscientas mesas* (two hundred tables, *mesas* being feminine/plural).
   Also, *uno* drops the *o* before a masculine/singular noun, as in *un niño* (never *uno niño*), and would change to the feminine, as in: *una niña*, or in the plural, both masculine and feminine: *unos niños, unas niñas*.

3. In English, both numbers are written separately while in Spanish they form one word.

4. In English, a comma is used to separate thousands from hundreds, as in: *2,147*, while in Spanish a period is used, as in: *2.147*.

5. In English, the word *and* is used between hundreds and tens, as in: three hundred and twenty, but not between tens and units, as in: fifty-seven, four hundred and forty-six. In Spanish, the *and> y* is only used between tens and units, but not between hundreds and tens, as in: *trescientos setenta y cuatro* (three hundred and seventy-four).

6. In everyday spoken English, between 1,000 and 9,999 is counted in hundreds, as in:
   2,700> twenty-seven hundred, 6,946> sixty-nine hundred forty-six. This never occurs in Spanish counting, always in thousands and hundreds, as in: 3,752> *tres mil setecientos cincuenta y dos*.

*Ciento*, which means *one/a hundred*, becomes *cien* before a noun, as in *cien libros* (one hundred books), but becomes *ciento* when followed by another number (101–199), as in *ciento dos libros* (one hundred and two books).

## BRAIN TICKLERS
### Set # 12

### Ejercicios

A. Answer these questions in English:
1. In numbers, when do you have to use the *y* in Spanish?
2. Is this correct or incorrect? 200> *dos cientos*. If incorrect, explain briefly why.
3. How would you say "five hundred and eight persons" in Spanish?

B. Write three sentences in Spanish using these numbers (make sure you write out each number). Use *tengo* to mean "I have."

100 _____

544 _____

951 _____

(Answers are on page 64.)

# DILO COMO YO
# SAY IT LIKE I DO

## Pronunciation of the *d* and *t*

In Spanish, these two consonants are called *dentales* (dentals) because they are pronounced with the tip of the tongue pressed against the back of the upper teeth. The basic difference between the two is that *d* is voiced (vibration of the vocal cords), and *t* voiceless; also, that the *t* is always occlusive (no air passing through), while the *d* can be occlusive and fricative (air passing through). Let's explain it further. Let's take this word as an example:

dedo

Here we have two *d*s; the first *d* is at the beginning of the word, after a pause, and the second between two vowels, without a pause. One is pronounced with the tip of the tongue pressed against the back of the upper teeth, with no air passing through (occlusive). The other is also pronounced with the tip of the tongue but slightly separated from the teeth, letting the air pass through. Try to say (we will put the occlusive *d* in bold, and the fricative *d* in italics):

**d**e*do*

How did it come out? Did you notice the difference?

It may be a bit difficult for you because the *d* in English is always occlusive, and therefore you would tend to say:

**d**e**d**o

This would be wrong.

As we said, the *t* is always occlusive, both in Spanish and English. In English, however, it is always explosive in initial position, while in Spanish it is not. Let's see these two words:

Tom – Tomás

Pronounce each one separately and see if you can notice the difference. If you don't, it means that you made both occlusive, which is wrong. Try it again and pronounce the Spanish *t* as in *step*. Got it now?

### Ejercicio

Read these words out loud:

| | | | |
|---|---|---|---|
| adiós | dama | tabla | tesoro |
| dado | decir | tanto | átono |

# ALMA HISPÁNICA
# HISPANIC SOUL

## Santa Teresa de Jesús

Santa Teresa de Jesús, also known as Santa Teresa de Ávila, is one of the greatest figures of Spanish literature, a doctor of the church, a mystic, and a profound, sensitive woman way ahead of her time. Her full name was Teresa Sánchez Cepeda Dávila y Ahumada, born in Ávila, in Old Castile, in 1515, and died at Alba de Tormes, 1582. She studied with the Augustinian nuns but due to illness left after 18 months and stayed with her father and relatives. An uncle acquainted her with the Letters of St. Jerome and she determined to give her life to God. In the years that followed she became very ill, but survived, and was greatly influenced first by the Dominicans and then by the Jesuits. Among her main works are the *Relations*, the *Book of Foundations*, and the *Interior Castle*, a spiritual biography often compared to the *Confessions of St. Augustine*. In 1562, she founded the convent of Discalced Carmelite Nuns, which rapidly expanded throughout Spain. The province of the Discalced Carmelites was established in 1580.

## The writings of Santa Teresa

This is just an excerpt from her book, *Camino de Perfección* (*Way of Perfection*). Here she is talking about the "water falling from heaven" (the rain) and some of its effects:

### Excerpt from *Camino de Perfección/ Way of Perfection*

Es la gran otra propiedad *limpiar cosas* que no limpias. (Si no hubiese *agua* para *lavar*, ¿qué sería del mundo?) ¿Sabéis qué tanto limpia este agua viva, este agua celestial, este agua *clara*, cuando no está *turbia*, cuando no tiene *lodo*, sino que se coge de la misma fuente? Que una vez que se *beba*, *tengo por cierto* que deja el *alma* clara y limpia de todas las *culpas*.

| | |
|---|---|
| *limpiar* | to clean |
| *cosas* | things |
| *agua* | water |
| *lavar* | to wash |
| *clara* | clear |
| *turbia* | muddy |
| *lodo* | mud |
| *beba* | drinks |
| *tengo por cierto* | I know it as true |
| *alma* | soul/spirit |
| *culpas* | sins |

# PLUMA EN MANO
# PEN IN HAND

### *Nuestra casa de Villafranca del Bierzo/*
### *Our house in Villafranca del Bierzo*

Villafranca del Bierzo es un pueblecito de la provincia de León, España, con una vieja e ilustre historia que se remonta (dating back) a los tiempos de los romanos. Allí nació casi toda la familia de mi padre, incluyéndolo a él en el año 1906. Nuestra casa, mejor dicho (better yet), nuestro piso, estaba en la plaza, en el centro del pueblo y a poca distancia estaban también las casas de mis tías Consuelo e Isabel. Nuestro piso era pequeño pero muy hermoso, con su balcón en el que nos sentábamos después de cenar a ver pasar a todos los amigos y conocidos. En la parte de atrás (in the back), pasada la cocina, había un patio que cuidaba mi abuela, con una fuente en el medio hecha (made of) de piedra y en la que jugueteaban pececillos multicolores. El suelo era de azulejos (tiles) y las paredes y techo de cal. Las puertas y ventanas eran de gruesa (thick) madera y todos los muebles, los de la sala, comedor y dormitorios de estilo castellano viejo. A la entrada había dos jarrones de cobre (copper) enormes con muchas flores. Por todas partes (everywhere) colgaban cuadros y fotos de la familia, de mis abuelos y bisabuelos y descendencia. Y cuando mi abuela se metía (got into) en la cocina, ¡ay!, sólo el olor de lo que cocinaba nos contentaba los corazones (made our hearts happy). ¿Que si nos gustaba comer? Tres veces al día más las meriendas y el picar (snack) y siempre con nuestra copita de vino. Tiempos felices que guardaré (will keep) siempre en mi alma…

# BRAIN TICKLERS
## *Set # 13*

### *Ejercicios*

A. List ten words from the previous passage that you have already learned; then, write what each one means.

B. List the cognates (words that look and mean the same in English and Spanish).

(Answers are on page 64.)

### ¡OJO!—WATCH OUT!

Do you know what *piso* means? It is the name given in Spanish to an apartment or flat, usually a condo or co-op, a place you own. The word also means floor (also *suelo*, in Spanish) or story, as in: *Ese edificio tiene cinco pisos* (that building has five stories). A *plaza* is typical of every Hispanic city and town, a square, usually with trees, benches, and perhaps a monument or fountain. These words, plus *patio*, are key in Spanish. Learn them well!

# ASÍ SOMOS
# THIS IS WHO WE ARE

## The early history of the Americas

Long before Christopher Columbus discovered America, four major civilizations had flourished to our south: The Aztec, the Maya, the Inca, and also the Chibcha. They were far superior in their accomplishments to any of the ones found in North America, such as the Pueblos. When the Spaniards came and saw for the first time the magnificent roads, majestic cities and buildings, and imposing pyramids, they stood in awe of something they had never before seen in all of Europe. They were particularly struck by the city of Tenochtitlán, the capital of the Aztecs, built on the same site where Mexico City stands today. They were also amazed by many of their customs, colorful attire, courtesy, exceptionally good manners, and cleanliness. No less amazed were the Spaniards with the city of Cuzco, the capital of the Incas.

### ¿Sabías que?

Did you know that Tenochtitlán was built on an island in a lake? It is the lake Texcoco, and the city was built around 1370 A.D. Why that site? The Aztecs' god, Huitzilopochtli, had told them to build their capital on an island in Lake Texcoco, where they would find an eagle perched on a cactus eating a snake. They found the eagle and built their city there.

# BRAIN TICKLERS—THE ANSWERS

## Set # 10, page 48

**A.**

1. V       2. F       3. F       4. V

**B.**

1. segundo piso    2. plantas y flores    3. blanca

## Set # 11, page 52

**A.**

1. Answers will vary.      4. amarillo (or anaranjado)
2. Answers will vary.      5. verdes
3. rojas, verdes

**B.**

1. B       2. C       3. D       4. E    5. A

**C.**

Answers will vary.

## Set # 12, page 57

**A.**

1. between tens and units, but not between hundreds and tens
2. incorrect; doscientos (one word)
3. quinientas ocho personas

**B.**

Tengo cien libros.
Tengo quinientas cuarenta y cuatro pelotas.
Tengo novecientos cincuenta y un dólares.

## Set # 13, page 62

**A.**

Answers will vary, but could include familia – family; padre – father; año – year; casa – house; tías – aunts; hermoso – pretty; la cocina – kitchen; abuela grandmother; fuente – fountain; puertas – doors; sala – living room; comedor – dining room; dormitorios – bedrooms; flores – flowers.

**B.**

provincia, ilustre, historia, romanos, familia, plaza, centro, distancia, balcón, parte, patio, multicolores, enormes, muchas, fotos, descendencia.

# El buen comer
# es un arte

# Good eating
# is an art

En todas partes *del mundo* hay muchos restaurantes, muchas cafeterías, infinidad *de lugares* para *comer un bocado*, sobre todo en las grandes *ciudades* como París, Roma, Madrid, Nueva York. *Así y todo*, para mí *no hay nada como la comida* de casa, la *comida casera*, la preparada con interés y mucho *amor*. *Piénsese* en una *mesa* con su *mantel* blanco y bien puesta, con sus buenos platos y *cubiertos* y adornada con unas flores. Como *aperitivos* hay *camarones rebozados* en salsa verde, unas *rebanadas de chorizos*, *papas fritas a la juliana* y *aceitunas rellenas*. Como plato del día hay *bistec de solomillo a la parrilla, ensalada de lechuga y tomate y arroz amarillo*, mucho *pan de barra, cortado* en *trozos* y *mantequilla* y algo bueno de beber. De *postre* hay *flan* y *arroz con leche*.

## Vocabulario básico

| | |
|---|---|
| del mundo | of the world |
| lugares | places |
| comer | to eat |
| un bocado | a bite (to eat) |
| ciudades | cities |
| Así y todo | Even though |
| no hay nada como la comida | there is nothing like the meal |
| comida casera | home-cooked food |
| amor | love |
| Piénsese | Think |
| mesa | table |
| mantel | tablecloth |
| cubiertos | covered |
| aperitivos | appetizer |
| camarones | shrimp |
| rebozados | breaded |
| rebanadas | slices |
| chorizos | sausages |
| papas fritas a la juliana | julienne fries |
| aceitunas rellenas | stuffed olives |
| bistec de solomillo a la parrilla | grilled filet mignon |
| ensalada de lechuga y tomate y arroz amarillo | lettuce and tomato salad and yellow rice |

| | |
|---|---|
| pan (de barra) | (French) bread |
| cortado | cut |
| trozos | pieces |
| mantequilla | butter |
| postre | dessert |
| flan | Spanish custard |
| arroz con leche | rice with milk |

### ¡OJO!—WATCH OUT!

In Spain and in most Hispanic countries there are three basic meals a day: *desayuno* (breakfast), *almuerzo* o *comida* (lunch), and *cena* o *comida* (dinner.) The main meal of the day is lunch, and dinner is relatively light. Breakfast is also very light—coffee and a roll or something similar. Lunch is usually between 1:30 and 2:30 P.M., and dinner late at night, between 8 and 10 P.M. *Comida* in Spanish can mean several things, including lunch or dinner, and food in general. Throughout Spain, and almost on every corner, there are eating places called *tapas* where people go to have a bite to eat and to have a good time with friends.

# BRAIN TICKLERS
## Set #14

### Ejercicios

A. Traduce (translate) la palabra o las palabras entre paréntesis:

1. No hay nada como (<u>home-cooked food</u>).

2. Camarones (<u>breaded</u>) en salsa verde son aperitivos.

3. Flan y (<u>rice with milk</u>) son postres.

B. What time do you usually eat breakfast, lunch, and dinner? Compare this to Hispanic countries.

(Answers are on page 81.)

### ¡OJO!—WATCH OUT!

*Aceitunas* (olives) *y* (and) *aceite de oliva* (olive oil) are among the main exports of Spain, rivaling those from Italy and Portugal. Leather goods from Spain and Argentina are among the finest in the world, and Chile is the world's largest exporter of copper and copper-made products.

# PIÉNSALO BIEN
# THINK IT THROUGH

## The interjection. La interjección

The interjection doesn't constitute a part of speech, as the noun, verb, or adjective do. In fact, it constitutes a sentence all by itself. It is used to express an emotion, such as surprise: *¡oh!*, pain: *¡ay!*, amazement: *¡bravo! ¡caramba!* (Good heavens!) *¡ándale!* (Get going!) If I say *¡ah!*, it would mean almost the same as using a whole sentence, such as: *Me encanta la buena noticia* (I love good news), *Me admira tu valentía* (I admire your courage). *¡Ni a la fuerza!* (No way!)

The meaning of most interjections largely depends on the intonation, or how they are expressed. For example, *¡ah!* can mean either surprise or a threat, as in: *¡Ah, fantástico!*, *¡Ah, si pasa algo, yo no respondo!* (Ah, if anything happens, I will not be held responsible!). There are other interjections, however, that have a fixed meaning, such as: *¡Ojalá!*, expressing a hope, or *¡Bravo!*, expressing amazement or satisfaction.

Also, there are many nouns, verbs, adjectives, and adverbs that can be used as interjections, such as *¡Madre!* (My goodness!) *¡Ojo!* (Watch out!), *¡Vaya!* (Well done!, Fantastic!), *¡ya!* (Right now!/Enough!), etc. Likewise, many phrases or expressions can also be used as interjections, such as: *¡Ni loco!* (No way!), *¡Que si me gusta!* (Of course, I like it!), etc. Notice that in all of these examples the intonation is what makes them interjections.

---

### ¿Sabías que?

If you like pineapples you have to thank the Spaniard Francisco de Paula Marín, who in 1813 proposed growing them on a large scale in Hawaii.

---

## BRAIN TICKLERS
### Set # 15

*Ejercicios*

A. Here are five interjections. Translate them to English.

1. ¡Ojo, _____!
2. ¡Ya _____!
3. ¡Caramba, _____!
4. ¡Ni a la fuerza _____!
5. ¡Ándale, _____!

(Answers are on page 81.)

---

### ¿Te acuerdas?

If you want to say *nowadays* in Spanish you would say *hoy en día.*

---

# MÁS ES MEJOR
# MORE IS BETTER

## Nouns

| | |
|---|---|
| la servilleta | napkin |
| el salero | saltshaker |
| la azucarera | sugar bowl |
| la sopa | soup |
| las papas fritas | French fries |
| el puré de papas | mashed potatoes |
| la leche | milk |
| el jugo | juice |
| el aceite | oil |
| la comida congelada | frozen food |

**71**

| | |
|---|---|
| el pescado* | fish |
| la langosta | lobster |
| el marisco | seafood |
| la carne | meat/beef |
| el pollo | chicken |
| el puerco/cerdo | pork |
| el huevo | egg |
| los vegetales/legumbres | vegetables |
| el arroz con pollo | chicken and rice |
| el arroz con frijoles | rice and beans |
| el sabor/gusto | taste |
| el café | coffee |
| el té | tea |
| la fruta | fruit |
| el tenedor | fork |
| el cuchillo | knife |
| la cuchara | spoon |

## Verbs

| | |
|---|---|
| poner la mesa | to set the table |
| quitar la mesa | to clear the dishes from the table |
| freír | to fry |
| asar | to roast |
| calentar | to heat up |
| cocer/hervir | to boil |
| comer | to eat |
| beber | to drink |
| masticar | to chew |
| probar | to taste |
| preparar | to fix |

*¡Ojo! There are two words in Spanish for *fish*. When the fish is alive and in the water, it is called *pez*; when caught and served or eaten, it is called *pescado* (which literally means *caught* in Spanish, derived from the word *pescar* > to fish). In other words, *pescado* can mean the noun fish (caught), or tho adjoctivo (caught), or the past participle of the verb *pescar* (to fish, caught). You never eat *pez* but PESCADO.

# HABLA POPULAR
# EVERYDAY SPEECH

Here are more idioms, expressions, and sayings:

| | |
|---|---|
| a menudo | often |
| por lo tanto | therefore |
| además de | in addition to |
| aún así | even so |
| dar gusto | to please |
| en caso de que | in case of |
| en adelante | from now on |
| así es la vida | that's life |
| ¡caramba! | good heavens! |
| ¡vete a la porra! | go and take a walk! |
| No es oro todo lo que reluce. | All that glitters isn't gold. |

# BIEN VALE LA PENA
# IT'S WELL WORTH IT

## Números ordinales (Ordinal numbers)

For now, and at this level, knowing how to count from *first* to *tenth* will suffice.

| Spanish | English |
|---|---|
| primero | first |
| segundo | second |
| tercero | third |
| cuarto | fourth |
| quinto | fifth |
| sexto | sixth |
| séptimo (or sétimo) | seventh |
| octavo | eighth |
| noveno | ninth |
| décimo | tenth |

The abbreviated forms in Spanish, which in English equal 1st, 2nd, 3rd, and after that *th* following the number, are formed in Spanish simply by adding a small *o* after the number and a period:

1o.  2o.  3o.  4o.  5o.  6o.  7o.  8o.  9o.  10o.

If they refer to a feminine noun, then it would be *a*, as in *8a*.

*Primero* and *tercero* drop the *o* before a masculine singular noun, as in:

| | |
|---|---|
| el primer mes | first month |
| el tercer año | third year |

The ordinal numbers agree in Spanish in gender and number with the nouns they are modifying, as in:

| | |
|---|---|
| el segundo piso | the second floor |
| la segunda parte | the second part |
| los primeros meses del año | the first months of the year |

Above *décimo*, Spanish ordinal numbers are rather difficult and seldom used; for example: *diecisieteavo* (seventeenth), *sexagésimo* (sixtieth).

---

# BRAIN TICKLERS
## Set #16

### Ejercicios

A. Translate the underlined words into Spanish:

I live in a three-story <u>house</u>. My <u>bedroom</u> is on the <u>third floor</u>, and my brother's is on the <u>first</u>.

B. Using the abbreviated and written form, fill in the blanks with the appropriate ordinal number:

En mi trabajo, mi oficina está en el (fifth floor) **1** _____
_____ y la de mi amiga Dolores está en el (eighth
floor) **2** _____. La cafetería
está en el (third floor) **3** _____ y la
máquina copiadora en el (fourth) **4** _____.

(Answers are on page 81.)

# DILO COMO YO
# SAY IT LIKE I DO

### ¡OJO!—WATCH OUT!

In Spain, the *ce* and *ci* are pronounced similarly to the
English *th* in *think, three*. This is mainly in the north of
Spain, and particularly in the region of Castile. In the south,
in the region known as Andalucía, the *c* is pronounced as
*s*. Which pronunciation is best? Here in America it is better
to pronounce it *s*. In any event, it really doesn't make that
much of a difference.

## Pronunciation of the *c, q*

The *c* with the vowels *a, o, u*, sounds like *k*, and so does the *q*,
which in Spanish can only be used combined with *ue* and *ui*,
as in: *queso, quinto*. Important: In these combinations of the
*que* and *qui*, you never pronounce the *u*. In English you do; in
Spanish you DON'T. The *c* combined with the other two vowels,
*e* and *i*, is pronounced similarly to the *s*, as in *cero, cinco*. The
reason for the *que* and *qui* is a simple one: Because the *ce* and *ci*
would be pronounced as *s*, not as *k*. Don't forget that the *q* would
never be used by itself in Spanish but only followed by *ue* and
*ui*. As we said, in English it is different, and that is why Spanish

speakers have difficulty pronouncing such words as *quantity* or *question*, because they would not pronounce the *u*.

---

### ¿Te acuerdas?

Remember—*que* sounds like "kay"; *qui* sounds like "key"; *c* before an *e* or *i* sounds like *s*; *c* before any other vowel sounds like the *c* in cat.

---

# BRAIN TICKLERS
### Set #17

### Ejercicios

A. Say these words out loud in Spanish:

| | |
|---|---|
| que | (kay) |
| química | (**key**-me-cah) |
| aunque | (ah-**oon**-kay) |
| cuota | (**kwōh**-tah) |
| carbón | (car-**bone**) |
| acequia | (ah-say-**key**-ah) |
| coco | (**co**-co) |
| cesta | (**say**-stah) |
| ciprés | (see-**prase**) |
| clave | (**clah**-bay) |

*Note: Bolded syllables get extra stress when pronounced.

(Answers are on page 81.)

## ¡OJO!—WATCH OUT!

Watch out for the word *cup* in Spanish. The way it is used in English, as in *a cup of coffee*, is *taza* in Spanish, as in *una taza de café*. On the other hand, *copa* translates into English as *glass*, as in:

| | |
|---|---|
| *una copa de vino* | a glass of wine |
| *una copa de champán* | a glass of champagne |

It would make absolutely no sense in Spanish to say *una copa de café*. The way you say it, again, is *una taza de café*. Keep in mind, however, that glass also translates into Spanish as *vaso*, as in *un vaso de agua* (a glass of water). To be safe, always use *copa* when referring to an alcoholic beverage, especially wine or champagne. A *glass of beer* would be *un vaso de cerveza*.

# ALMA HISPÁNICA
# HISPANIC SOUL

## José Martí

Here we have a true giant of Spanish letters, as well as a great patriot and political figure. José Martí was a writer, a poet, and a revolutionary, a man to whom Cuba owes much of its independence from Spain. His father was a Spaniard, but Martí was born in Cuba. José Martí was determined to see his land free and to that cause gave his life, literally, for he was killed on horseback, fighting, "facing the sun," as history reminds us. Some of the literary figures of the

Spanish *Generación del 98*, such as Miguel de Unamuno, had much praise for and greatly admired José Martí as a writer.

He was born in Havana in 1853 and died in military action during the Battle of Dos Ríos in 1895. In 1869, he published his first newspaper, *La Patria Libre* (Free Fatherland), for which he was arrested but freed soon after. He went into exile, first in Spain where he published *El Presidio Político de Cuba* and also studied at the universities of Madrid and Zaragoza. From 1891 to 1895, he resided mainly in New York, where he continued with his writings, returning to Cuba in 1895. In 1892, he founded the Cuban Revolutionary Party. He was a consummate writer of magazine articles, children's books (*La Edad de Oro*), and poetry (*Versos Sencillos*). The great Nicaraguan poet, Rubén Darío, said this of him: "Martí belonged to an entire race, an entire continent." He is called by Cubans "El Apóstol" (the Apostle).

## The writing of José Martí

Read and enjoy this poem from José Martí:

> Cultivo una rosa blanca
>
> Cultivo una rosa blanca
> en junio como en enero
> para el amigo sincero
> que me da su mano franca.
>
> Y para el cruel que me arranca
> el corazón con que vivo
> cardo ni ortiga cultivo
> cultivo una rosa blanca.

To help you better understand the poem, *cardo* is a *thistle*, and *ortiga* is a *nettle*.

# PLUMA EN MANO
# PEN IN HAND

## *El restaurante "Tío Pepe" de Nueva York/*
## *Tío Pepe restaurant in New York*

En la ciudad (city) de Nueva York, como
en toda la zona alrededor, hay muchos
restaurantes españoles de categoría.
Entre ellos (among them), y uno de los
más importantes y conocidos (known),
y de los más antiguos (oldest), es "Tío
Pepe" y cuyos dueños se llaman Jimmy
y Rocío. Aparte de (Besides) la comida,
que es deliciosa y muy variada, lo que
más llama la atención (what attracts the
most) es el ambiente, sobre todo pasada
(past) la medianoche (midnight). Allí
se reúne gente (people) muy alegre (happy) y simpática, toca la
guitarra, cantan (sing) y bailan (dance) y hablan por los codos.

## BRAIN TICKLERS
### *Set #18*

### *Ejercicios*

A. Contesta estas preguntas en
   oraciones completas:

   1. ¿Cómo se llaman los dueños
      del restaurante (names of
      owners)?

   2. ¿Cuál es la mejor hora para
      estar allí (best time to be there)?

   3. ¿Cómo se siente el autór sobre
      este restaurante (author's feelings
      on this restaurant)?

(Answers are on page 81.)

# ASÍ SOMOS
# THIS IS WHO WE ARE

### Early education in the Americas

After the Spaniards completed their first phase of conquest and exploration, a wave of missionaries from various religious orders (Franciscans and Dominicans at the beginning) made their way to America. They came with one purpose only—to convert the natives to Catholicism and to educate them according to Western beliefs and traditions.The cross and The Book spread to all corners of the Americas, changing it forever. Churches, cathedrals, schools, convents for sick and abandoned women, and hospitals sprung up everywhere, laying the foundation of a new civilization. In less than 50 years, houses were built, roads opened, universities were founded, books were written and printed, institutions, libraries, botanical gardens, industries, and arts established, as well as laws enacted, called *regulamientos*. In total, seven universities were founded in the Americas before Harvard.

In North America, the Spanish missionaries led by Friar Junípero Serra founded a string of missions (21 in total) that would later become some of our greatest cities, such as Los Angeles and San Francisco. They taught the native peoples how to read and write, different methods for cultivating the land, and techniques of arts and crafts. Of our present 50 states, Spain discovered and settled almost half of them, and of the original 13 colonies, Spain was the first in establishing settlements in three of them, Virginia, South Carolina, and Georgia; of the others, it was also the first in Alabama, Arizona, Arkansas, California, Florida, Louisiana, Minnesota, New Mexico, Tennessee, and Texas.

### ¿Sabías que?

The Spaniards Álvar Núñez Cabeza de Vaca, Hernando de Soto, Francisco de Coronado, and Father Juan Crispi, trekked over 100,000 miles in North America by mule or by foot.

# BRAIN TICKLERS—THE ANSWERS

## Set # 14, page 69

**A.**

1. comida casera
2. rebozados
3. arroz con leche

**B.**

Answers will vary, but generally Hispanic countries eat later than people in the United States.

## Set # 15, page 71

**A.**

1. Watch out!
2. Right now!
3. Good heavens!
4. No way!
5. Get going!

## Set # 16, page 74

**A.**

house – casa; bedroom – habitación or dormitorio; third floor – tercer piso; first – primero

**B.**

1. quinto piso (5o.)
2. octavo piso (8o.)
3. tercer piso (3o.)
4. cuarto piso (4o.)

## Set # 17, page 76

oral exercise

## Set # 18, page 79

1. Jimmy and Rocío
2. past midnight
3. Answers will vary. Author has a very positive tone, and seems to have enjoyed the dining experience at Tío Pepe.

# Vestir bien nos ayuda a triunfar en la vida

# Dressing well helps us succeed in life

En estos tiempos modernos *cada cual viste como le parece*, *a su manera*, sin importarle *en lo más mínimo* la opinión de los demás. *"Soy quien soy y como soy; al que le guste bien, y al que no, que se fastidie"*. Con un *pantalón*, una *camisa* o *blusa*, y unos tenis basta. Los tiempos de los *trajes* y *corbatas*, de los *vestidos* y *zapatos de tacones quedaron muy atrás*. *Hubo un tiempo* en el que vestir bien reflejaba *el buen gusto* y elegancia de una persona, *hasta el punto de que* se decía "tal vistes, tal eres", como igual se decía "tal hablas, tal eres". También se busca, y se insiste, en una sociedad "unisexo", en la que no hay distinción, o la hay muy poca, entre el hombre y la mujer. Pero, como nosotros *pecamos de* tradicionales, de gente a la antigua, *aferrada a* sus buenas costumbres y tradiciones, seguimos prefiriendo el buen vestir, sin importar el sexo o la edad, ni aun la condición económica de la persona, pues el que tiene gusto con *dos trapitos* sabe lucir como un rey o una reina.

Vístase cada cual *como le dé la gana*; sí recomendamos que para la próxima entrevista de trabajo que se tenga se vista uno de forma presentable y digna. *De lo contrario*, ¡adiós trabajo!

## Vocabulario básico

| | |
|---|---|
| cada cual | everybody/each of us |
| viste como le parece | dresses as one wishes or wants to |
| a su manera | to his/her own liking |
| en lo más mínimo | in the least |
| "Soy quien soy y como soy; al que le guste bien, y al que no, que se fastidie" | I am who I am and how I am; those that likc it, good, those that don't, too bad. |
| pantalón | pants |
| camisa | shirt |
| blusa | blouse |
| trajes | suits |
| corbatas | ties |
| vestidos | dresses |
| zapatos de tacones | high heels |
| quedaron muy atrás | are far behind |

| | |
|---|---|
| Hubo un tiempo | There was a time |
| el buen gusto | good taste |
| hasta el punto de que | to the point that |
| pecamos de | we are at fault of |
| aferrada a | holding tight to |
| dos trapitos | with two rags |
| como le dé la gana | as he/she pleases |
| De lo contrario | Otherwise |

# BRAIN TICKLERS
## Set # 19

### Ejercicios

A. Contesta estas preguntas en oraciones completas.

1. En general, ¿cómo te vistes tú?

2. ¿Cuál es tu color favorito de ropa?

3. ¿Te consideras tú una persona tradicional?

B. Basado en el pasaje, dinos si cada una de estas afirmaciones es *verdadera o falsa*:

1. En cuanto al vestirse, a la gente de hoy le importa la opinión que de ella tienen los demás.　　　　　　　　V　F

2. La gente de antes no estaba aferrada a sus costumbres y tradiciones.　　　　V　F

3. Cuando vamos a una entrevista de trabajo debemos vestirnos bien.　　　　V　F

(Answers are on page 109.)

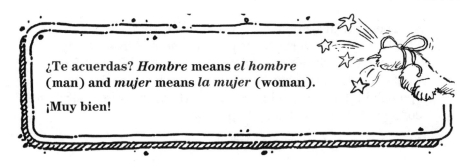

¿Te acuerdas? *Hombre* means *el hombre* (man) and *mujer* means *la mujer* (woman).

¡Muy bien!

### ¡OJO!—WATCH OUT!

*Lucir* in Spanish means *to look,* in the sense of *looking good*—the way you are dressed, your appearance, etc. *Looks* has of late been incorporated into the Spanish language and has the same meaning as in English.

# PIÉNSALO BIEN
# THINK IT THROUGH

## The verb, Part 1. El verbo, Parte 1

Here we are going to cover all that is important and basic about the Spanish verb.

We have already said that the verb is one of the most important parts of a sentence. It denotes action, or movement, just like the engine of a car. There are many similarities in the use of verbs between English and Spanish. Here are a few:

- They form the predicate.
- They are conjugated.
- They have different moods and tenses.
- The conjugation of each verb has six persons, three in the singular and three in the plural.
- They can be both regular and irregular.

There are also some basic differences. Here are a few:

Most Spanish verbs, in any tense, and referring to any person, have a different ending. This is quite different from English. In fact, verbs in English are much easier than in Spanish in that sense—let's take a verb, such as "to walk," and conjugate* it in English and Spanish:

*Conjugate means to change the ending of a verb.

| to walk | caminar |
|---|---|
| I walk | (yo) camino |
| you walk | (tú) caminas |
| he/she/it walks | (él/ella/usted) camina |
| we walk | (nosotros) caminamos |
| you walk | (vosotros) camináis |
| they walk | (ellos/ellas/ustedes) caminan |

In comparing both, notice that in English, you form the infinitive (name) of the verb by placing *to* before it. In the previous example, *to walk* is an English infinitive. The verb *caminar* is a Spanish infinitive. As you can see, each of the endings of the six persons is different, while in English the name of the verb, *walk*, remains invariable with the exception of the third person singular to which we add -*s*. On the other hand, in Spanish, there is really no need to use the personal pronouns since each ending tells us who the person is, except for the third person singular and plural. But there is more: In Spanish there are three main conjugations depending on the vowel used in the infinitive; those vowels can be *a*, *e*, or *i*, which are followed by the letter *r*; thus: *ar*, *er*, *ir*, as in *cant-ar* (to sing*)*, *com-er* (to eat*)*, *viv-ir* (to live). Let's conjugate the three verbs mentioned above in the three conjugations:

| **to sing** | **cant-ar** |
|---|---|
| I sing | (yo) cant-o |
| you sing | (tú) cant-as |
| he/she/it sings | (él/ella/usted) cant-a |
| we sing | (nosotros) cant-amos |
| you sing | (vosotros) cant-áis |
| they sing | (ellos/ellas/ustedes) cant-an |

| **to eat** | **com-er** |
|---|---|
| I eat | (yo) como |
| you eat | (tú) comes |
| he/she/it eats | (él/ella/usted) come |
| we eat | (nosotros) com-emos |
| you eat | (vosotros) com-éis |
| they eat | (ellos/ellas/ustedes) com-en |

| **to live** | **viv-ir** |
|---|---|
| I live | (yo) vivo |
| you live | (tú) vives |
| he/she/it lives | (él/ella/usted) vive |
| we live | (nosotros) viv-imos |
| you live | (vosotros) viv-ís |
| they live | (ellos/ellas/ustedes) viv-en |

Look at all the endings and you will notice that the main difference between each lies in the last vowel. With the exception of the *i* form, the last vowel for the first verb conjugation is *a*, for the second verb *e*, and for the third verb also *e*, excluding the *we* form and the *you* form in the plural, which is *i*. Notice that all the consonants following each of the vowels are the same for all three. Knowing this you will be able to conjugate any regular verb in the present tense. Just remember the vowels of each conjugation.

Now, to conjugate any verb in Spanish, once you know its infinitive (name), you must first separate the stem or root from the ending, as we did above, and then add to it the corresponding endings of the desired tense. This is for all of them.

# BRAIN TICKLERS
## Set # 20

### Ejercicios

A. Answer these questions in English: What are the three basic similarities between Spanish and English verbs?

B. Now write the most important difference between the two.

C. Conjugate the verb *caminar* in the present tense. When you are done, explain briefly the steps you took to do it.

(Answers are on page 109.)

## ¡OJO!—WATCH OUT!

In the previous conjugations you noticed the second person plural, or the *you* (*vosotros*) form. Today, many people leave it out, claiming that it is used only in Spain and there is really not a need for it. In a way this is true, and you have that option. However, keep in mind that this form is not used only in Spain but also in certain parts of South America, such as Argentina.

# The verb, Part 2. El verbo, Parte 2

## *Modos (Moods)*

There are four moods in Spanish:

| | |
|---|---|
| *Indicativo* | Indicative |
| *Potencial/Condicional* | Conditional |
| *Subjuntivo* | Subjunctive |
| *Imperativo* | Command/Imperative |

Why four?
Each of these moods has a purpose, a specific function:

- The indicative tells us what is, what is real.
- The conditional tells us what could be or should be.
- The subjunctive tells us what may be.
- The command tells someone to do something.

Of the four, the subjunctive is the one requiring the most attention, mainly because it is used in Spanish far more frequently than in English, and also because it has almost as many tenses as the indicative. The conditional* has only two tenses, and the command only one, which is always in the present. So, the two moods of greatest concern are the indicative and the subjunctive. The indicative has a total of 8 tenses, 4 simple and 4** compound. The subjunctive has a total of 6 tenses, 3 simple and 3 compound. In this lesson, we will cover only the indicative.

The 4 simple tenses of the indicative* are:

1. Present
2. Past or Preterite
3. Imperfect
4. Future

The 3 compound tenses** are:

1. Present perfect
2. Past perfect
3. Future perfect

(*) Some people make the conditional part of the indicative; others make it a separate mood. We prefer the latter.
(**) In this book we will use only 3, leaving out the Pretérito anterior, which is rarely used.

We already saw the present tense. With the past (preterite) tense, we have to go through the same process and separate the stem or root from the ending of the infinitive, to which the different past tenses are added. The endings of the past tense for all three conjugations are

| cant-ar (to sing) | com-er (to eat) | viv-ir (to live) |
|---|---|---|
| cant-é (I sang) | com-í (I ate) | viv-í (I lived) |
| cant-aste | com-iste | viv-iste |
| cant-ó | com-ió | viv-ió |
| cant-amos | com-imos | viv-imos |
| cant-asteis | com-isteis | viv-isteis |
| cant-aron | com-ieron | viv-ieron |

Notice that the endings of the -er and -ir verbs are the same. Also, the *you singular* forms end in *-ste* for all three conjugations; the *we* form ends in *-mos*; the *you plural* ends in *-steis*; and the *third plural* ends in *-ron*. In other words, the only difference is in the thematic vowel of the ending—a to i.

### OJO!—WATCH OUT!

A *simple tense* uses one conjugated verb; a *compound tense* uses two verbs, a conjugated one, which is called a helping or auxiliary verb, and a past participle, which is invariable. We will explain it further in lesson 13.

The endings for the imperfect tense are

| cant-ar | com-er | viv-ir |
|---|---|---|
| cant-aba (I sang) | com-ía (I ate) | viv-ía (I lived) |
| cant-abas | com-ías | viv-ías |
| cant-aba | com-ía | viv-ía |
| cant-ábamos | com-íamos | viv-íamos |
| cant-abais | com-íais | viv-íais |
| cant-aban | com-ían | viv-ían |

Notice that the endings of the -er and -ir verbs are identical. Also notice that the endings of the first and third person singular are the same in all three conjugations. The difference is determined in the context.

Looking at the conjugations of the past and the imperfect, you may become confused since both appear to mean the same in English. They do not. Here is the difference:

The past tense denotes a past action, which in the mind of the speaker is concluded, as in

*I played basketball yesterday.*

Here, the playing of basketball is an action with a definite end—yesterday.

However, in this other sentence

*I played basketball when I was in high school.*

the playing of basketball in the mind of the speaker is a continuous action with an indefinite ending. In other words, I played basketball for as long as I was in high school. Said differently, the playing of basketball is dependent upon my being in school. I could say it differently this way:

*I used to play basketball when I was in high school.*

When English and Spanish are compared in terms of the use of the imperfect, the difference is that in English the imperfect is implied, while in Spanish it is expressed by a specific tense that is different from the past tense. In English, the past tense is used for both, as in *played*. In other words, English has no imperfect tense.

Here is how we would say the sentences in Spanish:

*Jugué\* baloncesto ayer* (I played basketball yesterday).

*Jugaba baloncesto cuando estaba en la escuela secundaria* (I played/used to play basketball when I was in high school).

Many times, both the past and imperfect tenses are used in the same sentence:

While I (watched) was watching television, the phone rang.

Here, there are two expressed actions: one, *I watched/was watching television*, was in progress at the time; the other, *the phone rang*, occurred or took place. In Spanish, we would say

Mientras miraba la televisión sonó el teléfono.

\*The verb *jugar* is irregular in the past tense of the first person singular form; it doesn't follow the regular endings mentioned in the chart on page 92.

# BRAIN TICKLERS
## Set # 21

### Ejercicios

A. Answer these questions in English.
   1. How many moods are there in Spanish?
   2. For what specific purpose is the Indicative Mood used?
   3. Explain briefly what simple and compound tenses are.
B. Conjugate the verb trabajar in the imperfect tense.

(Answers are on page 109.)

# MÁS ES MEJOR
# MORE IS BETTER

## Nouns

| | |
|---|---|
| los zapatos | shoes |
| la blusa | blouse |
| la falda | skirt |
| el cinturón | belt |
| los calcetines | socks |
| las medias | stockings |
| la ropa interior | undergarments |
| el sombrero | hat |
| la gorra | cap |
| el suéter | sweater |
| la chaqueta | jacket |
| las botas | boots |
| las sandalias | sandals |
| los guantes | gloves |
| la bufanda | scarf |
| la talla | size (*la talla* is applied almost exclusively to clothes; otherwise it would be *el tamaño*) |
| la tintorería | dry cleaners |
| la lavandería | laundromat |
| las zapatillas | slippers |
| la camisa | shirt |
| el vestido | dress |

## Verbs

| | |
|---|---|
| llevar | to wear |
| ponerse | to put on |
| quitarse | to take off |
| probarse | to try on |
| abrochar | to fasten/button up |
| planchar | to iron |
| peinarse | to comb (one's hair) |
| cepillarse | to brush (one's hair) |
| maquillarse | to put on one's makeup |

**¿Cuánto sabes?**

Do you know what *quedar bien/mal* means?

It means to fit well/badly.

## El cuerpo humano (the human body)

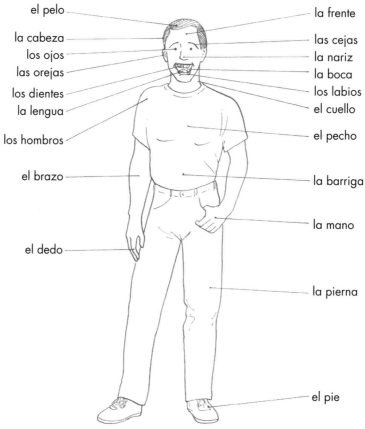

el pelo — la frente
la cabeza — las cejas
los ojos — la nariz
las orejas — la boca
los dientes — los labios
la lengua — el cuello
los hombros — el pecho
el brazo — la barriga
el dedo — la mano
la pierna
el pie

| | | | |
|---|---|---|---|
| la cabeza | head | las orejas | ears |
| el pelo | hair | el cuello | neck |
| la frente | forehead | los hombros | shoulders |
| los ojos | eyes | el pecho | chest |
| las cejas | eyebrows | el brazo | arm |
| la nariz | nose | la mano | hand |
| la boca | mouth | el dedo | finger |
| los labios | lips | la barriga | belly |
| los dientes | teeth | la pierna | leg |
| la lengua | tongue | el pie | foot |

# HABLA POPULAR
# EVERYDAY SPEECH

## Here are more idioms, expressions, and sayings.

| | |
|---|---|
| es decir | that's to say |
| por encima de todo | above all |
| siempre y cuando | provided |
| al contrario | to the contrary |
| por supuesto | of course |
| ¡manos a la obra! | let's get going! |
| ¡ni modo! | no way! |
| ¡adelante! | let's go!/let's move on! |
| no sólo de pan vive | man doesn't live by |
|    el hombre |    bread alone |
| la curiosidad mató al gato | curiosity killed the cat |

---

### ¿Sabías que?

The first European women and children arrived in North America in the expedition of Lucas Vázquez de Ayllón in 1512.

---

# BIEN VALE LA PENA
# IT'S WELL WORTH IT

## Telling the weather in Spanish

*Weather* in Spanish is *el tiempo*. This word, *tiempo*, as we saw earlier, is a problematic word for you because it can mean different things: time, hour, weather. When it refers to the time of the day, you already know that it is *hora*. When it refers to time in general, it is *el tiempo pasa muy rápido* (time goes by very fast), *en aquel tiempo yo era muy inocente* (at that time I was very innocent), *no me gusta perder el tiempo* (I don't like to waste time). *Tiempo* is also used with this same meaning in many expressions, such as: *a tiempo* (on time), *al mismo tiempo* (at the same time), *con tiempo* (in good time). It is also the word for weather, as in *¿Cuál es el tiempo para mañana?* (What's the weather for tomorrow?), *Con mal tiempo no podemos salir* (With bad weather we can't go out). However, when you use this word describing the condition of the weather, the verb to use is *hacer* and always in the third person singular> *hace*. For example:

## Question

*¿Qué tiempo hace hoy?* (What's the weather today?)

## Answer

*Hace frío.* (It is cold.)
*Hace calor.* (It is hot.)
*Hace viento.* (It is windy.)
*Hace sol.* (It is sunny.)

Notice that in English you use a totally different verb, also in the third person singular: *to be> it is*.

Of course, we can describe the weather in many other ways, saying, *It is raining, It is snowing, It is drizzling*. Here, as with the verb *hacer*, you also use the verb in the third person singular, and if you say it at the very same time that the weather condition is happening, you use the present participle to indicate that it is occurring as you speak. In such cases, the verb in Spanish is *estar*, plus the present participle, or you can simply use the main verb, to rain, to snow, to drizzle, in the third person singular. Here are some examples:

It is raining.   *Está lloviendo.* or *Llueve.* (from *llover*> to rain)
It is snowing.   *Está nevando.* or *Nieva.* (from *nevar*> to snow)
It is drizzling. *Está lloviznando.* or *Llovizna.*
    (from *lloviznar*> to drizzle)

Is there any difference between the verb itself in the third person singular and the use of the helping verb *to be* and the past participle?

Yes, there can be a difference, in this way:

It is raining.                  *Está lloviendo.* or *Llueve.*
In Florida it rains every day.  *En la Florida llueve todos los días.*

In other words, in Spanish *llueve* could mean that it is raining right now, or it can refer to a rainy condition unrelated to the time it is occurring. In English, you could say *It is raining* or *It rains*, but you would not say *Is it raining? Yes, it rains*. In Spanish, it is correct and it conveys the same meaning.

## Additional weather-related vocabulary

| | |
|---|---|
| la estación | season |
| la primavera | spring |
| el otoño | fall |
| el verano | summer |
| el invierno | winter |
| el clima | climate |
| el clima cálido | hot climate |
| el clima templado | mild climate |
| el clima frío | cold climate |
| la temperatura | temperature |
| el pronóstico del tiempo | weather forecast |
| la condición del tiempo | weather condition |
| el buen tiempo | good weather |
| el mal tiempo | bad weather |
| el hielo | ice |
| la niebla/la neblina | fog/mist |
| el rayo | bolt/ray |
| el relámpago | bolt of lightning |
| la atmósfera | atmosphere |
| la humedad | humidity |
| nublado | cloudy |
| húmedo | humid |
| lluvioso | rainy |
| nevoso | snowy |
| soleado | sunny |
| la nevada | snowfall |
| el copo de nieve | snowflake |
| la gota de lluvia | raindrop |
| el huracán | hurricane |
| la tempestad | storm |
| la brisa | breeze |

| | |
|---|---|
| el ventarrón | strong wind |
| aclarar | to clear up |
| escampar | to stop raining |
| mojarse | to get wet |
| empaparse | to get soaked |
| helarse | to freeze (over) |
| nublarse | to get cloudy |
| la bola de nieve | snowball |
| el hombre de nieve | snowman |
| claro | clear |
| obscuro (or oscuro) | dark |

## ¡OJO!—WATCH OUT!

*Llover* and *nevar* are irregular verbs in the present indicative and also in the present subjunctive:

| Present indicative | | Present subjunctive |
|---|---|---|
| *llover* | *llueve* | *llueva* |
| *nevar* | *nieva* | *nieve* |

However, the present participle is regular for both: *llover> lloviendo, nevar> nevando*, and so are the past participles: *llover> llovido, nevar> nevado*. With the present participle, as we said, you use *estar* as a helping verb, *está lloviendo, está nevando*, always in the third person singular. The past participle is always used with *haber* to form the present perfect, also the third person singular: *ha llovido* (it has rained), *ha nevado* (it has snowed). No matter what the verb tense is, whether simple or compound, the third person singular form is always used: *habrá llovido* (it will have rained), *había llovido* (it had rained), etc.

**Important note:** *Calor* (heat) is a noun, not an adjective, which is *caliente* (hot), as in: *El café está caliente* (The coffee is hot). Here's an example of *calor* used as a noun:

*No me gusta el calor.* (I don't like the heat.)

# BRAIN TICKLERS
## *Set # 22*

### *Ejercicios*

A. Traduca la palabra o las palabras entre paréntesis:

1. No me gusta el día porque (it is not sunny).

2. Cuando fui a Chicago (it was very windy).

3. Es una lástima; en estos momentos (it is raining).

4. En el Polo Norte siempre (it snows).

5. En Boston hace tanto (wind) como en Chicago.

B. Match the descriptions in column A with the word/words in column B:

| Column A | Column B |
|---|---|
| 1. Cuando el cielo se obscurece (*or* escurece) y no hace sol | a. abril |
| | b. nublado |
| 2. Es la época del año cuando más llueve | c. hace viento |
| | d. el paraguas |
| 3. Cuando uno se quema mucho por estar bajo él | e. el sol |
| 4. Quiere decir *it is windy* en español | |
| 5. Lo que usamos para protegernos de la lluvia | |

C. Contesta estas preguntas en oraciones completas:

1. ¿Qué te gusta más, cuando hace frío o cuando hace calor?

2. ¿Cómo es el clima donde tú vives?

3. ¿Tú miras el pronóstico del tiempo en la televisión todos los días? ¿A qué hora?

4. ¿Está nevando ahora?

(Answers are on page 109.)

### ¡OJO!—WATCH OUT!

*Cuánto* means how much, in the singular, and how many, in the plural. Used as an adjective, it must agree in gender and number with the noun, as in: *¿Cuántos libros hay en la mesa?* (How many books are on the table?) *¿Cuántas casas hay en esa cuadra?* (How many houses are on that block?) But, *¿Cuánto dinero tienes?* (How much money do you have?)

# DILO COMO YO
# SAY IT LIKE I DO

## Pronunciation of the *g, j*

The *j*, in combination with any of the five vowels, is always pronounced similarly to the *h* in *ham*, although not as strong, and without the aspiration typical of the English sound. It is never pronounced like the *j* in *jam* or *jelly*. Examples of the *j* in Spanish are *jamón* (ham), *jardín*, *jefe*, *joya*.

The *g* has the same sound as the *j* followed by the vowels *e* and *i*, as in *gente*, *gigante*. With the other three vowels, *a, o, u*, it is pronounced like the English *g* in *goat*, as in *gato*, *gota*, *gusto*. Problems with pronunciation usually occur with vowel sounds. Practice, Practice, Practice. When the *g* is followed by *u* and the vowels *e* and *i* > *gue, gui*, the *u* is never pronounced, unless it has a diaeresis over it, as in *agüita*, *güiro*; otherwise it would sound like a *j*. The diaeresis is the two dots placed over the "u" indicating its usual pronunciation.

## Pronunciation of the double consonants *ch, ll, rr*

These are the only double consonants in Spanish that cannot be separated. They form one letter and one sound.

The *ch* is pronounced similarly to the English *ch* in *chocolate*, although not as explosive: *noche, chaleco*.

The *ll* is generally pronounced like the English *y* in *yes*. There are variations in Spain and other Spanish-speaking countries (Peru, Bolivia). It is never pronounced as it is in English as two *ls*. Examples: *caballo, pollo*.

The *rr* is the pronunciation to watch, but for speakers of English, it is very hard. Nonetheless, even if you mispronounce it, you will be understood, unless it happens to be a word such as *pero* (but), which can also be *perro* (dog), or *caro* (expensive), which can also be *carro* (car), leading to some confusion. The *rr* is always trilled, as in *burro*; the *r* also is trilled at the beginning of a word or following *n*, as in: *rama* and *honra*.

---

**¿Sabías que?**

*El sistema métrico* (metric system) is used throughout the Hispanic world and in most countries (except the United States). It is applied to measurements based on meters, grams, and liters.

---

# BRAIN TICKLERS
### *Set # 23*

### *Ejercicios*

A. Say these words out loud:

| | |
|---|---|
| general | Camagüey |
| gitano | góndola |
| guitarra | guagua |
| joven | jirafa |

B. Answer these questions in English:

1. In Spanish when is the *g* pronounced like *j*?
2. What is the purpose of the *u* in the combinations *gue* and *gui*?
3. What is a diaeresis?

(Answers are on page 110.)

---

**¿Sabías que?**

You will be surprised at the new Spanish word for *blue jean*. Any guesses? It is *bluyín*, a Spanish phonetic transcription based exactly on its English pronunciation. That proves how popular the term has become worldwide! For some it continues to be *vaqueros* (cowboys), but it doesn't even come close in popularity to the other.

---

# ALMA HISPÁNICA
# HISPANIC SOUL

## Azorín

*Azorín* was his pseudonym; his real name was José Martínez Ruiz, a great contemporary Spanish writer and essayist, a key figure of the famous *Generación del 98*. He saw the little things in life that are common and ordinary, that we seldom notice or pay attention to, and wrote about them in a wonderful, poignant, and simple style. He was also a penetrating, profound observer of Spanish history and culture who helped us understand and appreciate it better. He wrote about many of the Spanish classics, including Miguel de Cervantes and his *Don Quijote*. His essay, *El artista y el estilo* (The Artist and Style) is a must-read for those interested in stylistics. His book *Castilla* describes the landscape, cities, and people of Old Castile, a region of Spain he loved dearly. He was born in Alicante in 1873 and died in Madrid in 1967. If you are interested in knowing and understanding the true Spanish soul throughout the ages, Azorín is the source.

## The writing of Azorín

This is an excerpt from his book *Castilla*. Azorín describes in his unique style a little town in Old Castile.

En la plaza de la ciudad se levanta un *caserón* de piedra; cuatro grandes balcones se abren en la fachada. Sobre la puerta, resalta un recio *blasón*. En el primer balcón de la izquierda se ve sentado en un sillón un hombre; su cara está pálida, *exangüe*, y remata en una *barbita* afilada y gris. Los ojos de este *caballero* están *velados* por una profunda tristeza; el *codo* lo tiene el caballero puesto en el brazo del sillón y su cabeza descansa en la *palma de la mano*.

To help you better understand this passage, here is the meaning of some key words:

| | |
|---|---|
| *caserón* | big house |
| *blasón* | coat of arms |
| *exangüe* | exhausted |
| *barbita* | little beard |
| *caballero* | gentleman |
| *velados* | fogged |
| *codo* | elbow |
| *palma de la mano* | palm of his hand |

# PLUMA EN MANO
# PEN IN HAND

## La moda de hoy/Today's fashion

Toda época tiene su moda propia que trata de ser distinta de las demás. La de estos tiempos, tal como la vemos a diario, es la que podríamos llamar a lo que salga (whatever works) y lo más barato y cómodo. Los grandes modistos italianos y las finas telas inglesas son para una minoría selecta, para la gente de posición (people of means) y para los que cuentan con tiempo suficiente. Parte también de la moda actual, al menos (at least) en la mujer, tira a (leans toward) lo natural y lo ligero. Las telas de más uso parecen ser (seem to be) el algodón, la seda y la lana y también el cuero, principalmente en las chaquetas y abrigos. En cuanto a las tallas, las más comunes son las medianas y grandes. Referente a los precios, y como casi toda la ropa está hecha en la China, son por lo general asequibles, aunque siempre hay que saber (one must know) dónde comprar para no gastarse una millonada. Las tiendas de descuento son las más baratas y populares pero no siempre las más atractivas.

## BRAIN TICKLERS
### Set # 24

### *Ejercicios*

A. Contesta estas preguntas en oraciones completas:

1. ¿Qué piensas (think) tú de la moda de hoy?

2. ¿Cuentas tú con tiempo y dinero suficientes para vestirte bien?

3. ¿Cuál es tu talla en zapatos y pantalones?

4. ¿Qué clase de telas te gustán más?

B. En no más de tres oraciones, describe la ropa que tienes puesta (llevas) hoy.

(Answers are on page 110.)

---

### ¡OJO!—WATCH OUT!

Is there a difference between the Spanish words *aun* and *aún* and *solo* and *sólo*? Yes, there is a difference:

*aun*, without an accent mark, is an adverb and means *even*, as in: *aun así, lo llamaré* (even so, I will call him).

*aún*, with an accent mark, is also an adverb, but it means *still*, as in: *aún está trabajando* (he's still working).

*solo*, without an accent mark, is an adjective and means *alone*, as in: *Me siento solo* (I feel alone).

*sólo*, with an accent mark, is an adverb and means *only*, as in: *Yo sólo hablo inglés* (I speak only English).

---

# ASÍ SOMOS
# THIS IS WHO WE ARE

## The Hispanic heritage of the United States

To most people the Western Hemisphere is divided into two main parts: the English to the north, and the Spanish to the south. The one to the north is called America, and the one to the south, South America or Latin America.

After the discovery of America, and for the next 100 years, America was called the Indies. What is called today a state, such as Louisiana or Florida, was then called a country, an immense piece of land with no known boundaries, and covering a big chunk of North America, extending all the way down to the Strait of Magellan. That vast territory, even Brazil for some time, was under Spanish domain. Then, after those first 100 years, other

Europeans arrived—the English, Dutch, and also the French, to the northeast, and the Russians to the northwest. The Dutch left quickly, the French stayed a bit longer, and the British longer than the French. The country that stayed the longest, up to 1812, to be precise, was Spain—almost 300 years. But if we count Mexico, which was part of Spain until it became independent in 1821, and the vast territory it possessed in the Southwest and ceded to the United States in 1848, and Cuba and Puerto Rico, which were also part of Spain until 1898, the Spanish presence in America lasted more than 406 years, counting from the year of discovery.

¿Sabías que? **Some of the Spanish firsts in North America:**

- **First European flag (Castile and León) carried by Juan Ponce de León in 1513 when he landed in Florida. In fact, it is considered the first U.S. flag.**
- **First European language, Spanish.**
- **First colony, San Miguel de Guadalupe, founded in 1526 by Lucas Vázquez de Ayllón, on a site 32 miles from the second colony, Jamestown, founded by the British 95 years later.**
- **First city, San Augustín (Saint Augustine) in Florida, founded by Pedro Menéndez de Avilés in 1565.**
- **First printing press established in Mexico by Juan Pablos in 1535, and the first book published in that year by the same person.**
- **First universities, Santo Tomás de Aquino, founded in the Dominican Republic in 1538, and the University of Mexico, founded in 1551, 85 years before Harvard, and 195 years before Princeton.**
- **First to discover the Pacific Ocean, the Gulf of Mexico (called earlier the Spanish Sea), and the Caribbean Sea.**

# BRAIN TICKLERS—THE ANSWERS

## Set # 19, page 86

**A.** Answers will vary.

**B.**
1. F    2. F    3. V

## Set # 20, page 90

**Piénsalo bien**

**A.** Answers will vary.

**B.** Answers will vary.

**C.**

| | |
|---|---|
| camino | caminamos |
| caminas | camináis |
| camina | caminan |

Answers will vary.

## Set # 21, page 94

**A.**
1. 4
2. what is, what's real
3. Single tense uses one conjugated verb; compound tense uses two verbs.

**B.**

| | |
|---|---|
| trabajaba | trabajábamos |
| trabajabas | trabajabais |
| trabajaba | trabajaban |

## Set # 22, page 101

**A.**
1. no está soleado
2. hacía mucho viento
3. está lloviendo
4. nieva
5. viento

**B.**

1. b    2. a    3. e    4. c    5. d

**C.**

Answers will vary.

## Set # 23, page 103

**A.** Pronunciation

**B.**

1. when followed by "e" or "i"

2. so it doesn't sound as in "ge" "gi"

3. the two dots over the "u"

## Set # 24, page 106

**Pluma en mano**

**A.** Answers will vary.

**B.** Answers will vary.

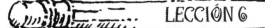

# Estudiamos para mejorar nuestra condición humana

# We study to become better people

¿Para qué estudiamos? Lo hacemos para *aprender*, para adquirir *conocimientos*, para ampliar nuestros horizontes, para honrar a nuestra familia y a nuestro nombre, para *mejorar de posición* y *llevar una vida* más *segura y cómoda*. Lo hacemos también para humanizarnos, para ser más comprensivos y nobles, para ser más personas. No lo hacemos, o no deberíamos hacerlo, *por el mero afán* de *ganar dinero* y adquirir y poseer cosas.

*Hace muchos años* sólo *asistía a* la universidad el que tenía vocación y capacidad en algún *campo del saber*. Hoy, *afortunadamente*, las *puertas* de las universidades están abiertas de *par en par* para acoger a toda persona que quiera estudiar sin tener necesariamente una vocación definida. Eso, por lo general, *viene después*, cuando el estudiante adquiere más conciencia de lo que quiere *llegar a ser* el día de mañana, de cuál *habrá de ser* su carrera profesional.

## Vocabulario básico

| | |
|---|---|
| aprender | to learn |
| conocimientos | knowledge |
| mejorar de posición | better our position |
| llevar una vida | lead a life |
| segura y cómoda | secure and comfortable |
| por el mero afán | just to/merely to |
| ganar dinero | to earn money |
| Hace muchos años | Long ago |
| asistía a | attended |
| campo del saber | field of knowledge |
| afortunadamente | fortunately |
| puertas | doors |
| par en par | wide open |
| viene después | comes later |
| llegar a ser | to become |
| habrá de ser | will be |

# BRAIN TICKLERS
### Set # 25

*Ejercicios*

A. Fill in the blanks, choosing the appropriate word(s) from the list below. You may need a Spanish/English dictionary or computer.

| | |
|---|---|
| asistir | beca |
| llegar a ser | escuela |
| ganar | costo |
| estudiar | estudios |
| bachillerato | |

Yo **1** _____ a una universidad en el sur de California.

Yo **2** _____ pues quiero **3** _____ un/una maestro/a. Cuando estaba en el segundo año de

**4** _____ me gané una **5** _____ de $5,000 de

mi **6** _____ Thomas Jefferson. Así el **7** _____

de mis **8** _____ será más económico.

B. The following verbs are all regular. Translate the words in parentheses using the correct form of the present tense:

1. Ellos (estudiar) italiano.

2. Nosotros (aprender) mucho en la escuela.

3. Ella no (ganar) lo suficiente.

4. Yo (llegar) siempre tarde (late) al trabajo.

C. Look at all these academic subjects in Spanish and write the English equivalent. Notice the similarity between the Spanish and English.

1. las matemáticas
2. la arquitectura
3. la ingeniería
4. la sociología
5. el cálculo
6. la historia
7. las ciencias políticas
8. las ciencias sociales
9. la filosofía
10. el arte

11. la medicina
12. las leyes/el derecho
13. la geografía
14. la psicología
15. el comercio
16. la biología
17. la economía
18. la literatura
19. la química
20. la astronomía

(Answers are on page 139.)

## ¡OJO!—WATCH OUT!

*To attend,* as you have seen, in the sense of attending school, is not *atender* in Spanish, which means something totally different. In this case, you must use *asistir.* Also, *bachillerato* is the name in Spanish for high school. It is not bachelor. And *colegio* is not college, but school, either primary or secondary. The word in Spanish for college is *universidad.* Campus is *recinto universitario,* although you can use campus in Spanish as well since it happens to be a Latin word, but with a different meaning of open space or field.

# PIÉNSALO BIEN
# THINK IT THROUGH

## The verb, Part 3. El verbo, Parte 3

Here you will learn about the future and conditional tenses and reflexive verbs. We will also explain the subjunctive and the command.

The future and conditional are the only tenses in Spanish formed by keeping the infinitive form of the verbs as is, without removing their respective endings. In other words, here you do not have to worry about the stem or root; you add the future and conditional endings to the whole infinitive, so the endings are the same for all three conjugations.

The endings for the future are

*-é, -ás, -á, -emos, -éis, -án.*

| **caminar** | **vender** | **escribir** |
|---|---|---|
| *caminaré* (I will walk) | *venderé* (I will sell) | *escribiré* (I will write) |

Notice how the ending *-é* is added to the whole infinitive of all three verbs. Notice also the accent mark on all endings with the exception of the "we" form.

For the conditional simple, we follow the same process, adding the endings to the infinitive of all three conjugations.

The endings for the conditional are

*-ía, -ías, -ía, -íamos, -íais, -ían* (which are the same for the imperfect verbs that end in *-er* or *-ir*, as we saw previously).

| **caminar** | **vender** | **escribir** |
|---|---|---|
| *caminaría* | *vendería* | *escribiría* |
| (I would walk) | (I would sell) | (I would write) |

You can look at it this way: The future endings correspond to the English *will*, and the conditional endings correspond to the English *would*.

The reflexive verb means, simply, that the subject performs the action and receives it at the same time, as in a boomerang—you throw it and it comes right back to you. Both Spanish and English have reflexive verbs, the only difference being that in

English it is mostly implied, while in Spanish it is expressed. If I say *I wash my hands*, it is implied that I am the one doing and receiving the action. It would be uncommon for me to say *I wash my hands myself*, for it is implied that you yourself do it. In Spanish we would have to say *me lavo las manos*, from the infinitive *lavarse*. The *me* is the reflexive pronoun, and the *se* at the end of the infinitive denotes that the verb is reflexive. However, using that same verb, *lavar*, I could also say *lavo el carro*, in which case I perform the action but it is received by the car, not by me.

The reflexive pronouns in Spanish are

| | | |
|---|---|---|
| *me* | myself | |
| *te* | yourself | (use for the familiar singular) |
| *se* | himself, herself, itself | (also use for the polite singular) |
| *nos* | ourselves | |
| *os* | yourselves | (also use for the familiar plural) |
| *se* | themselves | (also use for the polite plural) |

## Positioning of the reflexive pronouns

If it is a conjugated verb, put the reflexive pronoun before the verb, *me lavo las manos* (I wash my hands).

If it is an infinitive or a present participle, put it before the first verb or attached to the main verb,
*me voy a lavar las manos* ( I am going to wash my hands), *voy a lavarme las manos* (same)
*me estoy lavando las manos* (I am washing my hands), *estoy lavándome las manos* (same).

If it is a compound tense, put it before the helping verb, *me he lavado las manos* (I have washed my hands).

The same reflexive pronouns are also used in reciprocal verbs, as in *nos escribimos a menudo* (we write to each other often), *se hablan todos los días* (they speak to each other every day). As we will see later, in the case of the command, all reflexive pronouns are attached to the verb, as in *¡lávate las manos!* (wash your hands!).

## The subjunctive

The subjunctive is really the mood of choice in Spanish, and it is used much more frequently than in English. It expresses life as it should be, rather than as it is, as Don Quijote felt it.

The typical use of the subjunctive in Spanish requires two subjects and two verbs. The first verb expresses any of the following: hope, desire, possibility, doubt, preference, request, fear, sorrow, among others, and, when this happens, the second verb is always used in the subjunctive, as in:

> *Espero que Manuel vaya a la fiesta* (I hope (that) Manuel goes to the party).
> *Es probable que Manuel vaya a la fiesta* (It's probable that Manuel will go to the party).
> *Dudo que Manuel vaya a la fiesta* (I doubt that Manuel will go to the party).

All of the three sentences show:

two subjects (Manuel and I)
two verbs (to hope and to go: *esperar* and *ir*)
something that is not certain, but rather a hope, a probability, a doubt
the use of *que*

You could also say that you need two clauses, the second one depending on the first. The first clause takes the indicative, and the second the subjunctive.

This is the perfect formula in Spanish for the use of the subjunctive. Again, let's put it this way: We all look at life in two different ways: 1. what to us is certain, real, factual as in *I see the tree, tomorrow is my birthday*; and 2. what we wished or hoped would be true and real, as in *I hope she loves me, I wish she would look at me*. In English, the subjunctive is expressed in numerous ways; it is rather implied than expressed with specific verb tenses, which is quite opposite to Spanish. In Spanish, we have specific subjunctive tenses and a formula that is easy to follow, as indicated above.

Let's go back to the two verbs, and here is the other formula:

- If the first verb (main clause) is in the present or future, the second verb (second clause) takes the present subjunctive.

- If the first verb is in the preterite, the imperfect, or the conditional, the second verb takes the imperfect subjunctive.

There are other verb tenses in the main clause that would take either the present or imperfect subjunctive, but let's leave that out for now.

Let's give some examples of the first two:

*Quiero que María me llame* (I want Maria to call me).
*Espero que Bernardo salga bien del examen* (I hope [that] Bernard passes the exam).

*Quería que María me llamara* (I wanted Maria to call me).
*Esperaba que Bernardo saliera bien del examen* (I hoped that Bernard had passed the exam).

This would work both in affirmative and negative expressions, as in

*No quiero que María me llame* (I don't want Maria to call me).
*No espero que María me llame* (I don't expect Maria to call me).

*No quise/quería que María me llamara* (I didn't want Maria to call me).
*No esperé/esparaba que María me llamara* (I didn't expect Maria to call me).

Finally, the subjunctive is also used with certain expressions not requiring two subjects or two verbs. Some examples are:

*Es una lástima que no pueda ir* (It is a pity I can't go).
*¡Ojalá que pueda ir!* (I hope/wish I can go!)
*Es necesario que Roberto lo haga* (It's necessary for Robert to do it).
*Es probable que llueva mañana* (It's probable that it will rain tomorrow).

Notice that in all of these sentences *que* is also used.

In the previous chapter we said that the subjunctive has a total of 6 tenses, 3 simple and 3 compound. So far, we have seen 2 simple ones: the present and imperfect. Of the compound ones, the only ones that should concern us are the present perfect and the past perfect, which we will cover in Lesson 13 along with the other compound tenses of the indicative.

Endings of the present and imperfect subjunctive for the three types of verbs:

## Present

| AR | ER | IR |
|------|-------|-------|
| -e | -a | -a |
| -es | -as | -as |
| -e | -a | -a |
| -emos | -amos | -amos |
| -éis | -áis | -áis |
| -en | -an | -an |

Notice that for the ER verbs and IR verbs, the endings are the same. Notice also that in the AR, the vowel is *e* while in the ER/IR the vowel is *a*. Also notice, as with the indicative, the use of the same letters after the *e* or *a*.

## Imperfect

| AR | ER | IR |
|--------|---------|---------|
| -ara | -iera | -iera |
| -aras | -ieras | -ieras |
| -ara | -iera | -iera |
| -áramos | -iéramos | -iéramos |
| -arais | -ierais | -ierais |
| -aran | -ieran | -ieran |

Notice the switch of the vowels from the *e* to the *a* in the AR of the present and imperfect, and that the endings of the ER and IR are the same, and so are the letters after the *a* and the *e*.

The command is another troublesome mood in Spanish. First, you have the affirmative and negative command; second, it has only five persons minus the *I* form; third, the only true command forms are the *you* familiar singular and the *you* familiar plural; the other three are taken from the subjunctive, which has only one tense, the present. Let's see an example using the verb *cantar*:

| | |
|---|---|
| canta | command form |
| cante | subjunctive form |
| cantemos | subjunctive form |
| cantad | command form |
| canten | subjunctive form |

### ¡OJO!—WATCH OUT!

As with many other tenses, verbs in the subjunctive can be regular or irregular. A good tip to remember is that, usually, when a verb is irregular in the first person of the indicative, it will also be irregular in the present subjunctive. Not only that, but the other five persons of the subjunctive will follow the same irregular form. Let's take these verbs as examples, *tener* and *hacer*:

| | **Present Indicative** | **Present Subjunctive** |
|---|---|---|
| tener | tengo | tenga |
| | tienes | tengas |
| | tiene | tenga |
| | tenemos | tengamos |
| | tenéis | tengáis |
| | tienen | tengan |
| hacer | hago | haga |
| | haces | hagas |
| | hace | haga |
| | hacemos | hagamos |
| | hacéis | hagáis |
| | hacen | hagan |

For the negative command, all of the forms are taken from the subjunctive. The negative *no* always precedes the verb, as in *no cantes*. All pronouns: reflexive, direct, and indirect objects, are always attached to all affirmative forms of the verb, as in

| | |
|---|---|
| *¡Lávate!* | Wash (yourself)! |
| *¡Dame!* | Give me! |
| *¡Dámelo!* | Give it to me! |

For the negative command, the order is
negative + pronoun + verb, as in

*¡No te laves!*      Don't wash (yourself)!

Therefore, in the affirmative, the pronouns are attached to the verb. In the negative, they are placed between the *no* and the verb.

All of the negative command forms are taken from the subjunctive, as in

| | | |
|---|---|---|
| *¡No cantes!* | Don't sing! | you, familiar singular |
| *¡No cante!* | Don't sing! | you, formal singular |
| *¡No cantemos!* | Let's not sing! | we |
| *¡No cantéis!* | Don't sing! | you, familiar plural |
| *¡No canten!* | Don't sing! | you, formal plural |

**Note:** In most of Hispanic America the *you* formal plural is the same as the *you* familiar plural; in other words, there is only one form for both. In Spain they use both forms.

You must also be aware that many verbs in the command are irregular, especially verbs such as:

*ir, hacer, poner, salir,* and *ser* in the affirmative informal both singular and plural, as in

| | | |
|---|---|---|
| *ir* | | |
| *¡Ve!* | Go! | you, familiar singular |
| *¡Vayan!* | Go! | you, both formal and informal plural |
| *hacer* | | |
| *¡Haz!* | Do/Make! | you, familiar singular |
| *¡Hagan!* | Do/Make! | you, both formal and informal plural |
| *poner* | | |
| *¡Pon!* | Put! | you, familiar singular |
| *¡Pongan!* | Put! | you, both formal and informal plural |
| *salir* | | |
| *¡Sal!* | Leave! | you, familiar singular |
| *¡Salgan!* | Leave! | you, both formal and informal plural |
| *ser* | | |
| *¡Sé!* | Be! | you, familiar singular |
| *¡Sean!* | Be! | you, both formal and informal plural |

The following pointers may prove useful in using the command forms.

## Formal affirmative singular and plural commands

correspond to the same forms of the subjunctive, as in:

| | |
|---|---|
| *¡Hable primero con la maestra!* | Talk with the teacher first! |
| *¡Vayan después al parque!* | Go to the park later! |

## Informal affirmative singular commands

correspond to the third person singular of the indicative, as in:

| | |
|---|---|
| *¡Estudia!* | Study! |
| *¡Come!* | Eat! |

The *we* form corresponds to the *we* form of the subjunctive, as in:

| | |
|---|---|
| *¡Salgamos a pasear!* | Let's go out for a walk! |
| *¡Escribamos el ejercicio!* | Let's write the exercise! |

As for the negative, the informal singular and plural forms correspond to the present subjunctive, as in:

| | |
|---|---|
| *¡No corras tanto!* | Don't run so much! |
| *¡No hagan eso!* | Don't do that! |

# BRAIN TICKLERS
### Set # 26

### Ejercicios

A. Completa los espacios en blanco con el presente de subjuntivo según (according to) el verbo que se da (that is given) en paréntesis:

1. Deseo que Ana (lavar) _____ el carro.

2. No es seguro que mi padre (trabajar) _____ mañana.

3. Te ruego (I beg you) que lo (escribir) _____ ahora.

4. ¡Ojalá que ellos (hablar) _____ con el maestro!

**123**

5. Es verdad que hoy (ser) _____ martes.

*(No. 5 is tricky. Is it real? Or is it how something should be? Real—use indicative, should be—use subjunctive.)*

B. Answer if *true* (V) or *false* (F). The statements are given in English.

1. The subjunctive is used more frequently in Spanish than in English.                                    V    F

2. Compared to the indicative, the subjunctive expresses general emotions rather than facts.    V    F

3. The typical subjunctive construction in Spanish requires only one subject and one verb.             V    F

4. The subjunctive is used only in affirmative expressions and never in negative ones.            V    F

5. The relative pronoun *que* is generally used in all subjunctive constructions.                            V    F

C. Completa los espacios en blanco con la forma correcta del imperativo familiar (familiar command) según se da en paréntesis:

1. Emilio, (study!) ¡_____ para el examen!

2. María, (buy it! – a dress) ¡_____ en esa tienda!

3. ¡Por qué están sentados! (Let's dance!) ¡_____!

4. Josefina y Magdalena, (speak!) ¡_____ con el profesor!

5. Ustedes no tienen que escribir la composición. (Don't write it!) ¡_____!

(Answers are on page 139.)

## ¡OJO!—WATCH OUT!

The use of the pronoun *se* and a verb in the third person also indicates that the action is not attributed to a determined subject, but that it is impersonal, as in *Se dice que el profesor renunció* (It is said that the professor resigned).

Regarding transitive and intransitive verbs, a transitive verb always takes a direct object to complete the meaning, while the intransitive doesn't. Here is an example:

## Transitive verb

*Compré un vestido para mi madre.* (I bought a dress for my mother.) Here, *comprar* (to buy) is a transitive verb because it takes a direct object, which is *vestido* (dress).

## Intransitive verb

*Juan salió tarde.* (John left late.) Here, there is no direct object.

# MÁS ES MEJOR
# MORE IS BETTER

## Nouns

| | |
|---|---|
| la clase | class |
| la sala de clase | classroom |
| el curso | course |
| la asignatura | subject |
| la tarea | homework |
| el horario | schedule |
| la prueba | test |
| el libro | book |
| el estudiante | student |
| el maestro | teacher |
| el profesor/la profesora | professor |
| el ejercicio | exercise |
| el examen | exam |
| el libro de texto | textbook |
| la nota | grade |
| la matrícula | tuition/registration |
| el título | title |
| el lápiz | pencil |
| la pluma | pen |
| el bolígrafo | ballpoint pen |
| la pizarra | chalkboard |

| | |
|---|---|
| el pupitre | student's desk |
| el repaso | review |
| los apuntes | notes |

## Verbs

| | |
|---|---|
| aprender | to learn |
| aprobar | to approve |
| suspender | to fail (an exam, etc.) |
| pasar | to pass |
| graduarse | to graduate |
| repasar | to review |
| inscribirse/matricularse | to register/enroll |
| entender/comprender | to understand |
| repetir | to repeat |
| leer | to read |
| escribir | to write |
| tomar notas/apuntes | to take notes |
| explicar | to explain |

# HABLA POPULAR
# EVERYDAY SPEECH

## Here are more idioms, expressions, and sayings:

| | |
|---|---|
| hasta la fecha | up to now |
| en lo sucesivo | hereafter |
| de suerte que | so that |
| dejar tranquilo/en paz | to leave alone/not to bother |
| con mucho gusto | gladly |
| a través de | through/throughout |
| a fin de que | so that |
| a fin de cuentas | in the final analysis |
| por si las moscas | just in case |
| sin ton ni son/sin comerlo ni beberlo | for no reason |
| Dime con quién andas y te diré quién eres. | You're judged by the company you keep. |

# BIEN VALE LA PENA
# IT'S WELL WORTH IT

## Profesiones (professions)

| | |
|---|---|
| el médico/la médica | physician, doctor |
| el/la abogado/a | lawyer, attorney |
| el/la arquitecto/a | architect |
| el/la ingeniero/a | engineer |
| el/la psiquiatra | psychiatrist |
| el/la psicólogo/a | psychologist |
| el/la dentista | dentist |
| el/la periodista | journalist |
| el/la publicitario/a | publicist |
| el/la artista | artist |
| el/la técnico/a de computadoras | computer technician |
| el/la programador/a de computadoras | computer programmer |
| el/la diplomático/a | diplomat |
| el/la contador/a | accountant |
| el/la farmacéutico/a | pharmacist |
| el/la diseñador/a | designer |
| el/la juez | judge |
| la/el secretaria/o | secretary |
| la/el enfermera/o | nurse |
| el/la maestro/a | teacher |
| el/la empresario/a | businessperson |
| el/la ejecutivo/a | executive |
| el/la bibliotecario/a | librarian |
| el/la arqueólogo/a | archeologist |
| el/la científico/a | scientist |
| el/la astronauta | astronaut |
| el/la funcionario/a público/a | public official |
| el/la escritor/a | writer |
| el/la agente de bienes raíces | real estate broker |
| el/la editor/a | editor, publisher |
| el/la modisto/a | fashion designer |

## Telling the time in Spanish

Key words you should know:

| | |
|---|---|
| la hora | time/hour |
| el minuto | minute |
| el segundo | second |
| y | plus |
| menos | to (or minus) |
| el cuarto | quarter |
| quince | fifteen |
| en punto | o'clock sharp |
| pasada/pasadas | past |
| media | half |
| treinta | thirty |
| son las/es la | it is |
| el reloj | watch/clock |
| el reloj de pulsera | wristwatch |
| el reloj de pared | wall clock |
| el reloj despertador | alarm clock |
| la aguja del reloj | hand of the clock |
| el minutero | minute hand |
| el segundero | second hand |
| am (de la mañana) | A.M. |
| pm (de la tarde) | P.M. |

### Questions

| | |
|---|---|
| ¿Qué hora es? | What time is it? |
| ¿A qué hora…? | At what time…? |

Notice the use of *hora* for time. *Hora* means hour, not time. In both instances, *¿Qué hora es?* and *¿A qué hora?* you always reply this way:

With any time, **except one**, you say:

*son las/a las*    it is/at

Referring to **one only**, you say:

*es la/a la*    it is/at

Some examples:

| | |
|---|---|
| *María, ¿qué hora es?* | Mary, what time is it? |
| *Son las cuatro en punto.* | It is four o'clock. |
| *Juan, ¿qué hora es?* | John, what time is it? |

| | |
|---|---|
| *Es la una en punto.* | It is one o'clock. |
| *Pedro, ¿a qué hora vas a la escuela?* | Peter, at what time do you go to school? |
| *Voy a las ocho de la mañana.* | I go at eight in the morning. |
| *Rosa, ¿a qué hora vas al trabajo hoy?* | Rose, at what time do you go to work today? |
| *Voy a la una de la tarde.* | I go at one in the afternoon. |

Notice the use of *¿A qué hora?* in the question, meaning *At what time?*, and how you answer: *a la* or *a las* (at).

When it is past the hour up to the half hour, you use *y*, which means *past* (also *and*), as in:

| | |
|---|---|
| *Son las dos y veinte.* | It is twenty past two. (It is two and twenty.) |
| *Es la una y diez.* | It is ten past one. (It is one and ten.) |

From the half hour to the next hour, you use *menos*, which means *to* (also *minus*), as in:

| | |
|---|---|
| *Son las tres menos cinco.* | It is five to three. (It is three minus five.) |
| *Es la una menos cuarto.* | It is a quarter to one. (It is one minus a quarter.) |

You could also say it, as in English, although it is much longer:

| | |
|---|---|
| *Son las dos y cincuenta y cinco.* | It is two fifty-five. |
| *Son las doce y cuarenta y cinco.* | It is twelve forty-five. |

Therefore,
   *y* after the hour up to the half hour
   and
   *menos* after the half hour to the next hour.

And,
   *it is* can be either *es la* (only for one) or *son las* (for any other time);
   *at* can be either *a la* (only for one) or *a las* (for any other time).

Remember: *son las, es la, a las, a la.*

Here is additional vocabulary relating to time:

*mañana*   morning

*Mañana* can be a noun or an adverb, meaning morning (noun) or tomorrow (adverb). Used as a noun, it needs the article, whether definite or indefinite, *la* or *una*.

*tarde*        afternoon

As with *mañana*, *tarde* can be a noun or an adverb. As a noun it means *afternoon*, and it needs the article; as an adverb, it means *late*, no article.

*la noche*    night

In Spanish, before dark is *tarde*, and *noche* is from dark up to midnight. In reality, it is any time after 12 midnight.

| | |
|---|---|
| *temprano* | early |
| *el mediodía* | noon |
| *la medianoche* | midnight |
| *la madrugada* | early morning/dawn/daybreak |
| *el atardecer* | dusk |
| *el anochecer* | nightfall |
| *el amanecer* | daybreak/dawn |

# BRAIN TICKLERS
## Set # 27

### Ejercicios

A. Traduce la palabra o las palabras entre paréntesis:

1. Te veo en (five minutes).
2. Pregúntale (the time) a Margarita.
3. La clase empieza en unos (seconds).
4. Me gusta tu (watch).
5. Llámalo en (half hour).

B. Match the description in column A with the word in column B:

| Column A | Column B |
|---|---|
| 1. It is used for "past the hour." | a. menos |
| 2. It means half. | b. y |
| 3. It means o'clock. | c. media |
| 4. It is used for "to the hour." | d. en punto |

(Answers are on page 140.)

### ¡OJO!—WATCH OUT!

In Spanish, in the morning, in the afternoon is: *por la mañana, por la tarde.* Notice the use of *por* instead of *en.*

# DILO COMO YO
# SAY IT LIKE I DO

## Pronunciation of the ñ and the b-v

The *ñ* is a letter unique to Spanish. Other languages, including English, have pretty much the same sound but not the symbol.

The first thing you have to learn is how to write it. The *n* has a curved (or straight) line or dash right over it, which is called a *tilde*; it is used in upper or lower case: ñ. If you leave it out, it is simply an *n* with a totally different pronunciation and often with a different meaning, as in: *peña* (rock/crag), *pena* (pity/sorrow). Concerning its pronunciation, you should have no major problem since it is quite similar to the English *ni* in *onion.* Your problem is not how to pronounce it, but leaving out the tilde, which often happens. The *ñ* cannot stand by itself, needing always to be followed by a vowel, and never separating the two.

131

# BRAIN TICKLERS
### Set # 28

*Ejercicios*

A. Say these words out loud:
   | español | niño | caña | puño |
   | año | otoño | señal | riña |

B. Divide these three words into syllables:
   1. viña
   2. uña
   3. cañón

(Answers are on page 140.)

## The pronunciation of the *b-v*

There is often confusion when writing a word with a *b* or *v* since both consonants are pronounced alike in Spanish. The following tips may help you avoid such a confusion.

### Written with a *b*

- All verb infinitives ending in *-bir* and their respective tenses: *escribir> escribo, escribí, escribía, escribiré; concebir> concebimos, concebíamos, concebiremos*
- The verbs *deber* and *beber*, and their respective tenses: *deben, debieron, deberán; beben, bebieron, beberán*
- All the endings of the imperfect tense of *-ar* verbs: *soñaba, bailábamos, cantaban*
- The imperfect tense of the verb *ir*: *iba, íbamos, iban*
- Words beginning with the syllables *bu, bus, bur*, and the sound *bibl*: *butaca, buscar, burocracia, bibliografía, biblioteca*
- Any word in which the *b* precedes another consonant: *subsistir, admirable, breve*

## Written with a **v**

- All adjectives ending in *ave, ava, avo, eve, eva, ivo, iva*: *suave, esclava, cóncavo, diecinueve, nueva, exclusivo, llamativa*
- Following the syllable *ad*: *adversidad, advertir, adverso*
- The present indicative, subjunctive, and command of the verb *ir*: *vamos, vayamos, vayan*

Remember! Both the *b* and the *v* are pronounced identically in Spanish—no difference whatsoever.

## The pronunciation of the *d* at the end of a word

There is also some confusion or hesitation regarding the correct pronunciation of the letter *d* at the end of a word. There are generally three different pronunciations:

1. It is totally dropped following a pause, as in: *pared> paré, usted> usté*.
2. It is pronounced similarly to the Spanish *z* in *lápiz*.
3. It is pronounced like the *d* in initial position: *doy, dolor* (dental/occlusive).

Which one is the correct pronunciation?

Either 1 or 2 is recommended as being the most common.

## Pronunciation Practice

A. Read these words out loud, paying special attention to the *b-v*:

| | | |
|---|---|---|
| avance | a la vez | avestruz |
| abanico | a lo bestia | bombero |
| bisonte | embudo | |
| verde | en vano | |

B. Read these words out loud, paying special attention to the final *d*:

| | | |
|---|---|---|
| ciudad | Simbad | obscuridad |
| haced | verdad | potestad |
| potestad | soledad | |
| multitud | realidad | |

# ALMA HISPÁNICA
# HISPANIC SOUL

## Juan Ramón Jiménez

Juan Ramón Jiménez is one of the most
gifted writers of contemporary Spain.
Although he wrote for newspapers
and translated several works, he is
best known for his poetry and for his
insightful perception of what this art is,
of its language and meaning. Although
he spent most of his early years in Spain,
when civil war broke out in Spain in
1936, he left, like many other Spaniards,
to try his fortunes in other lands. He
accepted an invitation to teach at the
University of Puerto Rico, then Cuba,
later the United States, and from here he traveled extensively
throughout South America. He was born in Andalucía, in the
village of Moguer, Huelva, in 1881, and died in 1958. Juan Ramón
was a prolific writer, and many of his works have been translated
into various languages. One of his most precious writings is the
story of *Platero y yo*, published in Madrid in 1914. Platero was
a donkey. Following is an excerpt of this most beautiful and
tender story.

## Platero y yo

Platero es pequeño, *peludo*, *suave*, tan *blando* por fuera, que se diría todo de algodón, que no lleva huesos. Sólo los espejos de *azabache* de sus ojos son duros cual dos *escarabajos* de cristal negro.

Lo dejo suelto y se va al prado, y acaricia tibiamente con su *hocico*, rozándolas apenas, las florecillas rosas, celestes y gualdas... Lo llamo dulcemente: "¿Platero?", viene a mí con un *trotecillo* alegre, que parece que se ríe, en no sé qué *cascabeleo* ideal.

Come cuanto le doy. Le gustan las naranjas mandarinas, las uvas moscateles, todas de ámbar; los higos morados, con su cristalina *gotita* de miel...

To better understand this passage, here is the meaning of some key words:

| | |
|---|---|
| *peludo* | hairy |
| *suave* | smooth |
| *blando* | soft |
| *azabache* | jet, as in jet black |
| *escarabajo* | beetle |
| *hocico* | snout |
| *trotecillo* | light trot |
| *cascabeleo* | jingling |
| *gotita* | little drop |

Describe briefly, in your opinion, the relationship between *Platero* and the author.

# PLUMA EN MANO
# PEN IN HAND

### *La universidad de Salamanca/*
### *The University of Salamanca*

La universidad de Salamanca es la más antigua de España y la cuarta más antigua de Europa. Fue fundada por Alfonso IX en 1218 y grandemente organizada por Alfonso X en 1254. El papa (Pope) Alejandro IV confirmó su fundación en 1255. Cuenta, pues, con 787 años de fundada. La universidad se encuentra situada en el noroeste (northwest) de Madrid, en la señera (unique) ciudad de Salamanca en la región de Castilla la Vieja. Cuando Cristóbal Colón andaba gestionando (negotiating) su gran viaje, se presentó ante un consejo (council) de geógrafos de la universidad de Salamanca que le rechazó (rebuffed) su ambicioso proyecto. Uno de los más destacados eruditos (scholars) de España, Antonio de Nebrija, inició allí sus estudios a los 15 años de edad, graduándose cuatro años después. En 1475 regresó ocupando una cátedra (professorship) de retórica (rhetoric). Fue Nebrija el célebre autor de la primera gramática de la lengua española, *Gramática de la lengua castellana*, publicada en 1492, así como de dos diccionarios latino-español.

## BRAIN TICKLERS
### Set # 29

*Ejercicios*

A. Below are three of the verbs you learned earlier in this lesson. Write a sentence in Spanish with each one in the present, and then write another sentence using the same verb in the past. All are regular verbs.

1. aprender:

2. estudiar:

3. asistir:

B. Based on the passage on the preceding page, fill in the blanks:

1. La universidad de Salamanca es la más antigua de _____.

2. Está situada al _____ de Madrid.

3. Antonio de Nebrija fue el autor de _____.

**¿Cuánto sabes?** Can you name two important cities of Spain?

(Answers are on page 140.)

# ASÍ SOMOS
# THIS IS WHO WE ARE

## Women in early America

If you look at any history of the Americas and read about some of the main events and deeds of people, you would hardly notice any women mentioned, especially when history was first recorded in the early sixteenth century. This does not reflect any disdain toward women in general, but simply the fact that

women, at that time, were dedicated almost exclusively to their families and homes. However, there were many women, actually hundreds and even thousands of them, who stood up and contributed in large measure to many of the discoveries and explorations, side by side with the men. The fact that they were left out of the pages of history is indeed an injustice. It should never be forgotten that the person almost solely behind the discovery of America, the one who really made it happen, was a woman, one of the greatest figures in history: Queen Isabella of Spain. Without her vision and support, no men would have ever crossed the Atlantic, at least as early as they did.

But there were others who followed her footsteps, and held high positions of leadership, such as María de Toledo, wife of Diego Colón, son of Christopher Columbus, first woman governor of the Americas, Isabel de Bobadilla, wife of Hernando de Soto, first woman governor of Cuba, Isabel Barreto y Quirós, first and to this day only woman admiral in the Spanish navy, and many others.

# BRAIN TICKLERS—THE ANSWERS

## Set # 25, page 114

**A.**

1. asisto
2. estudio
3. llegar a ser
4. bachillerato
5. beca

6. escuela
7. costo
8. estudios

**B.**

1. estudian
2. aprendemos

3. gana
4. llego

**C.**

1. mathematics
2. architecture
3. engineering
4. sociology
5. calculus
6. history
7. political science
8. social sciences
9. philosophy
10. art

11. medicine
12. law
13. geography
14. psychology
15. commerce
16. biology
17. economics
18. literature
19. chemistry
20. astronomy

## Set # 26, page 123

**Piénsalo bien**

**A.**

1. lave
2. trabaje
3. escribas

4. hablen
5. es

**B.**

1. V
2. V
3. F

4. F
5. V

**C.**
1. estudia
2. cómpralo
3. Bailemos
4. hablen
5. No la escriban

## Set # 27, page 130

**A.** Pronunciation
1. cinco minutos
2. la hora
3. segundos
4. reloj (de pulsera)
5. media hora

**B.**
1. b
2. c
3. d
4. a

## Set # 28, page 132

**Bien vale la pena**
**A.** Pronunciation

**B.**
1. vi-ña
2. u-ña
3. ca-ñón

## Set # 29, page 137

**Pluma en mano**
**A.** Answers will vary.

**B.**
1. España
2. noroeste
3. "Gramática de la lengua castellana"

**¿Cuánto sabes?**
Answers will vary. Sample answer: Salamanca and Madrid.

# Sin economía no hay país

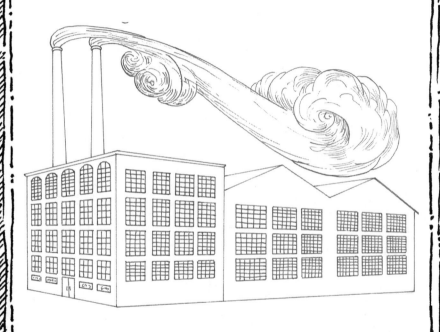

# The economy is vital to every country

Todo país depende de su comercio y economía para *mantenerse a flote*, para no caer en *bancarrota*, para el buen vivir de su *ciudadanía*. Unos *sobresalen* por su industria, otros por su agricultura, otros por su técnica y muchos de ellos por sus exportaciones. ¿Qué se *requiere* para que una economía *florezca* y *se desarrolle*? Veamos.

Lo primero es un sistema político estable, democrático y de *libre empresa*; lo segundo, una infraestructura al menos adecuada: *carreteras*, acueductos, buen sistema eléctrico; lo tercero, *recursos naturales* de toda clase: minas, petróleo, gas; lo cuarto, una *fuerza trabajadora* preparada y competente; y lo quinto, organización y buenos servicios públicos y de transporte. Buenos ejemplos *de tal* economía son los Estados Unidos, en primer lugar, seguido de algunos países europeos, el Japón y la China. Hablemos en particular de Norteamérica, de la tierra de Lincoln. José Martí se refirió a ella *como* "la mayor fábrica de trabajadores libres del mundo", *y si así era* hace cien años, mucho más lo es en la actualidad. Las grandes fábricas de todo tipo y las enormes corporaciones multinacionales han alcanzado un desarrollo *nunca visto antes*. Ahora bien, debido al *alto costo de vida* y a los grandes salarios que exige el trabajador muchos negocios se han visto obligados a trasladar sus operaciones manufactureras al *extranjero*, *buscando con ello* ahorrar dinero y mantener sus productos a precios *asequibles* al consumidor. *Así*, mucho de lo que se vende hoy aquí en las grandes *tiendas por departamentos* o de descuento, *está hecho* fuera del país, mayormente en China y países como Indonesia y Guatemala.

Este ha sido siempre el *sino* del emigrante hasta que, pasado el tiempo e innumerables sacrificios, logra *superarse* y llegar a una posición digna, por lo que será siempre *merecedor* del mayor *encomio* y admiración. *El de arriba* disfruta de complacencia y exige; *el de abajo* sueña y se conforma.

## Vocabulario básico

| | |
|---|---|
| mantenerse a flote | to stay afloat |
| bancarrota | bankruptcy |
| ciudadanía | citizenship |
| sobresalen | stand out |
| requiere | requires |
| florezca | flourishes |
| se desarrolle | develops |
| libre empresa | free enterprise |
| carreteras | roads |
| recursos naturales | natural resources |
| fuerza trabajadora | workforce/manpower |
| de tal | of such |
| como | as |
| y si así era | and if it was that way |
| nunca visto antes | never seen before |
| alto costo de la vida | high cost of living |
| extranjero | overseas/abroad |
| buscando con ello | looking to |
| asequibles | affordable |
| Así | Thus |
| tiendas por departamentos | department stores |
| está hecho | is made |
| sino | fate |
| superarse | to better onself |
| merecedor | worthy |
| encomio | praise |
| El de arriba | The one on top |
| el de abajo | the one under |

# BRAIN TICKLERS
### Set # 30

*Ejercicios*

A. By looking at these words, you should know what they mean. Write the meaning of each one:
   1. político
   2. acueductos
   3. transporte
   4. europeos
   5. operaciones
   6. relativamente
   7. común
   8. innumerables

B. Traduce la palabra o las palabras entre paréntesis:

1. Muchas de las grandes corporaciones estadounidenses tienen oficinas en el (overseas).

2. (I have never before seen) tantos automóviles en las (roads).

3. Gran parte de los productos que se compran hoy día (are made) en la China.

4. (The aqueduct) de Segovia fue construido por los romanos.

5. Muchos países occidentales tienen (political systems) democráticos.

C. Basado en el pasaje anterior, dinos si cada una de estas afirmaciones es *verdadera o falsa*:

1. Para no caer en bancarrota, todo país tiene que mantener una buena economía.  V  F

2. La estabilidad política es imprescindible para que un país se desarrolle.  V  F

3. La China no exporta sus productos a los Estados Unidos.  V  F

4. Norteamérica es la tierra de Lincoln.  V  F

(Answers are on page 168.)

**¡OJO!—WATCH OUT!**

The *Inc.* of a corporation corresponds to *S.A.* in Spanish, meaning Anonymous Corporation (the *S.* stands for Society), or stock company, as in: Consumer Products, Inc.> Productos del Consumidor, S.A. A corporation means that the ownership of the business belongs to an entity, not to the individual.

# PIÉNSALO BIEN
# THINK IT THROUGH

## The adjective. El adjetivo

Crucial in any language is the use of adjectives. The function of the adjective is to denote some degree of quality or way of being of a noun.

There are two kinds of adjectives—those that qualify the noun and those that determine it:

Qualifying the noun:

*mujer buena*          good woman

Determining the noun:

*dos lápices*          two pencils

As we said earlier, it is of the utmost importance to know that every single qualifying adjective in Spanish *must* agree in gender and number with the noun. If you want to really learn Spanish, this is one of those key things you must forever keep in mind. In terms of its positioning in a sentence, an adjective usually follows the noun in Spanish. In some cases, it may precede the noun, and by so doing, the quality of the subject is highlighted, as in

*buena mujer* instead of *mujer buena*

or

*mal hombre* instead of *hombre malo*

But, as we said, such use is infrequent. There are some masculine adjectives that when used in the singular drop their final *o*, such as: *malo, bueno, uno, alguno, ninguno*.

| | |
|---|---|
| *mal hombre* | bad man |
| *buen día* | good day |
| *un libro* | one book or a book |
| *algún año* | one year or some year |
| *ningún niño* | any child |

In addition to the ones above, there are other adjectives, such as *grande*, that drop their last syllable before a masculine singular noun, as in:

| | |
|---|---|
| *gran profesor* | great professor |

Another adjective, *ciento*, as we saw earlier, becomes *cien* before the noun, as in:

| | |
|---|---|
| *cien camiones* | one/a hundred trucks |

There are cases in which an adjective can be used as a noun by preceding it with the neuter article *lo*, as in:

| | |
|---|---|
| *lo bello* | the beautiful |
| *lo sublime* | the sublime |
| *lo necesario* | the necessary |

Adjectives can also be used to compare the quality of nouns in terms of being superior, inferior, or equal. I can say, for example:

Superior:

| | |
|---|---|
| *Esta flor es más bonita que ésa.* | This flower is prettier than that one. |

Inferior:

| | |
|---|---|
| *Esta flor es menos bonita que ésa.* | This flower is less pretty than that one. |

Equal:

| | |
|---|---|
| *Esta flor es tan bonita como ésa.* | This flower is as beautiful as that one. |

For the superior, we use:

| | |
|---|---|
| *más + adjective + que* | more + adjective + than |

For the inferior, we use:

| | |
|---|---|
| *menos + adjective + que* | less + adjective + than |

For the equal, we use:

| | |
|---|---|
| *tan + adjective + como* | as + adjective + as |

For the superlative, we use:

| | |
|---|---|
| *más + adjective + de* preceded by the definite article: *el más, la más, los más, las más* | the + the adjective ending in –est + of |
| *Este edificio es el más alto de la ciudad.* | This building is the tallest in the city. |
| *Estos árboles son los más antiguos del parque.* | These trees are the oldest in the park. |

When no comparison is made in expressing the highest quality of a noun, we can do it by using *muy* or by adding *ísimo–ísima–ísimos–ísimas* to the adjective, as in:

| | |
|---|---|
| *Esta comida está muy buena.* | This food is very good. |
| *Esta comida está buenísima.* | This food is very, very good. |

Notice how the adjective drops the final vowel before adding *–ísimo*.

---

**Tip:** *Más* in Spanish for the superior comparison equals the suffix *-er* in English, and *el/la/los/las más* for the superlative in Spanish equals the suffix *-est* in English. Just remember that for the superior you also use *que* in Spanish, meaning *than* in English, and for the superlative you also use *de*, meaning *of* in English. For the inferior comparison, in Spanish you use *menos*, or *less* in English. The *más*, *menos* come before the adjective followed by *que*. The *el/la/los/las más* come before the adjective followed by *de*.

Some adjectives have irregular forms for the comparative and superlative, such as: *mayor* (older, oldest), *menor* (younger, youngest), *mejor* (better, best), *peor* (worse, worst). They all have plural forms. Let's look at some examples:

| | |
|---|---|
| *Carlos es mayor que Juan.* | Charles is older than John. |
| *Carlos es el mayor.* | Charles is the oldest. |
| *Isabel es menor que Emilia.* | Isabel is younger than Emily. |
| *Isabel es la menor.* | Isabel is the youngest. |
| *Mi comida es mejor que la tuya.* | My food is better than yours. |
| *Mi comida es la mejor.* | My food is the best. |
| *Esta película es peor que la otra.* | This movie is worse than the other one. |
| *Esta película es la peor.* | This movie is the worst. |

*Mayor* and *menor* are only used when referring to age.

---

### ¿Sabías que?

When you are enjoying that juicy steak, thank the Spanish Franciscan missionaries for it. Christopher Columbus brought spotted Castilian range cattle to America. In 1579, a traveler in northern Mexico reported that some ranches had as many as 150,000 cows. In 1685, Spanish livestock operations had been established in East Texas, Arizona, California, and New Mexico. By 1860, Texas alone had more than three and a half million head of cattle.

# BRAIN TICKLERS
### Set # 31

### *Ejercicios*

A. Here you will see five nouns and five adjectives. Use the verb "son" (are) for plural nouns. Use the verb "es" (is) for singular nouns. Make up Spanish sentences using one of each:

| | | |
|---|---|---|
| la nieve | el papel | pequeño |
| las corbatas | blanco | rápido |
| la caja | cuadrado | |
| los caballos | largo | |

B. What is wrong with these sentences? One sentence is correct.
1. La mujer rubio llegó a la fiesta con vestido y zapatos negras.
   Write it correctly:
2. El altos hombre llevaba un botas negro.
   Write it correctly:
3. Cuando era niño mis padres me compraron una bicicleta roja y blanca.
   Write it correctly:

C. The comparative and the superlative. Write two Spanish sentences using: *más que* and *la más de*

D. Now, write two sentences using: *mayor* and *mejor*

E. Traduce la palabra o las palabras entre paréntesis:
1. Yo soy (prettier than) mi amiga Magdalena.
2. Esta blusa es (more expensive than) que aquélla.
3. Mi amigo Manuel es (the tallest) en la clase.
4. Esos niños son (the worst) del barrio.
5. Mi padre es (younger than) mi madre.

(Answers are on page 168.)

# MÁS ES MEJOR
# MORE IS BETTER

## Nouns

| | |
|---|---|
| el ingreso | income |
| la nómina | payroll |
| el valor | value |
| el pequeño negocio | the small business |
| el propietario | proprietor/owner |
| la tasa | rate |
| el mayoreo | wholesale trade |
| el menudeo | retail trade |
| el mercadeo | marketing |
| la publicidad | advertising |
| la contabilidad | accounting |
| la cuenta | account |
| la factura | invoice |
| las relaciones públicas | public relations |
| el banco | bank |
| la cuenta bancaria | bank account |
| el embarque | shipment |
| las finanzas | finances |
| el anuncio | advertisement |
| el archivo | file |
| el reciclaje | recycling |
| la conferencia | conference |
| la reunión | meeting |
| el puesto | job |
| el cajero automático | ATM |
| el depósito | deposit |
| el impuesto | tax |
| el descuento | discount |
| el pago | payment |

## Verbs

| | |
|---|---|
| negociar | to negotiate |
| descontar | to discount |
| fabricar | to manufacture |
| distribuir | to distribute |
| anunciarse | to advertise |

| | |
|---|---|
| valer | to be worth/to cost |
| delegar | to delegate |
| opinar | to give an opinion |
| traer | to bring |
| permitir | to allow/permit |
| conferenciar | to have a conference/to hold talks |
| confirmar | to confirm |
| aumentar | to increase |

# HABLA POPULAR
# EVERYDAY SPEECH

Here is an important and complicated Spanish verb: *tener* (to have).

*Tener* is used in very common expressions where English uses *to be*. In Spanish you don't say *I am hungry*, but *I have hunger*. Here are some other examples:

| | |
|---|---|
| *Tengo hambre.* | I am hungry. |
| *Tengo sueño.* | I am sleepy. |
| *Tengo frío/calor.* | I am cold/hot. |
| *Tengo miedo.* | I am afraid. |

When discussing how old you are in Spanish, you use *tener*, as in: *tengo veinte años* (I am twenty years old).

It doesn't help that *tener* is an irregular verb in the present, past, and future indicative, as shown below:

| Present | Past | Future |
|---|---|---|
| tengo | tuve | tendré |
| tienes | tuviste | tendrás |
| tiene | tuvo | tendrá |
| tenemos | tuvimos | tendremos |
| tenéis | tuvisteis | tendréis |
| tienen | tuvieron | tendrán |

Another troublesome verb in Spanish is *to be*, which can be either one of these two verbs: *ser* or *estar*.

Perhaps the best pointer we can give you is that *ser* is generally used to express permanent states, while *estar* is generally used for temporary states, as in:

| | |
|---|---|
| *Soy feliz.* | I am happy. |
| *Estoy feliz.* | I am happy. |

The difference here is that when I say *soy feliz*, I am denoting that I am a happy person, that it is my nature to be happy. On the other hand, *estoy feliz* denotes that I am happy about something that just happened, not that I am by nature a happy person. See if you can tell the difference in this example:

| | |
|---|---|
| *Soy un hombre feliz.* | I am a happy man. |
| *Estoy feliz porque mi hijo se casó.* | I am happy because my son got married. |

This may be the general rule, but there are exceptions, as, for example, when you say:

| | |
|---|---|
| *Él está muerto.* | He is dead. |

Being the ultimate state of permanency, here you use *estar* and not *ser*.

As indicated, *estar* is generally used with adjectives that are transitory, and also with the past participle acting as an adjective, as in

| | |
|---|---|
| *Estoy triste.* | I am sad. |
| *Estoy cansado.* | I am tired. |

*Estar*, as we already saw, is also used to form the present progessive, as in: *estoy corriendo* (I am running). *Ser* is also used as a helping verb to form the passive voice, as we saw earlier, as in *La casa fue construida por mi padre* (The house was built by my father). It is important to learn to conjugate these two verbs:

| ser | estar |
|---|---|
| soy | estoy |
| eres | estás |
| es | está |
| somos | estamos |
| sois | estáis |
| son | están |

Notice how irregular *ser* is and that *estar* is also irregular in the first person singular. *Ser* in the past tense is even worse, and it gets confused with the verb *ir* (to go), which is conjugated the same in the past:

| Past Tense: | **ser** | **ir** |
|---|---|---|
| | fui | fui |
| | fuiste | fuiste |
| | fue | fue |
| | fuimos | fuimos |
| | fuisteis | fuisteis |
| | fueron | fueron |

The difference, of course, between one and the other is in the context, as in:

*Fue una mujer amable.*     She was a kind woman.
*Fue a Europa el año pasado.*     She/He went to Europe last
     year.

## ¿Sabías que?

The U.S. dollar symbol ($) is derived from the Spanish *pillar* or milled dollar, the pillar or scroll design on the coin's reverse. It was used by a government clerk in 1788 and it came into general use soon thereafter. Also, during colonial times, specifically during Alexander Hamilton's era, the only legal tender generally accepted after three years was Spanish silver; in fact, you could hardly buy a loaf of bread or a bottle of milk at the time without paying in Spanish silver. That was in effect between 1792 and 1834, and after that, Spanish gold was the standard until 1857. By the way, all of that silver and gold came from the mines of Bolivia, Peru, and Mexico. What this means is that, although indirectly, we owe much to all three countries, as well as to their people for mining that silver and gold.

## BRAIN TICKLERS
### Set # 32

**Ejercicio**

For each sentence, choose *ser* or *estar* for the English verb "am" and "is."

1. Today I am happy because it is Friday.

2. Generally I am an optimist (*optimista*), but today I am sad (*triste*).

3. He is very busy (*ocupado*) with his work.

*For extra practice, translate the sentences to Spanish.

(Answers are on page 169.)

# BIEN VALE LA PENA
# IT'S WELL WORTH IT

## The curriculum vitae

You may be wondering what this means—it means *résumé*. In Spanish you could also use *la hoja de vida*, or *historial de vida*, although it would be applicable only in the United States. Of course, we recommend you use *el currículum vitae* (abbreviated *CV*), or simply *vitae*, especially in the academic community.

## How do you prepare your CV in Spanish?

Everybody has a different way of doing it; in other words, there is no set style in terms of contents, order, language, how long, or how short. It must include, however, certain basic information, such as personal data, education, and experience. We will give a model in Spanish, although we are mainly concerned with the information given rather than with the style used. You can change it around in any way you please.

Datos personales.

| | |
|---|---|
| Nombre: | Federico López Suárez |
| Domicilio: | Avenida Los Olmos 44, 5o. dcha. |
| | 00485 Salamanca, España |
| Teléf: | 469 612 995 |
| Fax: | 469 612 996 |
| Correo electrónico: | Lópezs@att.net.es |

Competencia principal y preferencia:

Gerencia de ventas de todo tipo a nivel nacional o internacional. Dispuesto a trasladarse a cualquier lugar de España o del extranjero.

Estudios.

Bachiller en Letras, Colegio La Asunción, Salamanca. Graduado en 1995.
Administración de Empresas, Universidad Alcalá de Henares. Graduado en 2000.
Parte de estos estudios fueron sufragados por dos becas concedidas en 1998.

Experiencia profesional.

Exportaciones Ibéricas, S.A. Miguel de Unamuno 92, Segovia. Sub-gerente de ventas, 2000–2003. A cargo de un departamento de cinco empleados. Supervisión total de toda actividad de ventas dentro y fuera de España.

Telecomunicaciones Nacionales, S.A. Avenida América 155, Valladolid.

Gerente de ventas de 2003 hasta la fecha. Asumió el puesto para montar, organizar y dirigir el departamento de ventas de esta nueva empresa. En menos de dos años se lograron ventas que sobrepasaron los diez millones de pesetas, muchas de ellas en distintos países europeos, como Alemania e Inglaterra. La empresa recientemente fue adquirida por una poderosa empresa francesa donde se transladarán todas las operaciones. Preferiría no vivir en Francia.

Otros datos.

Ha viajado por toda España y Europa. Siendo niño residió por cuatro años en Alemania donde su padre trabajaba. Dominio del español y buen dominio del inglés, con conocimientos básicos del alemán.

Referencias por solicitud.

## BRAIN TICKLERS
### Set # 33

**Ejercicio**

Contesta estas preguntas en oraciones completas:

1. ¿Cómo te llamas? Incluye nombre y apellido.
2. ¿Cuál es tu domicilio o dónde vives? Incluye el código postal.
3. ¿Cuál es tu número de teléfono? Incluye el código de la zona.
4. ¿Cuál es tu correo electrónico?

(Answers are on page 169.)

### ¡OJO!—WATCH OUT!

*Llamarse* in Spanish means literally *to be called*. It is a reflexive verb that means that it must be used with the reflexive pronouns, as in:

| | |
|---|---|
| *Me llamo Raimundo.* | My name is Raimundo. |
| *Ella se llama Maruja.* | Her name is Maruja. |

*Nombre* is name, especially referring to your first name, unless you are asked *¿Cuál es tu nombre completo?* (What is your full name?), in which case you would give your first and last names. You could also be asked *¿Cuál es tu nombre y apellido?* (What is your first and last name?). The question *What is your name?* in Spanish can be asked four ways:

| (familiar) | (polite) |
|---|---|
| *¿Cómo te llamas?* | *¿Cómo se llama?* |
| *¿Cuál es tu nombre?* | *¿Cuál es su nombre?* |

Notice the use of *cómo* with *llamarse* and of *cuál* with *nombre*. Both questions ask mainly for your first name, although *¿Cómo te llamas?* can also be asking for your full name.

# DILO COMO YO
# SAY IT LIKE I DO

## Pronunciation of the *h*

Never pronounce the *h* in Spanish. It is totally silent, as if it weren't there. It is purely an etymological letter, with no phonetic value; however, you can't leave it out in writing. It must be included always. So, these words, although written with *h*, are pronounced:

| | | | |
|---|---|---|---|
| humo> | umo | ahora> | aora |
| hambre> | ambre | hay> | ay |

Write it always, but never pronounce it.

## Pronunciation Practice

Say these words out loud:

| | | | |
|---|---|---|---|
| honor | historia | alcahuete | ahí |
| vehículo | búho | hermoso | hispano |

---

**¿Sabías que?**

In 1735, Spanish was taught for the first time in the New York public schools, and in 1751, the first Spanish textbook was published with the title *A Short Introduction to the Spanish Language.*

---

# ALMA HISPÁNICA
# HISPANIC SOUL

## Rómulo Gallegos

He is considered a master of modern Hispanic American literature and among its finest novelists. He was born in Caracas in 1884 and died there in 1969. He was married to Teotiste Arocha Egui, who died in Mexico City, where Gallegos had gone into exile. Educator, writer, and politician, he was named secretary of education in 1937 and proclaimed president of the republic in 1947, but he was overthrown by a military coup the following year. He wrote several novels— *Pobre Negro, El Último Solar, Canaima, Cantaclaro,* but his most celebrated work was *Doña Bárbara* (1929), which was translated into several languages and a movie was made by the same name, starring the famous Mexican movie star María Félix. In all of his works, but especially in *Doña Bárbara,* civilization and barbarism clashed in a struggle only too common in most Hispanic American countries. Gallegos is a true master in the description of typical landscapes and in the creation and development of his characters.

The writings of Rómulo Gallegos:

### Doña Bárbara (Excerpt)

Esta mujer se entretenía enamorando hombres que después *despojaba de* sus tierras y riquezas, o simplemente los mataba. Doña Bárbara comenzó a *comportarse* así *debido a* que cuando era joven había tenido un gran amor, Asdrúbal, al cual asesinaron, comenzando así los problemas de venganza contra los hombres. En uno de sus *enamoramientos* misteriosos, Doña Bárbara estuvo con Lorenzo Barquero con el que tuvo una hija, Marisela. Luego expulsó a su hija y *amante quedándose* con las tierras de él.

To help you better understand this passage, here is the meaning of some key words.

| | |
|---|---|
| *despojaba de* | stripped of |
| *comportarse* | to behave |
| *debido a* | owing to/because of |
| *enamoramientos* | infatuations |
| *amante* | lover |
| *quedándose* | taking over/keeping for herself |

# BRAIN TICKLERS
## Set # 34

### Ejercicio

Contesta estas preguntas en oraciones completas:

1. ¿Qué clase de mujer era Doña Bárbara?
2. ¿Por que se sentía así hacia (toward) los hombres?
3. ¿Con quién tuvo una hija?
4. ¿Qué le quitó a Lorenzo Barquero?
5. ¿Cómo se llamaba su hija?

(Answers are on page 169.)

# PLUMA EN MANO
# PEN IN HAND

## Mi primera carta en español/
## My first Spanish letter

### Key words to learn:

| | |
|---|---|
| la carta | letter |
| la carta personal | personal letter |
| la carta de negocios | business letter |
| la fecha | date |
| la firma | signature |
| Estimado/a | Dear (formal) |
| Querido/a | Dear (intimate) |

### Other related words:

| | |
|---|---|
| a | to |
| de | from |
| el remitente | sender |
| el sello/la estampilla | postage |
| correos | post office |
| el cartero | mailman/woman |
| la entrega | delivery |
| el correo regular | regular mail |
| la entrega especial | special delivery |
| el correo certificado | certified mail |
| el comprobante de entrega | proof of delivery |
| el papel | paper |
| el sobre | envelope |
| el paquete | package |
| PD | P.S. |
| ir a correos | to go to the post office |
| enviar una carta | to send a letter |
| recibir una carta | to receive a letter |
| envolver | to wrap |
| atar | to tie |
| pegar | to glue |
| el correo nacional | domestic mail |

| | |
|---|---|
| el correo extranjero | foreign mail |
| el código postal | zip code |
| por avión | air mail |
| por barco | by boat |

Modelo de una carta sencilla en español, dirigida a una persona amiga:

La Paz, 5 de julio de 2011

Querida Paulina:

Antes que nada quiero saludarte a ti y a tu familia. Espero que todos estén bien y gozando del buen clima de Puerto Rico.

La última vez que supe (knew) de ti te preparabas para hacer un viaje a Buenos Aires, donde tienes a tus tíos. ¿Hiciste por fin (finally) el viaje? ¿Cómo están tus tíos y primos? Me dicen (they tell me) que Buenos Aires es una gran ciudad, con excelentes avenidas y restaurantes. Me gustaría visitarla un día (one of these days).

Por aquí todo marcha (goes) como de costumbre. La Paz creciendo y empeorando (getting worse) de contaminación con más carros y más gente. Parece (it seems) que todo el país ha venido a parar (has come) a la ciudad y ya no se puede (and one cannot even) andar por las calles, aunque sigue siendo (continues to be) una ciudad encantadora y con mucha historia. ¡No la cambiaría por nada! (I wouldn't change it for anything!) Mi familia muy bien, unos trabajando y otros estudiando, como siempre (as always). Mi hermano José Alberto se gradúa pronto, y mi hermana Rosario pronto se casará, dentro de (within) unos seis meses. ¿Vienes a la boda (wedding)? Espero que sí porque tengo muchas ganas de verte.

Te dejo (I leave you) porque tengo que acompañar a mi madre al mercado.

Que estés muy bien y muchos abrazos y besos a todos de tu amiga que no te olvida (forgets you).

Marisol

PD - Espero que me escribas pronto.

**¿Cuánto sabes?**

If I sign off a letter to a friend saying *¡Recuerdos!*, what am I saying?
If you can't come up with the answer, it means: *Regards!*

## BRAIN TICKLERS
### Set # 35

*Ejercicios*

A. Answer these questions:

1. How would you address a letter in Spanish to your cousin Bernardo?

2. And to your friend Leticia?

3. What about to a dean of a college?

4. And to your Spanish teacher?

B. Write a letter in Spanish to a good friend, telling her:

a. that you miss her (echar de menos)

b. that you are studying very hard and that you have an exam tomorrow

c. that you are planning to go on vacation to Acapulco in the summer

d. that your family is fine

e. that you have a new dog

f. that you are hoping she can visit soon and spend some time with you

(Answers are on page 169.)

# ASÍ SOMOS
# THIS IS WHO WE ARE

## The treasures of Spain

When it comes to talking about the treasures of Spain, it is very hard to decide what treasures to include, since there are just too many of them.

Spain is very old and has seen many cultures cross over from the Mediterranean to settle there. Each one left many indelible marks that have survived the passing of centuries: the Phoenicians, Greeks, Romans, and Arabs, among others. They settled in Spain at the peak of their glory with some of the greatest minds in the arts, architecture, science, and warfare. Of a long list of treasures, we have chosen the following five:

1. The Aqueduct of Segovia
2. The Alcazar of Segovia
3. The Alhambra
4. The Prado Museum
5. The Escorial

## 1. The Aqueduct of Segovia. El acueducto de Segovia

Segovia, Spain

The Aqueduct is located in the city of Segovia, about one hour north of Madrid. It was built by the Romans during the time of Emperor Trojan between the second half of the first century and the first half of the second, making it about 2,000 years old. It consists of 320 arches and 20,400 solid granite stone blocks, and has a length of 1,615 feet (4922 m). To build it, the Romans did not use mortar or concrete, but laid the blocks one on top of the other in perfect balance. The three central arches rise to a height of 102 feet (31 m). The fact that it was built without any mortar is most amazing and a grand testimony to the Romans' architectural genius. The aqueduct still functions today, bringing water from a distance of about 6 or 7 miles (10–12 km), starting at Fuenfría through the Río Frío.

## 2. The Alcazar of Segovia. El alcázar de Segovia

Segovia, Spain

This is one of the great castles of Spain and Europe. It is said that Walt Disney was so impressed with it that he used it as a model for the one he built in Walt Disney World in Florida. Indeed, it is quite similar. The castle was built in the eleventh century as a palace and later served as a military fortress. A fire nearly destroyed it in 1862, and it was extensively renovated. The Catholic monarchs of Spain, Queen Isabella of Castile and King Ferdinand of Aragón, were married there in 1469. Most of the kings of Spain, but especially those of the Trastámara dynasty, lived there at one time or another, as well as Ferdinand III and Alfonso X the Wise. King Philip II took very good care of the castle and carried out major alterations. The castle sits on a high hill overlooking the Eresma and Clamores rivers. The keep, the most prominent part of the castle, was begun by John II and completed by his successor Henry IV, or perhaps even by Queen Isabella herself. The walls and ceilings are in the Mudéjar style.

## 3. The Alhambra of Granada. La Alhambra de Granada

Granada, Spain

This is one of the most revered and admired places in the world, a true marvel of Spain's Moorish or Islamic influence. The name *Alhambra*, from *Al Hamra*, means *The Red One* in Arabic. Washington Irving was so struck by it that he wrote his celebrated *Tales of the Alhambra* (1832) after residing in Spain between 1826 and 1829. And the Catholic monarchs of Spain, Queen Isabella and King Ferdinand,  spent their honeymoon there. Not a bad choice at all; in fact, they so admired it that Queen Isabella expanded it, building a palace adjacent to the Palace of the Lions, and so did Emperor Charles V who built his own palace in the sixteenth century designed by the renowned Pedro Machuca. Most of the original construction of the Alhambra, for example, the Royal Palace and the Alcazaba, was done in the thirteenth century by Mohammed V, together with his father Yusuf I. Its two huge square towers, the Torre del Homenaje (the Keep) and Torre de la Vela (Watchtower) are visible from far away. The Alhambra stands on hilly ground overlooking the city of Granada with the Sierra Nevada in the background. Inside, one stands in wonder, admiring, among many other intricate designs and decorations, the walls clad half in tiles and stucco. The gardens and courtyards, especially the Generalife, mostly built after the Reconquest, and Patio de los Leones add to the striking beauty of the complex. In the Sala de Embajadores it is believed that King Boaddil surrendered Granada to the Catholic monarchs in 1492.

## 4. The Prado Museum. El museo del Prado

Madrid, Spain

Unquestionably one of the world's finest museums, it houses the masterpieces of such classic greats as Velázquez, Goya, El Greco, Murillo, Zurbarán, Rembrandt, Rubens, Titian, and Botticelli, among many others. Part of the great Italian paintings collection was brought in by Velázquez himself from Rome and Venice, as he had pledged King Philip IV he would do. In all, eleven Spanish kings in a period of three centuries were instrumental in the acquisition of most of the collection, including Philip II. Despite Spain's great power all over the world, none of the paintings was looted or taken by force (as was the case in many other European museums), but each one was purchased or acquired as gifts or through inheritance. The gallery alone holds 8,600 paintings from all over the world, as well as thousands of sculptures, furniture, jewelry, and coins, from the sixth to the nineteenth centuries. The museum was begun under the reign of King Charles III, who was responsible for embellishing most of Madrid, and was inaugurated on November 19, 1819. It is located on one of Madrid's finest boulevards, El Paseo del Prado, from which the name of the museum was taken. Behind the museum is the Monastery of San Jerónimo el Real. Here at the Prado you can admire, for hours on end, the great works of Velázquez (widely considered one of the greatest painters of all time), such as *Las*

*Meninas* (The Maids of Honor), *Las Lanzas o La Rendición de Breda* (The Surrender of Breda), *Las Hilanderas* (The Fable of Arachne), the magnificent portraits of Prince Baltasar Carlos and the Infanta Margarita, and Goya, especially, his two Majas.

## 5. The Escorial. El Escorial

El Escorial, Spain

Often called the Eighth Wonder of the World, the Escorial is primarily a palace, church, monastery, mausoleum, college, library, and art gallery. It is located in the Sierra de Guadarrama, about 27 miles (45 km) northwest of Madrid. Its proper name is Real Monasterio de San Lorenzo de El Escorio, taking the name Escorial from the small town in the vicinity. It was built by King Philip II to commemorate the Spanish victory over the French at the Battle of San Quintín in 1557. The original architect was Juan Bautista de Toledo, who was succeeded by Juan de Herrera when he died in 1567. King Charles III built an addition to it. The structure was devastated by two fires and looted by French troops in 1807. It occupies an area of about 500,000 square feet with four main facades. The principal front is 744 feet long and 72 feet high ($227 \times 22$ m), and each of the four towers rises about 200 feet (61 m). Adjacent to it is the Monastery of Saint Laurence, served since 1885 by the Augustinians. Philip II, whose quarters were very small, died there. Through an opening in the wall he could see the celebration of mass when he was ill. In the mausoleum, or Crypt of Kings, are entombed every Spanish king since Charles V, as well as the only Queen, Queen Isabella II. Other members of the royal family are entombed in crypt rooms nearby. One of the greatest jewels of the Escorial is its library, housing some 7,000 engravings, 35,000 books, including 4,627 Greek, Latin, Arabic, and Hebrew manuscripts, among them an illuminated copy of the Gospels and the Apocalypse of Saint John. Many of the tapestries were designed by Goya, and its gallery holds masterpieces by such greats as Velázquez, Tintoretto, Pantoja, Zurbarán, and Titian.

# BRAIN TICKLERS—THE ANSWERS

## Set # 30, page 145

**A.**
1. politician
2. aqueducts
3. transportation
4. Europeans
5. operations
6. relatively
7. common
8. innumerable

**B.**
1. extranjero
2. Nunca he visto antes carreteras
3. están hechos
4. El acueducto
5. sistemas políticos

**C.**
1. V   2. V   3. F   4. V

## Set # 31, page 150

**Piénsalo bien**

**A.** Answers will vary.

**B.**
1. La mujer rubia llegó a la fiesta con vestido y zapatos negros.
2. El hombre alto llevaba unas botas negras.
3. Correct.

**C.** Answers will vary.

**D.** Answers will vary.

**E.**
1. más bonita que
2. más cara que
3. el más alto de
4. los peores
5. más joven que

## Set # 32, page 155

**Habla popular**

1. Hoy estoy contento porque es viernes. (estar)

2. Por lo general soy optimista, pero hoy estoy triste. (ser)

3. Está muy ocupado con su trabajo. (estar)

## Set # 33, page 157

**Bien vale la pena**

1–4. Answers will vary.

## Set # 34, page 160

**Alma hispánica**

1. Answers will vary.

2. Answers will vary.

3. Lorenso Barquero

4. sus tierras

6. Marisela

## Set # 35, page 163

**Pluma en mano**

**A.** Answers will vary.

**B.** Answers will vary.

# Cuatro ruedas para todo

# Four wheels for everything

Desde que se inventó *la rueda*, hace miles de años, *el ser humano* ha preferido *montar* en ella que caminar. Claro que *no fue* hasta entrado el siglo XIX que realmente *se valió de ella como medio de* transporte. Anteriormente era el camello, el caballo, hasta el burro y la llama; hoy lo es el automóvil, el autobús, el tren, el camión, hasta el avión con las que *despega y aterriza*. Se depende tanto de ellas que para *hasta ir* a la esquina a comprar comida, o a la farmacia, a comprar algún medicamento, preferimos hacerlo en cuatro ruedas.

Realmente, en los últimos cincuenta años la explosión del uso del automóvil ha sido extraordinaria. Hoy conduce todo el mundo, desde el más joven hasta el más anciano *y se hace*, mayormente, por la enorme *ventaja* de que el automóvil *nos libera*, nos da *alas* para transladarnos *de un lugar a otro* nosotros mismos, sin *contar* con nadie. Todo lo que tenemos que hacer es darle a la llave *y allá vamos* a donde *nos parezca* y tomándonos el tiempo que más *nos convenga*. Claro que el *conducir* requiere una gran responsabilidad, pues no sólo tenemos que *tener cuidado* de nosotros mismos, sino que *hay que* estar pendiente del otro *conductor*, del otro automóvil. Tenemos, además, que observar todas *las señales* de tráfico, conducir sensatamente, no marchar a alta velocidad y nunca, nunca, conducir si estamos cansados, con sueño, o si nos hemos tomado licor. De hacerlo, arriesgamos tener un accidente que puede ser fatal para nosotros y para otros. Conducir, también, *conlleva* un alto costo que nos *chupa* gran parte del dinero que ganamos, como son los pagos del automóvil que hay que hacer, sobre todo si es nuevo, seguro, gasolina, y mantenimiento.

## Vocabulario básico

| | |
|---|---|
| la rueda | wheel |
| el ser humano | human being |
| montar | to ride |
| no fue | it wasn't |
| se valió de ella | used it |
| como medio de | as a means of |
| despega y aterriza | takes off and lands |
| hasta ir | even to go |
| y se hace | and it is done |
| ventaja | advantage |
| nos libera | frees us |

| | |
|---|---|
| alas | wings |
| de un lugar a otro | from one place to another |
| contar | to rely |
| y allá vamos | there we go |
| nos parezca | pleases us |
| nos convenga | that is more convenient for us |
| conducir | to drive |
| tener cuidado | to be careful |
| hay que | one must |
| conductor | driver |
| las señales | signs |
| conlleva | to entail |
| chupa | takes away |

## ¡OJO!—WATCH OUT!

There are two verbs in Spanish for drive: *conducir* and *manejar*. In the present indicative, *conducir* is conjugated like *conocer* (to know someone), irregular in the first person singular: *conduzco* (I drive). For driver, you can use *conductor* or *chofer*.

## ¿Sabías que?

How much is Florida worth? The United States paid $15 million for Louisiana, $7 million for Alaska, and nothing for Florida, which was ceded by Spain in 1819. Although a treaty was signed to cede Florida for $5 million, Spain was never paid. But even if the $5 million had been paid, think of what $27 million bought—about one third of the continental United States! This is what a CEO of a large corporation makes in one year, or what a leading Hollywood star makes for one movie. And if you add to all this the big chunk of land ceded by Mexico to the United States, it becomes the biggest real estate deal in history!

# BRAIN TICKLERS
## Set # 36

### Ejercicios

A. By looking at these words, you should know what they mean.
   Write the meaning of each one:

   1. inventó
   2. transporte
   3. camello
   4. corporación
   5. accidente
   6. mantenimiento
   7. lujoso
   8. millonarios
   9. década
   10. bicicleta

B. Traduce la palabra o las palabras entre paréntesis:

   1. Yo también tengo (*four wheels*) sin las que no puedo vivir.

   2. En los aeropuertos se ven muchos aviones (*take off and land*).

   3. A mí no me gusta (*to drive*) en la ciudad.

C. Basado en el pasaje, dinos si cada una de estas afirmaciones es *verdadera o falsa*:

   1. El automóvil nos da mucha libertad de desplazamiento.                    V   F

   2. Hoy hay muchos más automóviles que hace un siglo (century).              V   F

   3. En las carreteras se ven hoy pocos camiones.                             V   F

   (Answers are on page 191.)

# PIÉNSALO BIEN
# THINK IT THROUGH

## The adverb. El adverbio

The adverb can modify the verb, just like an adjective modifies the noun, as in:

| | |
|---|---|
| *Él camina despacio.* | He walks slowly. |
| *Él no actúa bien.* | He doesn't act properly. |

That is their main function. However, they can also modify an adjective or another adverb, as in:

| | |
|---|---|
| *Él es muy alto.* | He is very tall. |

Here *muy* (very) is an adverb modifying an adjective, *alto* (tall) but in:

| | |
|---|---|
| *Él camina muy despacio.* | He walks very slowly. |

*Muy* (very), an adverb, modifies another adverb, *despacio* (slowly).

But again, as we said, the main function of an adverb is to modify a verb.

Many phrases also function as adverbs and are called adverbial phrases or clauses, as:

| | |
|---|---|
| *al amanacer* | at dawn |
| *en fin* | well |
| *por último* | at last |
| *tal vez* | perhaps |

There are several kinds of adverbs. Here are the most common:

## Of place

| | | | |
|---|---|---|---|
| *aquí* | here | *lejos* | far |
| *allí* | there | *dentro* | inside |
| *allá* | over there | *fuera* | outside |
| *cerca* | close | | |

## Of time

| | | | |
|---|---|---|---|
| *hoy* | today | *antes* | before |
| *ayer* | yesterday | *después* | after |
| *mañana* | tomorrow | | |

## Of manner

| | | | |
|---|---|---|---|
| *bien* | well | *fácilmente* | easily |
| *mal* | bad | *así* | thus |
| *despacio* | slowly | | |

## Of quantity

| | | | |
|---|---|---|---|
| *más* | more | *poco* | little |
| *mucho* | a lot/much | *tanto* | so/so much |
| *bastante* | enough | | |

## Of order

| | |
|---|---|
| *sucesivamente* | successively |
| *primeramente* | first of all |
| *últimamente* | recently/lately |

## Of affirmation

| | |
|---|---|
| *sí* | yes |
| *también* | also |
| *ciertamente* | certainly |

## Of negation

| | | | |
|---|---|---|---|
| *no* | no | *jamás* | never |
| *nunca* | never | *tampoco* | either |

## Of doubt

| | |
|---|---|
| *quizá/quizás* | maybe/perhaps |

Many adverbs in Spanish are formed by adding *-mente* to the adjective, as in

| | |
|---|---|
| *claramente* | clearly |
| *fácilmente* | easily |
| *normalmente* | normally/usually |

Thus *-mente* generally equals the English *-ly*. If the adjective is masculine, ending in *-o*, you must change the *o* to *a* as in *lento> lentamente* (slow/slowly).

## BRAIN TICKLERS
### Set # 37

**Ejercicios**

A. Give the adverbs for the following adjectives using the rules for *-mente*:
1. apurado
2. difícil
3. duro
4. igual
5. misteriosa

B. Using any of the adverbs given above (of place, time, etc.), make five sentences with each.

C. Tell how many adverbs are in this sentence and write them below:

*Salimos al amanecer para llegar muy temprano.*
A total of _____ adverbs.

(Answers are on page 191.)

# MÁS ES MEJOR
# MORE IS BETTER

### Nouns

| | |
|---|---|
| el volante/timón | steering wheel |
| el freno | brake |
| el freno de mano | hand brake |
| el acelerador | gas pedal |
| el cambio | shift |
| el asiento | seat |
| el cinturón de seguridad | seat belt |
| la bolsa de aire | air bag |

| | |
|---|---|
| el baúl/maletero | trunk |
| el parabrisas | windshield |
| la licencia de conducir | driver's license |
| la placa | plate |
| la matrícula/registración | registration |
| el semáforo | traffic light |
| la multa | fine/ticket |
| el peatón | pedestrian |
| el cruce | crossing |
| a la derecha | to the right |
| a la izquierda | to the left |
| la señal de alto | stop sign |
| la velocidad | speed |
| el peaje | toll |
| el choque | crash |
| el espejo retrovisor | rearview mirror |
| las luces | lights |
| el tablero | dashboard |
| la autopista | freeway |
| el parqueo/estacionamiento | parking |
| el garage | garage |
| la gasolinera | gas station |
| el asiento | seat |
| el mecánico | mechanic |

## Verbs

| | |
|---|---|
| acelerar | to accelerate/speed up |
| frenar | to brake |
| parar | to stop |
| retroceder | to back up/go backward |
| doblar/virar | to turn |
| seguir | to continue (ahead) |
| ceder | to yield |
| ceder el paso | to yield the right of way |
| aparcar/parquear/estacionarse | to park |

### ¡OJO!—WATCH OUT!

The word *parking* is commonly used in Spain's larger cities, just like *patio* and *plaza* are commonly used in the United States. Of the three Spanish words, *aparcar, parquear,* and *estacionarse,* the latter is the most commonly used. The same occurs with *car> carro, auto, automóvil, coche, máquina.* When in doubt, use *automóvil.* Another tricky word is *computer> computadora, computador, ordenador.* The first one is your best choice. *Carretera* in Spanish is any kind of a road, which in the United States is far from true— *road, roadway, freeway, speedway, highway, turnpike,* etc. *Autopista* is also used for what is in the United States a four-lane highway.

# HABLA POPULAR
# EVERYDAY SPEECH

Here are more idioms, expressions, and sayings:

| | |
|---|---|
| no sea que | or else |
| ni siquiera | not even |
| luego que | as soon as |
| junto con | together with |
| en realidad | as a matter of fact |
| el caso es | the fact is |
| en particular | especially |
| dado que | supposing/given that |
| por poco | almost |
| de segunda mano | secondhand |
| quedar en | to agree on |
| al rato | shortly |
| pagar a plazos | to pay in installments |
| no hay remedio | there's nothing we can do |
| tener agallas | to have guts |
| tener en cuenta | to take into account |
| andar por las nubes | to be on cloud nine |

¡socorro!/¡auxilio!          help!
Nunca es tarde
   si la dicha es buena.      Better late than never.

---

### ¿Sabías que?

Who discovered Hawaii? To the English it was James Cook in 1778. To the Spaniards, it was Juan de Gaitán in 1555, based on a map by Ortelius and Mercator where Hawaii is called *Desgraciada* (Unfortunate), and on a Spanish map (now at the Naval Museum in Madrid), noting that Hawaii was discovered by Juan de Gaitán. Also, when he got there, Cook found a piece of Spanish armor now preserved at the British Museum.

---

# BIEN VALE LA PENA
# IT'S WELL WORTH IT

## The job interview. La entrevista de trabajo

E> entrevistador (interviewer)
T> Tú (you)

T:  Buenos días.
E:  Buenos días.
T:  ¿Cómo está usted?
E:  Bien, ¿y usted?
T:  Muy bien, gracias.
E:  Usted es el Sr. Hernán Fernández, ¿no?
T:  Así es.
E:  ¿Y la posición que le interesa es la de gerente de ventas?
T:  Sí, señor.
E:  ¿Trajo su currículum vitae?
T:  Sí, señor. Aquí lo tiene.
E:  ¿Se graduó de la universidad?
T:  Sí, hace cuatro años.
E:  ¿Qué estudió?
T:  Administración de empresas.
E:  Veo que ha tenido bastante experiencia en este campo.

T: Más de diez años en total.

E: ¿Por qué dejó su último empleo?

T: La empresa se trasladó a Francia.

E: ¿Qué sueldo tiene pensado ganar?

T: ¿Cuánto paga esta posición?

E: $45,000 al año, más beneficios. ¿Qué le parece?

T: Más o menos lo que yo pensaba.

E: Déjeme darle algunos datos de esta empresa. La empresa se especializa en la manufactura, venta y distribución de artículos del hogar y lleva de fundada treinta años. Es una empresa de propiedad familiar, dirigida por el hijo del fundador, el Sr. Gutiérrez, que es el presidente de la Junta Directiva. Las ventas anuales sobrepasan los diez millones de dólares y sus productos se venden por todo el mundo, principalmente en Sur América. Contamos con sucursales en México, Puerto Rico, y Argentina. Ahora, en cuanto a su responsabilidad, dado que se le ofreciera este trabajo, sería la de administrar todo lo relacionado con las ventas, para lo cual tendría que viajar a menudo. ¿Tiene usted alguna objeción a esto?

T: No, señor, me encanta viajar y conozco muy bien esos países que ha mencionado más otros muchos. Durante un tiempo me pasé casi tres meses viajando por el continente.

E: Eso es algo a su favor. ¿Qué idiomas habla además del español?

T: Bien bien, el inglés, con algunos conocimientos de italiano.

E: ¿No habla portugués?

T: Algo, pero no mucho. También estuve en Brasil.

E: Me parece que es usted un buen candidato para esta posición, aunque no le puedo garantizar nada. Aún tenemos que entrevistar a otros candidatos.

T: Lo comprendo perfectamente. ¿Cuándo me avisarían?

E: Calcule en dos o tres semanas; se le llamaría por teléfono en caso de que la empresa estuviera interesada en sus servicios. ¡Ah, antes de que se me olvide! ¿Nos puede proporcionar algunas referencias?

T: Sí, señor. Aquí tiene los nombres.

E: Pues bien, Sr. Fernández, ha sido un placer en conocerle y ojalá que todo salga bien para usted. Le agradezco su interés en nuestra empresa y le deseo mucha suerte. Nos vemos pronto, espero…

T: El gusto ha sido mío. Quedo pendiente de sus noticias. Hasta luego.

# BRAIN TICKLERS
## Set # 38

### Ejercicios

A. Contesta estas preguntas en oraciones completas:

1. ¿Cómo se llama el solicitante (applicant)?

2. ¿Cuánto tiempo hace que se graduó el solicitante de la universidad?

3. ¿Por qué dejó su último empleo?

4. ¿A qué se dedica la empresa?

5. ¿Dónde tiene sucursales (branches)?

6. ¿Cree usted que el entrevistador está interesado en darle la posición al solicitante? ¿Por qué sí o por qué no?

7. ¿Cómo se le avisa al solicitante si se le va a ofrecer el puesto?

B. Give the meaning of these words/phrases:

1. Aquí lo tiene
2. Veo que
3. Más o menos
4. Junta Directiva
5. dado que

6. me pasé
7. Algo
8. en caso de que
9. perfectamente
10. semana

(Answers are on page 191.)

## ¡OJO!—WATCH OUT!

Even though many Hispanic countries have their own units of currency, others, such as Colombia, Chile, Argentina, Mexico, Cuba, the Dominican Republic, and Uruguay, use *peso* as their standard unit of currency. *Peso* means weight in Spanish, and during colonial times it consisted of a piece worth eight reales, which later became the *peso*.
Some of the units of currency of the other countries are: *sol* (Peru), *bolívar* (Venezuela), *balboa* (Panamá), *córdoba* (Nicaragua), *boliviano* (Bolivia), *colón* (El Salvador, Costa Rica), *lempira* (Honduras), *euro* (Spain). In Ecuador it used to be *sucre*, but it is now the dollar.

# DILO COMO YO
# SAY IT LIKE I DO

## Pronunciation of the x, y, z

The *x* in Spanish is pronounced as in English between vowels (ks), and as *s* before a consonant, as in: *examen, expreso*.

The *y*, before a vowel, is pronounced similarly to the English *y* in *yes*. The conjunction *y* (and), and the *y* at the end of a syllable are pronounced like *i*, as in: *Juana y Pedro*.

The *z* is always pronounced *s* in Hispanic America, while in most of Spain it is pronounced like the English *th* in *three, think: cruzar, zapato*.

## Pronunciation Practice

Say these words out loud:

| | |
|---|---|
| yodo | yerno y nuera |
| yuca | yogurt y yerba |
| yunque | caray |
| yegua | soy |
| yarda | batey |
| yo y tú | Camagüey |
| yema y yeso | estoy |

# ALMA HISPÁNICA
# HISPANIC SOUL

## Antonio Machado

Antonio Machado is a man who shines in Spanish letters. His work is the purest of pure lyricism, the language of the soul at its finest. If you appreciate poetry, Machado will forever be one of your favorites.

He was born in Seville in 1875 and died in a small town in France, Colliure, in 1939, near the end of the Spanish Civil War. In fact, he left Spain with his mother and other relatives (as well as many other Spanish refugees) that year, and died a few days before his mother. He lived in Paris where he worked at the Garnier House. He then returned to Spain, to Soria, where he married his beloved Leonor in 1909, when she was 16. In 1911, they traveled to Paris where Leonor fell ill and returned to Soria where she died in 1912. From that moment on, Machado was a different man. His life had been shattered by his wife's unexpected death. He longed for the years past and the love they both shared.

## The writings of Antonio Machado

*Señor, ya me arrancaste lo que más quería*
*oye otra vez, Dios mío, mi corazón clamar*
*tu voluntad se hizo, Señor, contra la mía,*
*Señor ya estamos solos mi corazón y el mar.*

*Ayer soñé que veía*
*a Dios y que a Dios hablaba;*
*y soñé que Dios me oía...*
*Después soñé que soñaba.*

*Anoche soñé que oía*
*a Dios, gritándome: ¡Alerta!*
*Luego era Dios quien dormía*
*y yo gritaba: ¡despierta!*

To help you better understand the poems, here is the meaning of some key words:

| | | | |
|---|---|---|---|
| *oye* | listen | *soñé* | dreamed |
| *clamar* | clamor | *oía* | heard |
| *voluntad* | wish | *gritándome* | yelling (to me) |
| *solos* | alone | *Luego* | later |
| *mar* | sea | *dormía* | slept |

## Review

A. Review the three poems. In the first poem, what is Machado inferring?

B. What about in the other two?

# PLUMA EN MANO
# PEN IN HAND

## *La contaminación ambiental/Air pollution*

Si nos ponemos a pensar, respiramos veneno (poison) en todo momento de nuestras vidas. A pesar de (despite) todo lo que digan, de todas las leyes y regulaciones (laws and regulations) de las que se habla (what they say), de todos los grupos que protestan, cada día la contaminación ambiental o polución se agrava. Nadie la puede contener (It can't be contained) y en poco la pueden mejorar (improve) por la sencilla razón (simply) del progreso que se nos viene encima (that overwhelms us). El hollín (soot) de las grandes fábricas, los gases que despiden (emit) los automóviles y otros vehículos de motor, la niebla tóxica (smog) que nos envuelve y poco a poco nos van acabando (doing us harm), contribuyendo enormemente a infinitas enfermedades y trastornos que nos aquejan (afflict us). Y no solamente debemos preocuparnos por lo que respiramos, sino de igual forma por lo que comemos, por lo que metemos en la boca (what we put in our mouth) y todo producto que compramos para limpiar, para desinfectar, para embellecernos, y no dejemos fuera (leave out) los materiales para la construcción, como pinturas, barnices, pegamentos (glues), etc.

# BRAIN TICKLERS
### Set # 39

*Ejercicios*

A. Choose five words/idioms from the list below and write a Spanish sentence with each:
pensar
en todo momento
contaminación ambiental
nadie
preocuparse

B. Give the infinitive forms of the following verbs from the passage:
   1. ponemos
   2. protestan
   3. pueden

C. Of the verbs from **Ejercicio B** above, give the *I* form (1st person singular) of the indicative for each.

D. Write three sentences in Spanish about the dangers of today's air pollution.

(Answers are on page 192.)

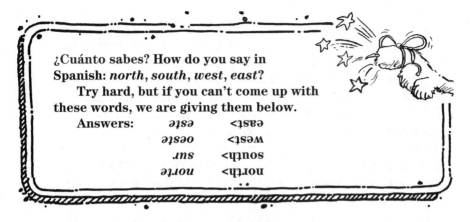

# ASÍ SOMOS
# THIS IS WHO WE ARE

## The treasures of Mexico

An imposing cathedral is in the heart of Mexico City in what is known as the *Zócalo*, the largest square in all of Hispanic America. The Zócalo was built by the Spaniards on what used to be the Aztec seat of government. More than 80 magnificent structures such as temples, buildings, and palaces were all built by the Aztecs when they settled there in the beginning of the fourteenth century. The cathedral was begun in 1572, and it took an amazing 250 years to complete, being one of the largest in the world. Adjoining the cathedral is the National Palace, built in 1693, where the president of Mexico resides. The National Palace occupies the same site as the former palace

of the emperor Moctezuma. The frescoes of Mexico's greatest painter, Diego Rivera, which took him six years to complete, can be seen everywhere within the palace's walls. Also adjoining the cathedral and palace is the church of *El Sagrario*, built in 1749, in a perfect Baroque style, or more specifically, Churrigueresque style, typical of many Hispanic American structures. If you go to some of the other cities, such as Guadalajara, Taxco, Cuernavaca, Jalisco, Oaxaca, you will also be transported in time and be totally convinced of Mexico's greatness; that includes also the food, and the customs, and most definitely, the people and their unique way of life. There are the pyramids of Teotihuacán and Tula, the ancient Toltec city, where the glory of pre-Columbus Mexico can be seen at its highest, and the Aztec calendar, one of the many calendars of Mesoamerica, consisting of a 365-day cycle and a 260-day ritual cycle, which combined formed a 52-year century. The solar calendar of 365 days consisted of 18 months of 20 days each, with an additional period of 5 to 6 days added at the end. It was discovered in 1790 near the Great Aztec Temple in the Mexican capital.

# BRAIN TICKLERS—THE ANSWERS

## Set # 36, page 175

**A.**

1. invented
2. transportation
3. camel
4. corporation
5. accident

6. maintenance
7. luxurious
8. millionaires
9. decade
10. bicycle

**B.**

1. cuatro ruedas
2. despegar y aterrizar
3. conducir/manejar

**C.**

1. V    2. V    3. F

## Set # 37, page 178

**Piénsalo bien**

**A.**

1. apuradamente
2. difícilmente
3. duramente

4. igualmente
5. misteriosamente

**B.** Answers will vary.

**C.**

3—al amanecer—muy—temprano

## Set # 38, page 183

**Bien vale la pena**

**A.**

1. El solicitante se llama Hernán Fernández.
2. Hace cuatro años que se graduó.
3. Dejó su último empleo porque la empresa se trasladó a Francia.
4. La empresa se dedica a la manufactura, venta y distribución de artículos del hogar.
5. Tiene sucursales en México, Puerto Rico y Argentina.
6. Answers will vary.
7. llamándole por teléfono.

**B.**

1. Here it is
2. I see that
3. More or less
4. Board of Directors
5. supposing/given that

6. I spent
7. Something
8. in case
9. perfectly
10. week

## Set # 39, page 188

**Pluma en mano**

**A.** Answers will vary.

**B.**

1. poner
2. protestar
3. poder

**C.**

1. pongo
2. protesto
3. puedo
4. pido
5. hago

**D.** Answers will vary.

# No hay mejor educación que el viajar

# Traveling is the best education

El mundo es amplio, maravilloso, *sorprendente*. Hay tanto que ver, tanto que aprender, que nadie puede permanecer entre las cuatro paredes de su pueblo o ciudad, *sin echar al menos un vistazo* a lo que está fuera de nuestra frontera. Pero, como todo en la vida, hay que saber viajar, saber *lo que se va a ver* y el porqué. Como primer paso, hay que apartarse de las grandes zonas metropolitanas y seguir una *pauta* distinta a la del turista común. *Nada de* hoteles de lujo o caravanas a los *lugares de interés* en los que *se ve y no se ve*, en los que se aprende y no se aprende. Tampoco hay que viajar como un *vagabundo*, con una maleta *a cuestas* y *deambular* de un lado para otro. No. Todo país, todo rincón de la tierra tiene su *encanto* y algo único que *mostrar*, y mejor es hacerlo con alguien querido al lado, *se quiere decir*, *mezclándose* con la gente y aprendiendo de ella *de viva voz* y no de un guía turístico, y contando con tiempo, el que sea, para poder absorber y apreciar lo que *se tiene delante* sin que nadie *nos lo empañe*.

Con el viajar se nos amplía nuestra perspectiva del mundo y de la vida, quizá *en mayor grado* que en la escuela, pues lo que aprendemos no es teoría ni *a través* de fotos o películas, sino que es el verdadero *aprendizaje* que nos entra por nuestros *propios* ojos y oídos. No es igual que se nos hable de México, que ver a México, como no es igual que se nos hable del Cañón del Colorado, que verlo. Y si lo que realmente nos interesa es aprender un nuevo idioma, el que sea, estando en el país que se habla por cierto tiempo, lo aprenderemos más rápido y mejor que en 100 horas en el laboratorio de lenguas. Adónde viajar?

## Vocabulario básico

| | |
|---|---|
| sorprendente | surprising |
| sin echar al menos un vistazo | without at least taking a look |
| lo que se va a ver | what one will see |
| pauta | norm |
| Nada de | No |
| lugares de interés | places of interest |
| se ve y no se ve | one can see and not see |
| vagabundo | vagabond |

| | |
|---|---|
| a cuestas | on one's shoulders |
| deambular | to wander |
| encanto | charm |
| mostrar | to show |
| se quiere decir | that's to say |
| mezclándose | mingling |
| de viva voz | personally |
| se tiene delante | one has in front/one can see |
| nos lo empañe | fogs it over for us |
| en mayor grado | to a greater degree |
| a través | through |
| aprendizaje | learning |
| propios | own |

## ¿Sabías que?

About 30 percent of U.S. geographical names are Spanish or were designated Spanish names when they were first discovered. And no less than 2,000 U.S. cities also have Spanish names.

# BRAIN TICKLERS
### Set # 40

### *Ejercicios*

A. By looking at these words you should know what they mean. Write the meaning of each one.

1. frontera
2. zonas
3. turista
4. único
5. guía
6. hamburguesas
7. regularmente
8. partes
9. frijoles
10. teoría

B. Traduce la palabra o las palabras entre paréntesis.

1. (There is so much to see) en México.
2. De vez en cuando hay que salir. No se puede estar siempre entre (four walls).
3. A mí no me gustan los (tourist guides).
4. (Where we live) hay muchos parques.
5. Para apreciar bien el Cañón de Colorado hay que (see it) en persona.
6. Una (custom) típica de España es dormir la siesta.

C. Give the Spanish for the following:

1. to travel
2. to see
3. to drink/take
4. to serve
5. to depend

(Answers are on page 210.)

---

### ¡OJO!—WATCH OUT!

*Ir de paseo* is a very common Spanish idiom meaning to go out for a walk, a stroll, a ride, anything that is fun and enjoyable. *Paseo*, a noun, can mean an avenue, as in *el Paseo del Prado*, a famous avenue in Havana, or *el Paseo de la Castellana*, a well-known avenue in Madrid.

# PIÉNSALO BIEN
# THINK IT THROUGH

## About the Spanish language

Spanish is a very old language, at least 1,000 years old. It is called a *Romance language* because it originated from Latin, just as French and Portuguese did. Why? Because for many years Spain was one of the key provinces of Rome and was greatly influenced by Rome's language, culture, and customs. Throughout most of the Middle Ages, Latin was the language spoken in Spain, until the thirteenth century, when King Alphonse X proclaimed it the official language of his kingdom of Castile. However, many medieval writers began to write in *romance*, or Spanish, early on, and by the sixteenth century most writers were already writing in Spanish. The father of the Spanish language, as he is commonly called, was Miguel de Cervantes, the author of *Don Quijote*, the one who largely made the language what it is today. Spanish was also influenced by many other languages, including Arabic, and, of course, Greek and Latin. When Spain discovered America in 1492, many of the languages spoken by the indigenous cultures, such as the Aztecs and Incas, also greatly influenced Spanish, especially in names of food and plants. Some people think that there are different kinds of Spanish, which is not really true. There is only one kind of Spanish, although there are differences in the use and pronunciation of certain words and sounds, and in the intonation. However, no matter how many different equivalents a word may have, there is always one standard word that everybody knows, which is the one you should use. For example, in the Caribbean, the word most commonly used for *bus* is *guagua*, and in Central America *camión*. However, the standard Spanish word is *autobús*, or *bus*. Either one should be your first choice.

# MÁS ES MEJOR
# MORE IS BETTER

## Nouns

| | |
|---|---|
| el metro | subway |
| la agencia de viajes/pasajes | travel agency |
| el cheque de viajeros | traveler's check |
| la tasa de cambio | exchange rate |
| la moneda nacional | national currency |
| el boleto/pasaje | ticket |
| el viaje de ida/el viaje de vuelta | one-way trip |
| el viaje de ida y vuelta | round trip |
| la aduana | customs |
| inmigración | immigration |
| a bordo | on board |
| la llegada | arrival |
| la salida | departure |
| el equipaje | luggage |
| la maleta | suitcase |
| el bolso de mano | handbag |
| al registro | search |
| el detector de metales | metal detector |
| el abordaje | boarding |
| la sala de espera | waiting room |
| el aeropuerto | airport |
| la visa | visa |
| el boleto | ticket |
| el viaje | trip |
| el vuelo | flight |

## Verbs

| | |
|---|---|
| volar | to fly |
| llegar | to arrive |
| partir | to depart |
| cargar | to carry |
| llevar | to take |
| abordar | to board |
| inspeccionar | to inspect |
| montar | to get on/ride |
| subir | to go up |

| | |
|---|---|
| bajar | to go down |
| esperar | to wait |
| apurarse | to hurry up |
| pesar | to weigh |

# HABLA POPULAR
# EVERYDAY SPEECH

Here are more idioms, expressions, and sayings.

| | |
|---|---|
| de ahí | hence |
| por aquí/por acá | around here |
| de aquí en adelante | from now on |
| por el/la presente | for now |
| siempre que | whenever |
| mientras que/en tanto que | whereas |
| por el/la/los/las que | whereby |
| en el/la/los/las | wherein |
| en cualquier parte/lado | wherever |
| a propósito | by the way |
| más bien | rather |
| tanto mejor | so much the better |
| mojarse los labios | to take a sip |
| tomar el pelo | to tease |
| sacar los trapos sucios | to air the dirty linen |
| Los ojos son el espejo del alma. | The eyes are the mirror of the soul. |

## ¿Sabías que?

A relative of Emily Da Silva Nathan, Emma Lazarus, a Sephardic Jew, was the author of the poem now inscribed on the Statue of Liberty: *Give me your tired, your poor, Your huddled masses yearning to be free.* Another Nathan, Annie Nathan Meyer, was the founder of New York's prestigious Barnard College. And another Sephardic family, the Seixas (later Saks), were the founders of the world-famous department store, Saks Fifth Avenue in New York. Sephardic Jews lived for centuries in Spain and were expelled in the fifteenth century. They contributed greatly to Spain and are an intrinsic part of Spanish culture. Today, many of them still speak Spanish and follow many of the Spanish customs.

# BIEN VALE LA PENA
# IT'S WELL WORTH IT

## Holidays. Días de fiesta

Here we will give only some of the national holidays of the
United States with their Spanish counterparts.

| | |
|---|---|
| La Navidad | Christmas |
| El Fin de Año | New Year's Eve |
| El Día de Fin de Año | New Year's Day |
| El Día de Martin Luther King, Jr | Martin Luther King, Jr's Day |
| El Día de San Valentín | Valentine's Day |
| El Día de los Presidentes | Presidents' Day |
| El Día de San Patricio | St. Patrick's Day |
| El Domingo de Ramos | Palm Sunday |
| El Viernes Santo | Good Friday |
| El Domingo de Pascua | Easter Sunday |
| El Día de los Inocentes | April Fools' Day |
| El Día de las Madres | Mother's Day |
| Día en que se celebra a los caídos en las guerras | Memorial Day |
| El Día de los Padres | Father's Day |
| El Día de la Independencia | Independence Day |
| El Día del Trabajo | Labor Day |
| El Día de la Raza | Columbus Day |
| El Día de las Brujas | Halloween |
| El Día de todos los Santos | All Saints' Day |
| El Día de las Elecciones | Election Day |
| El Día de los Veteranos | Veterans Day |
| El Día de Acción de Gracias | Thanksgiving Day |

### ¿Sabías que?

In addition to many other holidays, big celebration days for
Hispanics are *La Nochebuena* (Christmas Eve) and *El Día de
Reyes* (The Three Wise Men's Day) on January 6th. *El Día de la
Raza* is Columbus Day, and it means, literally, the *Day of the
Race*, honoring the great mosaic of Hispanic races and cultures.

# DILO COMO YO
# SAY IT LIKE I DO

## Pronunciation of the vowels

Generally speaking, Spanish has five vowels and five sounds. This works greatly to your advantage, as the student, especially when you are used to the same five vowels in English with multiple different sounds, some 27 in total. No matter what their position is within a word—whether they are stressed or not, whether they precede or follow a consonant, are used beginning or ending a syllable, or one same vowel following another—you can safely assume that each one of the five Spanish vowels are always pronounced the same. Nothing like the *oo* or *ee* in English at all, ever. We are giving you, below, the approximate sound of each one of the vowels:

*a*  close to the *a* in *father*, as in: *casa, calabaza, cama*

*e*  close to the *e* in *pen*, as in: *Pepe, pelele, bebé*

*i*  close to the *ee* in *seen*, as in: *sí, siglo, silla*

*o*  close to the *o* in *robe*, as in: *oro, ola, cosa*

*u*  close to the *oo* in *boot*, as in: *uno, luna, mucho*

## Pronunciation Practice

A. Say these words out loud:

| | | | | |
|---|---|---|---|---|
| mamá | mañana | barbacoa | camaleón | salga |
| enero | mes | este | mesero | nene |
| abril | minoría | silbido | asimismo | risa |
| lobo | como | solo | bobo | noto |
| pulso | susurro | puma | púrpura | tuba |

B. And now, say these words out loud:

| | | |
|---|---|---|
| papanatismo | pupilaje | abracadabra |
| cantaclaro | horrorosidad | cosmopolita |
| alibabá | cucurrucú | locomotora |
| fantasmagórico | | |

¿Cuánto sabes?

¿Cuánto sabes?

How is your sense of geography? See if you can do this: From New York City, match the Hispanic countries in column A with their correct direction in column B:

Column A          Column B

1. México         a. sudeste
2. España         b. sudoeste
3. Puerto Rico    c. este
4. Colombia       d. sur

Answers: 1-b, 2-c, 3-a, 4-d

And what about *el Mar Mediterráneo*? Circle the right location from New York City:

norte     este     oeste     sur

Answer: *este*

# ALMA HISPÁNICA
# HISPANIC SOUL

## Ricardo Palma

Ricardo Palma was one of the masters, perhaps the greatest one, of the *costumbrismo* (literary genre about local customs) in Peru, especially during colonial Lima in the eighteenth century (then the Americas' most majestic city). Many of the things we know today about that period are because of his *Tradiciones peruanas* (Peruvian Traditions). In an amusing picaresque style, he vividly portrays general life in Lima from the Incas to contemporary times. As writer Raúl Porras Barrenechea once wrote: He (Palma) "opened the eyes of colonial Lima during the period of the Viceroys." He was the consummate narrator, the storyteller who animated customs, folklore, and people alike, from viceroys to beggers, from ladies of high society to the typical women of the streets. About his *Tradiciones* he once confessed to a friend that "he was not the writer, the historian, but rather those we call the people." He began his *Tradiciones* in 1852 and completed six series from 1872 to 1883, followed by several others. One of the things that stands out about Palma is his belief that language must reflect evolution, that it is not up to scholars behind a desk, as he called members of the Spanish Royal Academy of Language, to dictate or at least limit the natural growth and development of a language. He was, thus, deeply concerned with linguistics and the use of his own language and style, which has been categorized as eminently popular and American. Palma is also revered for his total dedication to the National Library of Peru where he was the director from 1883 to 1912. He replenished some 4,000 volumes that were looted during the War of the Pacific, many of which he had himself donated, and many through donations from friends around the world.

## The writings of Ricardo Palma

### Tradiciones peruanas

### *Mujer Hombre*

No fue en América Doña Catalina de Erauzo, bautizada en la historia colonial con el *sobrenombre* de la "Monja alférez", la única hija de Eva, ni la sola *monja* que cambiara las faldas de su sexo por el traje y costumbres *varoniles*.

El 25 de octubre de 1803 se comunicó de Cochabamba a la *Real Audiencia de Lima* el descubrimiento de que un caballero, conocido en Buenos Aires y en Potosí con el nombre de Antonio Ita, no era tal varón con derecho de varonía, sino doña María Leocadia Álvarez, monja *clarisa* del monasterio de la villa de Agreda, en España… terminó por espontanearse declarando su verdadero nombre de María Leocadia Álvarez y su condición de monja escapada, no por *amoríos carnales*, sino por espíritu aventurero, como doña Catalina de Frauzo.

To help you better understand this passage, here is the meaning of some key words:

| | |
|---|---|
| *sobrenombre* | nickname |
| *monja* | nun |
| *varoniles* | manly, masculine |
| *Real Audiencia de Lima* | High Court of Lima |
| *clarisa* | Order of Saint Claire |
| *amoríos carnales* | love affairs |

## BRAIN TICKLERS
### Set # 41

*Ejercicios*

Answer these questions in English:

1. According to the story, how many women disguised themselves as men and what were their names?

2. What do you think was the reason for their behavior?

3. What is *Cochabamba*?

4. Where is the *Monasterio de Agreda*?

5. How would you translate *hija de Eva*?

(Answers are on page 210.)

---

### ¿Sabías que?

During the Spanish colonial period in South America, a total of 12,412 books were published as compared to only 500 in the U.S. colonial period.

# PLUMA EN MANO
# PEN IN HAND

## Mis vacaciones pasadas/My last vacation

He viajado mucho, visto muchos lugares y todos me han gustado. Pero hasta ahora (until now) no ha habido nada (nothing) comparable a mi viaje a Puerto Rico, mi primero y desde luego (of course) no el último (the last one). Le di la vuelta a la isla (around the island) y me quedé varios días en San Juan, la capital, en la playa de Luquillo. Me hospedé (I stayed) en el hotel Conquistador que ya no sé si sigue allí (if it is still there). De ahí, por carretera (by road) me fui a Ponce, en el extremo sur de la isla, y al regreso me quedé en Mayagüez el resto del tiempo, en casa de unos amigos que vivían cerca del ingenio (sugar mill) Igualdad, en un caserón viejo pero encantador (enchanting). Todas las mañanas, bien tempranito (very early), me levantaba y a pie (walking) me iba a la playa de Añasco. Allí, me tiraba en la arena (sand) debajo (under) una palma a disfrutar del paisaje y de la brisa (breeze) tropical y de un cielo tan claro y un sol (sun) tan intenso que me cegaba (blinded me). Al rato (in a little while) me levantaba y corriendo me tiraba (threw myself) en el mar respirando el olor (smell) incomparable de las aguas caribeñas—olor a mar, olor a limpio, olor a historia. Allí me estaba hasta el atardecer (dusk). Luego me iba (went) al hotel de Mayagüez que estaba cerquita (very close) y allí charlando y comiendo se me iban las horas volando (hours went flying by). Antes de regresar a casa, me daba otra vuelta (another walk) por la playa, ya de noche (already night) a ver las estrellas. El espectáculo ante (before) mis ojos me sobrecogía (overwhelmed me) sin poder creer que pudiera haber (that there could be) en el mundo tal (such) maravilla.¡Ay Dios mío! Luego a casa al banquetazo (great feast) que me esperaba, a la cama (to bed) a descansar y soñar…

# BRAIN TICKLERS
## Set # 42

### Ejercicios

A. Choose five words/idioms from the list below and write a Spanish sentence using each:

hasta ahora    hospedarse
temprano    olor
maravilla    isla
carretera    estrella

B. Taken from the passage on the previous pages, give the infinitive forms of the following verbs:

1. di _____

2. me quedé _____

3. fui _____

4. me tiraba _____

5. charlando _____

C. Match the definitions in column A with the words in column B:

Column A

1. es la capital de Puerto Rico

2. nombre de la playa donde está/ estaba el hotel Conquistador

3. ciudad de Puerto Rico que está al extremo sur de la isla

4. ciudad donde me quedé el resto del tiempo

5. nombre de la playa donde me gustaba ir

Column B

a. Mayagüez
b. Ponce
c. Añasco
d. San Juan
e. Luquillo

D. All of the verbs below are regular. Give the imperfect indicative of each according to the person given in parentheses (refer to Lesson 5):

1. disfrutar (yo):
2. ver (ellos):
3. charlar (tú):
4. correr (ella)
5. descansar (nosotros):

6. vivir (usted):
7. volar (él):
8. soñar (ustedes):
9. hospedarse (yo):
10. dar (vosotros):

(Answers are on page 210.)

# ASÍ SOMOS
# THIS IS WHO WE ARE

## The treasures of Peru

Sometimes we think that we must travel to Europe or Asia to see some of the great historical wonders of the world. Seldom do we think that right here, in America, especially in the countries to our south, there are as many such wonders as any other place on Earth. Take Peru, for instance: Step back in time and put yourself in the first half of the sixteenth century. Do you know what actually transpired there during that period? Think of the Incas and the Spaniards, of one of the most advanced civilizations that ever existed, the Incas, and a country at the peak of its glory, Spain, and how they came together in an epic of Homeric proportions. Think of Lima today, rightly called in the past *la Ciudad de los Reyes*, the City of Kings, founded on January 18, 1535, a great city indeed, and the Lima of the sixteenth and seventeenth centuries. It rivaled the greatest cities in Europe, and was one of the centers of the universe at the time, the absolute pride of the Spanish empire in America for more than two centuries. There is so much to see in Peru that you would be hard-pressed to decide where to begin. But let's concentrate on two places: Lima and Machu Picchu.

In Lima, the Plaza de Armas, or Plaza Mayor, is stunning, with the following major attraction: the cathedral, for which Francisco Pizarro himself placed the first stone on January 18, 1535; he also inaugurated the first church on March 11, 1540. The first mass was celebrated on August 15, 1622. The archbishop Jerónimo de Loayza wanted to make it like the cathedral of Seville, if not better. Other attractions in the Plaza are the Archbishop's Palace, the Government Palace, and Town Hall.

Machu Picchu, or as it is commonly called, the Lost City of the Incas, is one of the greatest marvels of the world in terms of its location and architecture. It is not really a city, but a country retreat for the Incas. It is located on a mountain above the Urubamba Valley at an elevation of 6,750 feet (2057 m). Machu Picchu was discovered, or perhaps rediscovered, in 1911 by Yale professor Hiram Bingham III. It is believed that the city was built by Sapa Inca in 1440; it mainly consists of a large palace, numerous temples, and other buildings for the staff. Some of the stone structures did not use mortar but precise cutting blocks aligned in unique shapes. People from around the world have been flocking into Machu Picchu ever since the magazine *National Geographic* devoted an entire issue (April 1913) to it. Besides Lima and Machu Picchu, the Amazonian basin that occupies almost half of Peru and the Peruvian Andes are sights to behold. We can't fail to mention also the city of Cuzco, the ancient Inca capital.

# BRAIN TICKLERS — THE ANSWERS

## Set # 40, page 196

**A.**

1. frontier
2. zones
3. tourist
4. unique
5. guide
6. hamburgers
7. regularly
8. parts
9. beans
10. theory

**B.**

1. Hay tanto que ver
2. cuatro paredes
3. guías turísticos
4. Donde vivimos
5. verlo
6. costumbre

**C.**

1. viajar
2. ver
3. tomar
4. servir
5. depender

## Set # 41, page 205

**Alma hispánica**

1. 2; Catalina de Erauzo and María Leocadia Álvarez
2. Answers will vary.
3. a city in Bolivia
4. España
5. daughter of Eve

## Set # 42, page 207

**Pluma en mano**

**A.** Answers will vary

**B.**

1. dar
2. quedarse
3. ir
4. tirarse
5. charlar

**C.**

1. d
2. e
3. b
4. a
5. c

**D.**

1. disfrutaba
2. veían
3. charlabas
4. corría
5. descansábamos
6. vivía
7. volaba
8. soñaban
9. me hospedaba
10. dabais

# Con buen gobierno avanzan los pueblos

# Nations advance with good government

Los gobiernos *promulgan* leyes que el pueblo *acata* u obedece. Si no fuera por ellas, caeríamos todos en *la barbarie*, en la anarquía, en nuestra propia destrucción. Pero hay gobiernos con muchas leyes que por lo general se ignoran, mientras que hay otros, *los menos*, en los que la ley *reina* victoriosa. Uno de estos países son los Estados Unidos, nación basada totalmente en un sistema de leyes inquebrantables que se *han mantenido* sin interrupción *por más de* doscientos años. A este sistema de leyes se le llama la Constitución de los Estados Unidos de América, ratificada en 1787. Un grupo de patriotas, un sueño y una feliz realidad que *nos ha llevado* por un largo camino hasta nuestros días, unas veces dando *vueltas y tumbos*, y otras muy derechito con un *rumbo* muy preciso.

Esta Constitución, la más antigua aún *en vigencia*, es el *amparo* y refugio de todo ciudadano estadounidense. En 7 artículos y 27 enmiendas, *se abarca* todo cuanto se necesita para dirigir un país por el camino de la democracia, por el camino del triunfo. En ella se establecen tres *poderes* federales: Legislativo, Judicial, y Ejecutivo, que representan *la balanza del poder*, es decir, que el poder no reside en *ninguno de ellos en particular*, sino en todos, uno pendiente y vigilante del otro y siempre *dispuestos* los tres a mantener el equilibrio. El Legislativo *lo compone* el Congreso, formado por el Senado y la Cámara de Representantes, legisladores, o diputados; el Judicial lo componen los nueve *jueces* del Tribunal Supremo; y el Ejecutivo un Presidente y Vicepresidente. A los componentes del Poder Legislativo *los elige* el pueblo, al igual que al Presidente y Vicepresidente del Poder Ejecutivo. A los nueves jueces del Tribunal Supremo los nombra el Presidente de la nación. O sea que los legisladores promulgan las leyes, el Presidente las ejecuta, y cuando hay *divergencias* o disputas decide el Tribunal Supremo. Este sistema de gobierno federal es el que siguen los estados de la Unión, así como las ciudades y pueblos aunque con nombres distintos. Por ejemplo, en ellos, el que dirige será un *alcalde*, y el legislador un comisionado, pero sus funciones son equivalentes aunque en muchísimo *menor grado*. Cada cuatro años se elige al Presidente, cada seis años a los senadores, y cada dos años a los representantes. Al Presidente sólo *se le puede* elegir dos veces pero en cuanto *a* los otros no hay límites. Al Presidente de la nación no lo elige el pueblo *sino* los electores que asignan los distintos estados. Es decir, que un candidato que obtenga la mayoría del voto popular puede *perder* las elecciones si no lo han elegido por mayoría los electores.

La estabilidad política logra la paz, bienestar y progreso de los pueblos, *a diferencia de* los sistemas de gobierno dictatoriales *en los que* el poder descansa en un individuo y en los que el pueblo, el verdadero *soberano*, poco influye. En otros gobiernos el poder descansa, por tradición mayormente, en una monarquía, aunque modernamente son *monarquías parlamentarias* y en los que el monarca o *rey*, o en algunos casos *la reina*, como en Inglaterra, son simplemente figuras a las que se venera y honra pero *carentes* de poder alguno. Así es el sistema español actual, aunque *hubo un tiempo* en que España estaba *regida* por un dictador, *como lo estaban* Italia y Alemania. La América hispana tuvo sus épocas de dictaduras, *golpes de estado* y revoluciones, pero *paulatinamente* se va imponiendo un sistema democrático que *augura* un futuro más seguro y progresivo.

## Vocabulario básico

| | |
|---|---|
| promulgan | promulgate/enact |
| acata | obeys |
| la barbarie | barbarism |
| los menos | the lesser number |
| reina | reigns |
| han mantenido | have maintained |
| por más de | for more than |
| nos ha llevado | has taken us |
| vueltas y tumbos | turns and jolts |
| rumbo | course/direction |
| en vigencia | in force |
| amparo | protection |
| se abarca | is covered |
| poderes | powers |
| la balanza del poder | balance of power |
| ninguno de ellos en particular | none of them in particular |
| dispuestos | ready |
| lo compone | is composed |
| jueces | judges |
| los elige | are elected |
| divergencias | differences |

| | |
|---|---|
| alcalde | mayor |
| menor grado | lesser degree |
| se le puede | can be |
| sino | but |
| perder | to lose |
| a diferencia de | in contrast to |
| en los que | in which |
| soberano | sovereign |
| monarquías parlamentarias | parliamentary monarchies |
| el rey | king |
| la reina | queen |
| carentes | lacking |
| hubo un tiempo | there was a time |
| regida | ruled |
| como lo estaban | as were |
| golpes de estado | coups |
| paulatinamente | gradually |
| augura | foretells/predicts |

# PIÉNSALO BIEN
# THINK IT THROUGH

## The pronoun. El pronombre, Part 1

Pronouns are very confusing as there are many of them with
different functions. For example, *se* can be a reflexive pronoun
or an indirect object pronoun, as in *él se baña* (he takes a bath),
reflexive pronoun, *se lo di* (I gave it to him), indirect object
pronoun. They are also confusing because of their placement
within a sentence, sometimes preceding the verb, while others
are attached to it, as in: *lo hago* (I do it), *¡hágalo!* (do it!), *lo voy a
hacer/voy a hacerlo* (I am going to do it), *lo estoy haciendo/estoy
haciéndolo* (I am doing it). As you can see, in those sentences,
the *lo* (it) is all over the place. And the same pronoun *me* can
have different functions, as in *me visto* (I get dressed), reflexive;
*me llamó* (he/she called me), direct object; *me lo compró* (he/she
bought it for me), indirect object. Notice that with the exception
of the reflexive pronoun, in English it is not that different: *me* used
as both a direct and indirect object pronoun.

First of all, a pronoun is used as a substitute for a noun. For example:

María estudia italiano.     Mary studies Italian.
Ella estudia italiano.      She studies Italian.

The *Ella* (She) pronoun replaces *María* (Mary), a noun/subject. In Spanish, there are five kinds of pronouns:

Personal pronouns
Possessive pronouns
Demonstrative pronouns
Relative pronouns
Indefinite pronouns

In this lesson we will first discuss the personal pronouns and possessive pronouns, and then the demonstrative pronouns, relative pronouns, and indefinite pronouns.

## Personal Pronouns

We have already seen the personal pronouns:

| | |
|---|---|
| *yo* | I |
| *tú* | you |
| *él, ella, usted* | he/she/you |
| *nosotros* | we |
| *vosotros* | you |
| *ellos, ellas, ustedes* | they/they (feminine)/you (plural) |

## Possessive Pronouns

The possessive pronouns are

| | |
|---|---|
| *mío/mía* | mine |
| *tuyo/tuya* | yours (familiar singular) |
| *suyo/suya/de usted* | his/hers/yours (*de usted*>polite singular) |
| *nuestro/nuestra* | ours |
| *vuestro/vuestra* | yours (familiar plural) |
| *suyo/suya/de ustedes* | theirs (*de ustedes*>polite plural) |

All of them have plural forms.

When they are placed before the noun, the forms: *mío/mía, tuyo/tuya, suyo/suya* change to *mi, tu, su,* respectively, for example:

| | |
|---|---|
| *la casa es mía* | the house is mine |
| *mi casa* | my house |
| *la casa es tuya* | the house is yours (familiar) |
| *tu casa* | your house (familiar) |

| | |
|---|---|
| *la casa es suya* | the house is his/hers/yours (polite) |
| *su casa* | his/her/your house (polite) |

All *three* have plural forms: *mi> mis, tu> tus, su> sus.* For example:

| Singular | Plural |
|---|---|
| *mi casa* | *mis casas* |
| *tu casa* | *tus casas* |
| *su casa* | *sus casas* |

Personal object pronouns can be used with or without a preposition.

| Without a preposition | | With a preposition |
|---|---|---|
| *me* | me | *mí* (when combined with *con> conmigo*) |
| *te* | you | *ti* (when combined with *con> contigo*) |
| *lo/la/le/se* | him/her/it/you | *él/ella/a usted* |
| *nos* | us | *nosotros* |
| *os* | you | *vosotros* |
| *los/las/les/se* | them/you (plural) | *ellos/ellas/a ustedes* |

To these we would have to add the reflexive pronoun *se* as an object without a preposition (himself/herself/itself), and *sí* when used with a preposition> *para sí* (for himself/herself/itself). Also, when combined with the preposition *con*, *sí* changes to *consigo*.

When the pronouns are used without a preposition, they are attached to the verb if it is a present participle, infinitive, or command. When the pronouns are used with a preposition, they generally follow the verb.

Before we go any further, let's have some examples of the object pronouns used without and with a preposition.

Without a preposition:

| | |
|---|---|
| *Me dijo que vendría.* | He told me he would come. |
| *Él está escribiéndonos una carta.* | He is writing us a letter. |

With a preposition:

| | |
|---|---|
| *Eso es para él.* | That is for him. |
| *Ellos vienen conmigo.* | They come with us. |
| *No quieren hablar contigo.* | They don't want to talk with you. |

# BRAIN TICKLERS
### Set # 43

### *Ejercicios*

A. First, answer these two questions:
   1. What does a pronoun do? Give an example in Spanish with the English equivalent.
   2. How many kinds of pronouns are there in Spanish? List them.

B. Traduce el pronombre entre paréntesis:
   1. (We) trabajamos en una fábrica de metales.
   2. No está bien que (them, masc.) lo hagan.
   3. ¿Dónde vas (you, sing., familiar)?
   4. ¿Hablan (you, plural pol.) ruso?
   5. (I) me despierto a las 7am.
   6. Nos gusta mucho (your, sing. pol) automóvil.
   7. Esa lámpara es (mine), no (yours, pl. pol.).
   8. (Our) abuelo se llama Miguel.
   9. (My) sillas son muy antiguas.
   10. ¿Quieres venir (with me) al teatro?
   11. Primero vamos a casa de (my) tía Consuelo.
   12. Sí, me gustaría ir (with you) a la playa.
   13. Esa carta es para (me).
   14. ¿A qué hora (do I call you, sing. fam.)?
   15. (He) me dijo que hablara con (her).

C. Translate these sentences into Spanish:

1. She is the mother of Leticia.

2. I love my job.

3. It is our duty to do it.

4. We are happy to go with you.

5. I don't want to go with them.

(Answers are on page 236.)

## The pronoun. El pronombre, Part 2

Here we will discuss:

- Demonstrative pronouns
- Relative pronouns
- Indefinite pronouns

## Demonstrative pronouns

In Spanish, the demonstrative pronouns are:

| mas. sing. | fem. sing. | masc. pl. | fem. pl. |
|---|---|---|---|
| *éste* (this one) | *ésta* (this one) | *éstos* (these ones) | *éstas* (these ones) |
| *ése* (that one) | *ésa* (that one) | *ésos* (those ones) | *ésas* (those ones) |
| *aquél* (that one over there) | *aquélla* (that one over there) | *aquéllos* (those over there) | *aquéllas* (those over there) |

**For the neuter:**

| | | | |
|---|---|---|---|
| *esto* (this one) | *eso* (that one) | *aquello* (that one over there) | no fem. form |

Notice that the neuter forms have no written accent.
How they are used:

éste/ésta/éstos/éstas: when the person/s or thing/s is/are near the person doing the speaking, as in *éste es mío* (this one is mine, referring to a book)

ése/ésa/ésos/ésas: when the person/s or thing/s is/are near the person who is listening, as in *ése es mío* (that one is mine, referring to a book)

aquél/aquélla/                when the person/s or thing/s is/are far
aquéllos/aquéllas:            from the person talking and the person
                             listening, as in *aquél es mío* (that one
                             over there is mine)

When the demonstrative pronouns are placed before the noun they become adjectives, since they help describe the noun, in which case they do not have a written accent mark, as in *este libro* (this book), *esos libros* (those books), *aquellos libros* (those books over there). Thus, when they replace the noun they are pronouns, and carry a written accent mark; when they are used with the noun, in front of it, they are adjectives and do not carry a written accent mark.

Here are some more examples:

*Mario, esta pluma es mía; ésa es de Dulce María, y aquélla es de Miguel Ángel.* (Mario, this pen is mine; that one is Dulce María's, and that one over there is Miguel Ángel's.)

—*Cecilio, ¿este carro es el tuyo?* (Cecilio, is this your car?)

—*No, el carro mío no es ése; es aquél.* (No, that is not my car; it is that one over there.)

—*¿De quiénes son estas flores?* (Whose flowers are these?)

—*Estas flores son para mi madre, ésas son para la tuya, y aquéllas son para tu abuela.* (These flowers are for my mother, those are for yours, and those over there are for your grandmother.)

## Relative pronouns

The relative pronouns replace a noun that has been named previously, an antecedent. For example: *Los niños que vimos anoche son mis sobrinos* (The children that we saw last night are my nephews). Here we have two phrases: one, *Los niños que vimos anoche* (The children that we saw last night), and the other, *son mis sobrinos* (are my nephews). In this case, the relative pronoun *que* replaces *los niños* (the children) who were named before.

The relative pronouns in Spanish are:

*que*     This refers to persons or things and serves for the singular or plural (that, which, who, or whom).

*cual*    It is used with the definite article in all of its forms: el/la/los/las, often to clarify or determine the gender and the number of *que: el cual, la cual, los cuales, las cuales* (who, that, whom, which, the one that, the ones that, the one who, the ones who).

*quien*    It is only used referring to persons, and it uses the plural *quienes* (who, or whom).

*cuyo*    Besides being a relative pronoun, it is also a possessive, and it has feminine and plural forms: *cuyo, cuya, cuyos, cuyas* (whose, of which).

In interrogative and exclamatory phrases, the relative pronouns always carry a written accent mark, and are called interrogative pronouns: *¿Qué has comprado?* (What have you bought?); *¿Cuál prefieres?* (Which one do you prefer?); *¿Quién nos llamó?* (Who called us?); *¡Qué lástima!* (What a pity!)

## Indefinite Pronouns

The indefinite pronouns are those that vaguely designate persons or things without determining them. The main ones are: *alguien* (somebody, someone), *algo* (something, anything), *nada* (nothing, anything), *cualquiera* (either, referring to two or more persons and things); *quiera* (any one, referring to two or more things); *quienquiera* (whoever). *Cualquier* is a shortened form of *cualquiera* used before nouns, and it means any. It is invariable in its gender.

Here are some more examples:

*Esa mujer, a la cual conozco muy bien, es muy simpática.* (That woman, whom I know very well, is very nice.)

*Tienes que ser tú mismo quien les hable.* (It has to be you who speaks to them.)

*Esos hombres, de cuyos nombres no me acuerdo, trabajan con mi padre.* (Those men, whose names I can't remember, work with my father.)

*Necesito a alguien que me ayude.* (I need someone/ somebody to help me.)

*¿Quieres algo de comer?* (Do you want something/anything to eat?)

*Lo que haces es mejor que nada.* (What you do is better than nothing.)

*Pregúntale a cualquiera.* (Ask anybody/anyone.)

*Quienquiera que lo haya hecho* (Whoever may have done it)

# BRAIN TICKLERS
## Set # 44

### Ejercicios

A. Traduce la forma correcta del adjetivo demostrativo según se da en paréntesis:
1. (This is) el maestro de mis hermanos.
2. (That) camisa no te queda bien.
3. A mí me gustan más (those) pantalones que los otros.
4. Por favor, alcánzame (those over there) platos.
5. (These) exámanes son muy difíciles.

B. Traduce la forma correcta del pronombre demostrativo según se da en paréntesis:
1. Dame (that one) y quédate con los otros dos.
2. No es (this one) el que pedí, sino el de color azul.
3. (That one over there) es el vestido que nos gusta a todos.
4. Los más caros son (those) cerca de ti.
5. Llévate (those over there) que son las plantas que más le gustan a tu padre.

C. Los adjetivos y pronombres. Traduce la forma correcta de cualquiera de los dos según se dan en paréntesis:
1. Referring to *relojes*:
(This) reloj es de oro; (that one) es de plata.
2. Referring to *maletas*:
(Those over there) maletas son las mías; (those) son las de Isabel.
3. Referring to *autobuses*:
(That one) autobús te lleva a Nueva York; (that one over there) te lleva a Chicago.

4. Referring to *cuadros*:
   (That one over there) cuadro lo pintó Dalí; (that one) lo pintó Goya.

5. Referring to *botas*:
   Me gustan (these) botas porque son negras; no me gustan (those over there) porque son grises.

D. Interrogative pronouns. Traduce la forma correcta según se da en paréntesis:

1. ¿(What) vas a hacer mañana?

2. ¿(What) hora es?

3. De esos dos que tienes en la mano, ¿(which one) te vas a comprar?

4. Hace rato que estoy mirando a ese muchacho. ¿(Who) es él?

5. ¿(Which ones) de esos carros son los más bonitos?

E. Translate this sentence into Spanish.
   Those three teachers, whose names I forgot, teach history.

F. Write four Spanish sentences using for each: a demonstrative adjective; a demonstrative pronoun; a relative pronoun; and an indefinite pronoun.

(Answers are on page 236.)

# MÁS ES MEJOR
# MORE IS BETTER

## Nouns

| | |
|---|---|
| el alcalde | mayor |
| el senador | senator |
| el congresista | congressperson |
| las elecciones | elections |
| el votante | voter |
| el ministro/secretario | minister/secretary |
| el voto | vote |
| la boleta electoral | ballot |
| el candidato político | political candidate |

| | |
|---|---|
| el partido político | political party |
| el colegio electoral | electoral college |
| el decreto | decree |
| la máquina de votar | voting machine |
| el estatuto | statute |
| el gobernador | governor |
| la primaria | primary |
| el proyecto de ley | bill |
| el gobernante | governor/ruler |
| el cargo público | public office |
| el funcionario público | public official |
| los derechos civiles | civil rights |
| los derechos humanos | human rights |
| el juramento | oath |
| la orden de arresto | arrest warrant |
| el arma | weapon |
| la celda | cell |
| la prueba | proof |
| el cargo | charge |
| el interrogatorio | interrogation |
| el sospechoso | suspect |
| el demandante | plaintiff |
| el demandado | defendant |
| la demanda | lawsuit |
| el indulto | pardon |
| el cómplice | accomplice |
| los antecedentes penales | criminal record |
| la denuncia | complaint |
| el testigo | witness |
| el ladrón | thief |
| el asesino | murderer |
| la libertad condicional | parole |
| la apelación | appeal |

## Verbs

| | |
|---|---|
| votar | to vote |
| elegir | to elect |
| legislar | to legislate |
| postularse | to run (for public office) |
| nominar | to nominate |
| asignar | to assign |

| | |
|---|---|
| juramentar | to swear |
| gobernar | to govern |
| ejercer presión para conseguir algo | to lobby |
| acusar a un funcionario público | to impeach |
| arrestar | to arrest |
| denunciar | to report/denounce |
| testificar | to testify |
| soltar | to release |
| perseguir | to chase |
| dudar | to doubt |
| robar | to steal/rob |
| acusar | to accuse |
| alegar | to allege |
| apelar | to appeal |
| entregarse | to surrender |
| admitir | to admit |

# HABLA POPULAR
# EVERYDAY SPEECH

Below are some very common Spanish verb idioms/expressions:

| | |
|---|---|
| caer bien | to sit well |
| caminar con la frente alta | to walk tall |
| estar de capa caída | to be down |
| hablar sin rodeos | to get to the point |
| echar culpas | to blame someone for something |
| hacerse de la vista gorda | to turn the other way |
| meterse en camisa de once varas | to get into trouble |
| no pegar un ojo | to be awake all night |
| no saber nada | to know nothing/be ignorant |
| sabérselas todas | to know everything |
| tener mala pata | to not have luck |
| ser más bueno que el pan | to have a good heart |
| ser un as | to be the best at something/ an ace |

| | |
|---|---|
| sentar cabeza | to settle down |
| coger el toro por los cuernos | to grab the bull by the horns |
| crisparse de nervios | to get your nerves up |
| darse contra la pared | to hit the wall |

## Practice with idioms

From the list of idioms/expressions above, choose any five and make up a Spanish sentence with each.

# BIEN VALE LA PENA
# IT'S WELL WORTH IT

## The active and passive voices

In Spanish, the active voice is used far more frequently than the passive, which is not the case in English. The passive voice simply means that the subject receives the action of the verb instead of being an agent of it. In the active voice the subject is the agent of the action but not its receiver. Let's see an example:

## Active voice

> *Cervantes escribió "Don Quijote"*. (Cervantes wrote *Don Quixote.*) Here, Cervantes is the subject and the agent of the action (*escribió*>wrote).

## Passive voice

*"Don Quijote" fue escrito por Cervantes. (Don Quixote* was written by Cervantes.) Here, the subject is no longer Cervantes but *Don Quijote* and Cervantes receives the action of the verb. The passive voice in English is formed with *to be* as a helping verb, plus a past participle. The same is true in Spanish, although *to be* is not *estar* but *ser*. If it were *estar*, as explained, the past participle would function as an adjective. Notice the use of the preposition *por* (by) in this passive construction.

As we said, the Spanish language generally rejects the use of the passive voice as described above. It is much better to do it in a different way, which is by using the pronoun *se* and a verb in the third person either singular or plural, as in:

> *Aquí se habla español.* (Spanish is spoken here.)
> *En esa tienda se venden productos mexicanos.*
> (In that store Mexican products are sold.)

# DILO COMO YO
# SAY IT LIKE I DO

## Diphthongs/Diptongos

Here is where English and Spanish truly diverge, or go in different directions.

A diphthong in Spanish is a combination of a weak and strong vowel, or two weak vowels, in one same syllable. The weak vowels in Spanish are *i* (also *y*) and *u*, and the strong are *a, e, o*. You must know this well, and remember it in order to better understand what follows.

**Golden Rule:** In Spanish you can *never* separate a diphthong, not in writing, not orally, unless one of the two weak vowels happens to have a written accent mark over it—then, and only then, is when that diphthong can be separated. If the written accent mark happens to be over any of the strong vowels, the diphthong remains intact, or together. And, when there are no written accent marks over any of the vowels, whether weak or strong, the stress is always placed over the strong vowel.

Here are two examples:

*cierto*   This word has two syllables: *cier* and *to*. In the first syllable there is a diphthong: *ie* (the *i* weak, the *e* strong). There are no written accent marks. The stress must then go on the *e*, so you pronounce it: *ciER-to*.

*día*   This word also has two syllables, only because there is a written accent mark over the *í* (weak vowel) and, therefore, the diphthong is split, both when you say it or write it. In other words: *dí-a*.

The problem with the diphthongs in English, and the reason why it is so different from Spanish, is that you almost always split the diphthongs, not in writing, but orally. Take this word:

*piano*   You split this word into two syllables, right at the diphthong, and say *pi-ano*. In Spanish, that word, a cognate, would also have two syllables but you would split it differently: *pia-no*, keeping the diphthong together. A big difference indeed.

There are just a few exemptions, words that traditionally or because of their etymology do not break or split a diphthong, such as in *cruel* and *ruido*, pronounced *cru-el* and *ru-i-do*. But, again, there are just too few for you to be concerned.

How many diphthongs are there in Spanish? Altogether there are 14 diphthong combinations and each one follows precisely what we have said before. In other words, each one adheres to the rules as explained.

### ¡OJO!—WATCH OUT!

The strong vowels, *a*, *e*, *o*, when together, each forms a syllable by itself; in other words, they are not fused together as in the case of the diphthongs. For example: *floreo* (*flo-re-o*), *aéreo* (*a-é-re-o*.)

## BRAIN TICKLERS
### Set # 45

*Ejercicios*

A. Say each one of these words out loud, keeping in mind the correct pronunciation of all the diphthongs. We are splitting the words into syllables to make it easier for you:

| | | | |
|---|---|---|---|
| ba*i*-le | ace*i*-te | he-r*oi*co | r*ui*-señor |
| r*au*-do | de*u*-da | lim-p*ia* | m*ie*-do |
| ri-p*io* | c*iu*-dad | len-g*ua* | f*ue*-go |
| con-ti-n*uo* | | | |

B. Now say these other words out loud:

| | | | | |
|---|---|---|---|---|
| búho | traspiés | decía | subirías | ¡huy! |
| averigüéis | Julián | navío | púa | oído |

C. How many syllables would you say these words have:

1. búho
2. decía
3. navío
4. púa
5. oído

(Answers are on page 237.)

# ALMA HISPÁNICA
# HISPANIC SOUL

## Federico García Lorca

He is among the world's greatest and best-known poets and writers throughout the world. One of the saddest losses during the Spanish Civil War, his life was cut short at the very young age of 38. He was an idol to most and an innocent victim in a country gone insane during one of its darkest periods. He is, undoubtedly, one of the most studied and admired literary figures in U.S. colleges, a testimony to his popularity and genius, perhaps because in 1929, he came to New York where he became deeply identified with Harlem and wrote *Poeta en Nueva York—Oda al Rey de Harlem* (Poet in New York—Ode to the King of Harlem).

He was born in Granada in 1898 (or 1899), and adored his mother, a gifted pianist. His father owned a farm not too far away from Granada. García Lorca attended Sacred Heart University, where he studied law but later gave it up, dedicating himself to his work in poetry and theater. He was greatly influenced by popular culture, particularly flamenco and gypsy themes, which is mirrored in most of his writings. The *Romancero Gitano* (Gypsy Ballads) catapulted him to world fame. He was a key figure of La Barraca, a traveling theater that performed in public squares all over Spain, and that produced some of his finest tragedies: *Bodas de Sangre* (1933), *Yerma* (1934), and *La Casa de Bernarda Alba* (1936). While at his country home in 1936, at the beginning of the Spanish Civil War, he was arrested by Franco's soldiers and later killed with the butt of a rifle then shot numerous times. Soon after, his books were burned in the Plaza of Granada and banned in all of Spain. No one knows to this day what happened to his body or where he was buried, if he was at all.

## The writings of García Lorca

From the *Romancero Gitano*.

*Verde que te quiero verde.*
*Verde viento. Verdes ramas.*
*El barco sobre la mar*
*y el caballo en la montaña.*
*Con la sombre en la cintura*
*ella sueña en su baranda,*
*verde carne, pelo verde,*
*con ojos de fría plata.*
*Verde que te quiero verde.*
*Bajo la luna gitana,*
*las cosas la están mirando*
*y ella no puede mirarlas.*

To better understand the poem, here is the meaning of some key words:

| | | | |
|---|---|---|---|
| *sombra* | shadow | *carne* | flesh |
| *cintura* | waist | *luna* | moon |
| *baranda* | banister | *cosas* | things |

## Review

In your opinion, what is the meaning of the use of the word *verde* in this poem?

# PLUMA EN MANO
# PEN IN HAND

### El Descubrimiento de América/
### The Discovery of America

Se cree (It is believed) que los vikingos fueron los primeros europeos que llegaron a América, y se da como fecha probable el año 1000 guiados por Leif Eriksson. Por descubrir se entiende (it is understood) dar a conocer, compartir con otros lo que se ha (what has been) descubierto. De nada vale que yo descubra algo si me lo callo (if I keep it quiet), si no vas más allá (if it doesn't go beyond) de mi persona. Esto precisamente fue lo ocurrido con el supuesto viaje de los vikingos. No fue, además, un viaje de descubrimiento ni de exploración, guiado exclusivamente por tales metas (objectives), sino más bien un viaje al azar (at random), un viaje casual. Puede ser (It could be) también que antes de los vikingos otras culturas hubiesen arribado (had arrived) a América, por ejemplo de Asia pero, de haber sido así (had it been so), nadie se enteró, quedó en la nada (led to nothing), en el anonimato total.

La persona que dio a conocer América (made America known) al mundo de aquella época, el occidental y en oriental, fue Cristóbal Colón, impulsado por el apoyo que le dio la corona española. O sea que, para bien o para mal (for better or for worse), el verdadero descubridor de América fue el almirante Colón. Pero Colón no viajó solo; el fue el de la idea, el que tuvo el plan, pero para llevarlo a cabo (to carry it out) tuvo que contar con marineros experimentados y con dineros para sufragar los gastos. Esos marineros, esos dineros, todos esos recursos (resources), se los dio España en momentos en que el país necesitaba más ser ayudado (be helped) que ayudar. España, enfrentaba por entonces (at the time) mil problemas internos que la llevaron muy cerca de la ruina total y, sin embargo, se dejó llevar (went after) por la quimera (illusion) de un desconocido, de un hombre al que los geógrafos de Salamanca consideraron un simple loco. Ciertamente fue más la reina Isabel que su consorte el rey Fernando, interesado principalmente en explorar África, más a la mano, más conocida (better known), que las distantes tierras de un mundo imaginario. En esto demostró el rey cariño y respeto por su mujer y decidió apoyarla (back her up).

Zarpó (Sailed) Colón con sus tres carabelas del puerto de Palos el 3 de agosto de 1492, y al cabo de (at the end of) tres meses, el marinero Rodrigo de Triana divisó (sighted) en el horizonte la tierra soñada el 11 de octubre, desembarcando al día siguiente. Ese momento, ese instante, selló (sealed) para siempre el futuro de la humanidad y abrió un mundo y unas perspectivas que nos cambiarían a todos para siempre.

# BRAIN TICKLERS
### Set # 46

### *Ejercicios*

A. Choose five words/idioms from the list below and write a Spanish sentence with each:

| | | |
|---|---|---|
| probable | de nada vale | metas |
| cultura | nadie | época |
| pueblo | quimera | |

B. Taken from the passage, give the infinitive forms of the following verbs:

1. cree
2. descubra
3. entiende
4. impulsado
5. viajó

C. Write three sentences in Spanish about the discovery of America.

D. All of the verbs below are regular. Give the future tense indicative of each according to the person given in parentheses (refer to Lesson 6):

1. llegar (yo):
2. descubrir (él):
3. callar (nosotros):
4. explorar (ellos):
5. ser (ella):
6. dar (yo):
7. cambiar (usted):
8. viajar (vosotros):
9. enfrentar (él):
10. considerar (nosotros):

(Answers are on page 237.)

# ASÍ SOMOS
# THIS IS WHO WE ARE

### "Hello, I am a Hispanic!"

What is a Hispanic? When we think of people south of the border, all the way down to Patagonia, on the very tip of Argentina, excluding Brazil, what do we call them? Is it Spanish, Latins, Latinos, Hispanic Americans, South Americans? Is there a single, proper name that embraces them all? And, if not, what is the proper name that would best apply to them?

To explain this would take a long time. We can, however, point you in the right direction. It can't be Spanish because there are other cultures involved, from ancient times all the way to the present, such as the Aztecs, Incas, Mayas, and others. It can't be Latins or Latinos, because this word, Latin, refers to a culture and a language, not to a people. The country, nation, or empire was Rome, and their people the Romans. It can't be Hispanics because that name comprises only Spain, to which the Romans gave the name of *Hispania*, although at the time it comprised the entire Iberian Peninsula, including Portugal. We are then left with Spanish Americans, or Hispanic Americans, and South Americans. These three names are somewhat proper, but the first two leave out many other modern cultures, such as Portuguese, Italian, German, Asian, and Arab, and even the English in Argentina. Thus, we are left with one single name: South Americans. The problem with this name is that it totally leaves out the European heritage, principally of Spain. The other problem is that South America is not one country but many, which includes the Portuguese-speaking country of Brazil and other non-Hispanic islands and colonies of English, French, and Dutch heritage.

**Then, what name to use?**

As you can see, there is not really one single historically or culturally correct name applicable to them. But, if we had to choose, we would say South American, which is the name used in Spanish (*suramericano*), in contrast to North American (*norteamericano*), and Central American (*centroamericano*). Finally, we need to say this:

### Who are the Americans?

For the United States, it means all its people, and no one else, which is very, very improper. Ask someone from the United States this question: What is your nationality? The answer, inevitably, will be "I am an American." There is no valid justification to monopolize a name that was meant to identify all cultures, all nations, and all the people of the Western Hemisphere. By the way, the name America is really a misnomer, a name given to someone totally undeserving of such recognition. Amerigo Vespucci was an obscure explorer who had nothing to do with the discovery of America or with any of its major discoveries or explorations. His name was printed erroneously on a map and it stuck. When the mistake surfaced, it was already too late to change it. A lucky man indeed!

# BRAIN TICKLERS—THE ANSWERS

## Set # 43, page 218

**Piénsalo bien**

**A.**

1. It replaces a noun. Example will vary.
2. 5:
   - personal pronouns
   - possessive pronouns
   - demonstrative pronouns
   - relative pronouns
   - indefinite pronouns

**B.**

1. Nosotros
2. ellos
3. tú?
4. ustedes
5. Yo
6. su
7. mía – suya/de ustedes
8. Nuestro
9. Mis
10. conmigo
11. mi
12. contigo
13. mí
14. te llamo?
15. Él – ella

**C.**

1. Es la madre de Leticia.
2. Me encanta mi trabajo.
3. Es nuestro deber hacerlo.
4. Nos alegra ir contigo.
5. No quiero ir con ellos.

## Set # 44, page 222

**Piénsalo bien**

**A.**

1. Éste es
2. Esa
3. esos
4. aquellos
5. Estos

**B.**

1. ése
2. éste
3. Aquél
4. esos
5. aquellas

**C.**

1. Este – ése
2. Aquellas – ésas
3. Ése – aquél

4. Aquel – ése
5. estas – aquéllas

**D.**

1. ¿Qué
2. ¿Qué
3. ¿cuál

4. ¿Quién
5. ¿Cuáles

**E.**

Esos tres maestros, cuyos nombres no me acuerdo, enseñan historia.

**F.** Answers will vary.

## Set # 45, page 229

**Dilo como yo**

**A.** Pronunciation

**B.** Pronunciation

**C.**

1. 2   2. 3   3. 3   4. 2   5. 2

## Set # 46, page 233

**Pluma en mano**

**A.** Answers will vary.

**B.**

1. creer
2. descubrir
3. entender

4. impulsar
5. viajar

**C.**

Answers will vary.

**D.**

1. llegaré
2. descubrirá
3. callaremos
4. explorarán
5. será

6. daré
7. cambiará
8. viajaréis
9. enfrentará
10. consideraremos

# El arte es maravilloso

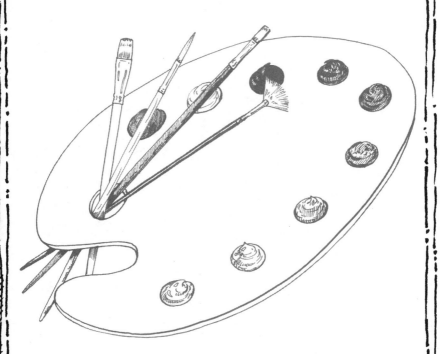

# Art is wonderful

El ser humano siempre ha sentido la necesidad *imperiosa* de expresarse, y lo hace con *la palabra viva*, con la pluma, o con *el pincel*. Estos *medios* le valen para comunicar sus más íntimos *pensamientos y sentimientos*, con el deseo y esperanza de que gusten y le sean *comprendidos*, de que otros vean la vida y la interpreten de la misma forma.

En los países hispánicos el arte se ha manifestado siempre de forma extraordinaria, desde los tiempos más antiguos hasta nuestros días, sobre todo *las artes plásticas*, como son la cerámica, *el grabado*, la escultura, *la joyería* y la pintura. Todas las civilizaciones, la Inca, la Maya, la Azteca se han caracterizado por poseer grandes artistas, por expresiones artísticas de distinta índole. *Desgraciadamente*, muchas de ellas *se han perdido*, quedando sólo *huellas* de una grandiosidad que *se perdió* en el pasado. *Al llegar* los españoles se fundieron, la occidental con la indígena, con la autóctona, produciendo verdaderas obras de arte expresadas mayormente en *la artesanía* popular. Así, en lugares como México, Perú, Guatemala, donde esa fusión entre las dos culturas *cobró más fuerza*, el arte del pueblo, el más puro y verdadero, ha estado siempre *a la cabeza* de los demás. En México, la ciudad de Taxco, entre otras, es donde se hace más visible, más aparente dicha expresión artística en todos *los órdenes*, principalmente en *la orfebrería*, es decir, trabajos *labrados* en oro o plata. En Chile, *por otro lado*, estos trabajos se hacen en *cobre,* mineral que abunda en ese país, y en la Argentina es en cuero o piel por la abundancia de *ganado* que hay allí en la región de Las Pampas. El oro, la plata, *la madera*, el hierro, el cuero, *el barro*, son los materiales usados por excelencia, *sin descontar* otros muchos. *Asombra* a veces los *tallados* que *se han hecho y hacen,* aun en *piedra*, como los hacían todas las culturas aborígenes y de los que permanecen hoy verdaderas *joyas* arquitectónicas aunque casi en ruinas, como son las pirámides y templos de las tres culturas *mencionadas*.

En la ciudad de Bogotá, Colombia, se halla el Museo del Oro en el que se pueden admirar maravillosos objetos tallados en oro que datan de los tiempos pre-Colombinos. La cerámica es otro trabajo *artesanal* de *gusto* exquisito como, por ejemplo, los llamados de Talavera en México, todos pintados *a mano* con un estilo único, *a semejanza de* los de España, los de Talavera de la Reina, en Toledo, de gran influencia árabe y que los misioneros españoles trasladaron a América. *Y ya* que mencionamos a

Toledo, vale destacar *la armería* toledana, sobre todo *las espadas* de limpio *acero* consideradas las mejores del mundo desde hace *siglos*.

Las *bellas artes*, entre las que se encuentra la música, y muchas de las artes plásticas mencionadas, entre las que se encuentran también *el grabado* y a joyería, le dan un carácter *inigualable e inolvidable* al mundo de habla española. *Por estar* más cerca, *vale la pena* visitar la infinidad de museos de toda clase que hay en México, empezando por el Museo Nacional de Arquitectura y el Museo Nacional de Antropología, *sin tomar a menos* los muchos que hay en casi todas sus ciudades. *Pero bueno*, para apreciar el arte hispánico, no es realmente necesario visitar un museo, aunque siempre es recomendable, pues Hispanoamérica en sí *es toda ella* un museo vivo de su historia y pasado. Las ciudades de La Habana, Cartagena, en Colombia, Santo Domingo, Cajamarca, en Perú, *entre otras muchas*, son testimonios *imperecederos* de una de las grandes culturas de la Humanidad. *A los que les guste* el arte, un viaje por la América hispana le resultará una experiencia difícil de olvidar y en el que aprenderá cosas *nunca soñadas*.

## Vocabulario básico

| | |
|---|---|
| imperiosa | pressing |
| la palabra viva | living word |
| el pincel | paintbrush |
| medios | means |
| pensamientos y sentimientos | thoughts and feelings |
| comprendidos | understood |
| las artes plásticas | plastic arts |
| el grabado | engraving |
| la joyería | jewelry making |
| Desgraciadamente | Unfortunately |
| se han perdido | have been lost |
| huellas | traces |
| se perdió | was lost |
| Al llegar | On arriving |
| la artesanía | craftwork/craftsmanship |

| | |
|---|---|
| cobró más fuerza | was more intense |
| a la cabeza | on top |
| los órdenes | all aspects |
| la orfebrería | goldsmith trade/ silversmith trade |
| labrados | carved |
| por otro lado | on the other hand |
| cobre | copper |
| ganado | cattle |
| la madera | wood |
| el barro | clay |
| sin descontar | without leaving out |
| Asombra | One is amazed |
| tallados | carvings |
| se han hecho y hacen | have been made and continue to be made |
| piedra | stone |
| joyas | jewels |
| mencionadas | mentioned |
| artesanal | craftwork |
| gusto | taste |
| a mano | by hand |
| a semejanza de | similar to |
| Y ya que | And since |
| la armería | armor |
| las espadas | swords |
| acero | steel |
| siglos | centuries |
| bellas artes | fine arts |
| inigualable e inolvidable | incomparable and unforgettable |
| Por estar | For being |
| vale la pena | it's worth |
| sin tomar a menos | without undermining |
| Pero bueno | But, well |
| es toda ella | it is itself |
| entre otras muchas | among many others |
| imperecederos | everlasting |
| A los que les guste | Those liking/appreciating |
| nunca soñadas | never dreamed |

# BRAIN TICKLERS
## *Set # 47*

*Ejercicios*

A. By looking at these words you should know what they mean. Write their meaning on a separate sheet of paper:

1. la necesidad
2. comunicar
3. forma
4. cerámica
5. escultura
6. pintura
7. caracterizado
8. abundancia
9. aborígenes
10. objetos

B. Traduce la palabra o las palabras entre paréntesis:

1. Yo siempre (have felt) ganas de viajar.
2. Yo tengo (the desire and hope) de que algún día habrá paz en el mundo.
3. (Unfortunately) el costo de vida ha subido mucho.
4. En el Museo Metropolitano de Nueva York hay muchas (masterpieces) de todas las culturas y épocas.
5. Los (carvings) en piedra son muy típicos de las culturas aborígenes americanas.
6. A mi me encantan las joyas de (gold and silver).
7. (The pyramids and temples) de los Incas, Aztecas y Mayas son impresionantes.
8. (The swords) toledanas son las mejores del mundo.
9. Mi viaje al Cañón del Colorado fue (unforgettable).
10. (For being) muy cerca de donde yo vivo, voy con frecuencia a Nueva York.

C. Contesta estas preguntas en oraciones completas:

1. ¿Por qué se han caracterizado siempre las culturas Inca, Maya y Azteca?

2. ¿En qué países fue mayor la fusión de las principales culturas americanas con la cultura española?

3. ¿En qué ciudad de México se hacen algunos de los mejores trabajos de orfebrería?

4. ¿En qué ciudad de Hispanoamérica se encuentra el Museo del Oro?

5. ¿Adónde debe viajar toda persona a la que le guste el arte?

D. Basado en el pasaje anterior, dinos si cada una de estas afirmaciones es *verdadera o falsa*:

1. La ciudad de Taxco está en Ecuador.           V     F

2. En Chile no se hacen trabajos de artesanía de cobre.           V     F

3. La cerámica de Talavera de la Reina en Toledo tiene una gran influencia árabe.     V     F

4. En México hay grandes museos de arquitectura y antropología.           V     F

5. La ciudad de Cajamarca está en Puerto Rico.           V     F

E. Da el equivalente de estas palabras en español:

1. testimony
2. to possess
3. pure
4. iron
5. almost
6. influence
7. character
8. there
9. pre-Columbian
10. to mention

(Answers are on page 260.)

---

**¿Sabías que?**

Tahiti was first explored by Domingo de Boenechea in 1772–1775, who named it *Isla de Amat* in honor of Manuel de Amat, Viceroy of Peru.

---

# PIÉNSALO BIEN
# THINK IT THROUGH

## The conjunction. La conjunción

Be aware. Some conjunctions are difficult, especially those consisting of more than one word. They go far beyond the simple *y* (and) and *o* (or), as you will soon see.

Frequently, sentences are linked or related to each other grammatically by relative pronouns, as well as by other words used with that specific function. These other words are called *conjunctions*. Examples: *El maestro hablaba y el estudiante escuchaba* (The teacher spoke and the student listened); *Queríamos salir pero estaba lloviendo* (We wanted to go out, but it was raining). Here, *y* (and) and *pero* (but) are conjunctions. When one or more sentences are linked by relative pronouns or conjunctions, they are called compound sentences, and they can be either *coordinated sentences* or *subordinated sentences*.

When one sentence does not depend on the other, when the meaning is complete in itself, it is called a *coordinated sentence*. When it does depend on another sentence to complete its meaning, it is called a *subordinated sentence*. Here are examples of each one:

Coordinated sentences:
*Queremos comprar el carro pero no
    tenemos dinero.*
(We want to buy the car, but we have
    no money.)

Here, each one of the sentences:
*Queremos comprar el carro* and *no tenemos
dinero*, can stand on its own with its own
complete, separate meaning.

Subordinated sentences:
*Te lo hago saber a ti para que estés enterado.* (I am telling
    you so you know.)

Here, obviously, *para que estés enterado* (so you know) would have no meaning without *Te lo hago saber* (I tell you). In other words, the second sentence depends on the first to complete the meaning.

There are a host of conjunctions in Spanish classified into two main categories, coordinants and subordinants, according to how one or the other relates to the sentences they unite. Some are just one word; some are a combination of words, making it difficult to distinguish between the two, especially when translating them into English. The translations of some of the following conjunctions are not complete, meaning that there are additional ways of translating them. We are just providing the basic translation for each, especially regarding conjunctions consisting of more than one word.

Here are some common one-word conjunctions:

| | | |
|---|---|---|
| y/e | and | (use *e* before a word beginning with *i* or *hi*) |
| o/u | or | (use *u* before a word beginning with *o* or *ho*) |
| pero/mas | but | |
| sino | but rather/on the contrary | |
| si | if | |
| ni | neither, nor | |
| que | that | |
| aunque | although | |
| porque | because | |
| luego | therefore/then | |
| pues | well | |
| porque/pues | because | |
| como | as, since | |
| menos | but | |
| antes | before | |
| así/como/siquiera | although, though, whether | |
| excepto | except | |

Here are some common multiple-word conjunctions:

| | |
|---|---|
| a causa de | because of |
| puesto que | since, although |
| no obstante | nevertheless/nonetheless |
| por lo cual/así pues/por tanto | therefore |
| de modo que | so/so that |
| siempre que/con tal de que | provided that, whenever |
| sin embargo | however |
| a fin de que | in order that, so that |
| con el fin de que | with the purpose of |
| ya que/bien/mal que | since |

### ¡OJO!—WATCH OUT!

Sometimes, conjunctions can be found within the same sentence, not related to another one, as in *La madre y el hijo* (the mother and the child), *Me desagrada éste o aquél* (I dislike this one or that one).

## BRAIN TICKLERS
### Set # 48

#### Ejercicios

A. Traduce la palabra o las palabras entre paréntesis:

1. Los libros (and) los cuadernos están sobre la mesa.

2. El padre de Lucila (or) el de Matilde nos van a acompañar.

3. Lo entendemos todo. (However) nos lo debes explicar una vez más.

4. No tengo puesto el reloj (because) lo perdí ayer.

5. (Before) de que se haga tarde, me llamas.

6. Te iré a buscar (provided that) vayas solo.

7. Estudiaremos todo el fin de semana (in order that) saquemos buenas notas.

8. No nos ayudó, (but rather) se fue a la fiesta de Jacinto.

9. Compré la entrada (so that) pudiéramos ir juntos.

10. (Nevertheless) lo voy a comprar porque es muy bueno.

B. The following paragraph contains several conjunctions. Underline each one that you find and rewrite them giving their meaning in English:

Celebramos el 4 de julio con una comida campestre. Fueron los jefes míos y los de mi compañera Adela. Al poco rato de estar allí, aunque estábamos bajo una tienda de campaña, comenzó a llover y nos empapamos de pies a cabeza. Pero, aún así, la pasamos muy bien. Sin embargo, uno de los jefes se enfermó de pronto y tuvimos que llevarlo a su casa a la carrera. Los demás, ya que estábamos allí, continuamos con la fiesta hasta entrada la noche. A eso de la medianoche, le dije a mi novio: —O me llevas a casa o me quedo a dormir aquí, puesto que es muy tarde y estoy muy cansada.

(Answers are on page 260.)

# MÁS ES MEJOR
# MORE IS BETTER

## Nouns

| | |
|---|---|
| el pintor | painter |
| el dibujante | artist/draftsman/draftswoman |
| la acuarela | watercolor |
| el lienzo | canvas |
| el caballete | easel |
| el aguarrás | turpentine |
| el dibujo | drawing |
| la galería de arte | art gallery |
| la tinta | ink |
| la exposición de arte | art exhibit |
| el/la escultor/tora | sculptor |
| la escultura | sculpture |
| el/la tallador/dora | carver |
| el artesano | artisan/craftsman/-woman |
| el premio | award |
| el borde | border |

249

| | |
|---|---|
| el fondo | background |
| el marco | frame |
| la naturaleza muerta | still life |
| la caricatura | caricature/cartoon |
| el/la caricaturista | caricaturist/cartoonist |
| el/la orfebre | silversmith/goldsmith |
| el acrílico | acrylic |
| el carboncillo | charcoal |
| el retrato | portrait |
| la fotografía | photograph |
| el diseño | design |
| la porcelana | porcelain |
| el yeso | plaster |
| la sombra | shadow |
| la perspectiva | perspective |
| el paisaje | landscape |
| el grabado | engraving |

## Verbs

| | |
|---|---|
| pintar | to paint |
| dibujar | to draw |
| exponer | to exhibit |
| tallar | to carve |
| plasmar | to give expression to |
| esculpir | to sculpt |
| premiar | to award |
| diseñar | to design |
| retratar | to paint a portrait/to photograph |
| enmarcar | to frame |
| fotografiar | to photograph |
| enyesar | to plaster |

¿**Cuánto sabes?** Do you know the last names of these two world-famous contemporary Spanish painters?

Pablo _____ and Salvador _____.

Answer: Picasso and Dali.

# HABLA POPULAR
# EVERYDAY SPEECH

Here are more common Spanish verb idioms/expressions:

| | |
|---|---|
| ser un Quijote | to be a dreamer |
| andar de coronillas | to be running around |
| abrirse paso | to get ahead |
| caerse de la mata | to be obvious |
| coger la baja | to get over (someone) |
| botar la pelota | to hit a home run |
| dar donde duela | to hit hard |
| estar como una cabra | to be crazy |
| lavar el cerebro | to brainwash (someone) |
| hacerle a alguien un número ocho | to get someone into trouble |
| levantarse con el pie izquierdo | to get up on the wrong side of the bed |
| ir viento en popa | to do well/at full speed |
| matar dos pájaros de un tiro | to kill two birds with one stone |
| mirar de reojo | to look at someone out of the corner of your eye |
| dejarse llevar | to be easygoing |
| pensar en las musarañas | to think nonsense |
| no pintar nada | to get ignored |
| romperse el lomo | to work too hard |
| ser una gallina | to be a coward/chicken |

## More Practice with Idioms

From the list of idioms/expressions above, choose any five and write a Spanish sentence with each.

### ¿Sabías que?

Today, the United States leads the world in agriculture. Much of this is owed to the Spanish Franciscan missionaries who pioneered some of the main agricultural industries, such as citrus, peaches, and vineyards.

# BIEN VALE LA PENA
# IT'S WELL WORTH IT

## The structure of the basic Spanish sentence

The basic Spanish sentence is made up of two elements: the subject and the predicate. The subject is the person or thing of whom/which we say something. The predicate is what we say about the subject. Every subject may have complements, and so may the predicate. Let's look at this sentence:

*Juan juega a baloncesto.* (John plays basketball.)

If we break it down into its basic elements, we have:

Juan                    subject (the person about whom we say
                         something)
juega a baloncesto   predicate (what we say about the person)

I could make the sentence longer by adding other elements to it as follows:

*Juan, el amigo de mi hermana, juega a baloncesto muy bien.* (John, the friend of my sister, plays basketball very well.)

Here, *el amigo de mi hermana* is a complement of the subject, and *muy bien,* a complement of the predicate. In fact, all that I say about the subject up to the verb is a complement of the subject, no matter how long it is. Thus, the structure of the basic Spanish sentence is as follows:

Subject + complements of the subject
Predicate + complements of the verb

In longer, more elaborate sentences, there might also be complements of the verb as follows:

direct + its complement
indirect + its complements
circumstantial + its complements

Keep in mind, however, that a Spanish sentence would rarely have this many elements. Finally, remember that every sentence must have a verb, and every verb forms a sentence.

What is important here is to know that every sentence needs a subject and a predicate, that the subject can be a person or a thing, and that the predicate is a verb that may be used with a variety of complements, just like the subject. No matter how short or how long I make a sentence, the basic structure would not change. Also, the subject can be a noun, or it can express a concept using more than one word to complete its meaning.

## BRAIN TICKLERS
### Set # 49

### Ejercicios

A. Based on the above, underline the subject and predicate in the following sentences:

1. La casa de mis padres está en California.

2. Los edificios de la ciudad son muy altos.

3. El reloj de plata es un regalo de mi novia.

4. Mi maestra de español es de Buenos Aires.

How did you do?

B. Now, rewrite those sentences taking out all the complements of the subject. Try it and see how well you do.

C. Let's take it a step further since we know how smart you are. Write three sentences using a basic subject and predicate, with no complements in either one:

1. _____

2. _____

3. _____

(Answers are on page 261.)

# DILO COMO YO
# SAY IT LIKE I DO

## Pronunciation of *b, v*

Before we start, you should take the pronunciation of Spanish sounds very seriously. You want to say them right and, above all, be understood. Although the pronunciation of certain consonants is similar in Spanish and English (such as the *m* or the *n*), there are many others, most, in fact, that are quite different.

## About the *b* and *v*

As we discussed in Lesson 6, both letters are pronounced identically in Spanish, which is quite contrary to English. In English, for example, you pronounce the *b* using both the upper and lower lips and keeping them tightly together. With the *v*, the lower lip makes contact with the upper teeth. Now say *boy* and *video*, and you will see it clearly.

In Spanish, on the other hand, both the *b* and the *v* are pronounced very close to the *b* in English, but only when either one is pronounced after a pause or before *m* or *n*. Otherwise, they will be pronounced with both lips (upper and lower) slightly open, letting the air flow out. Here are some examples:

*bobo*    Here, the first *b* is at the beginning of the word, and the second between vowels; the first is pronounced with the lips closed, and the second with the lips slightly open. Now say it: *bobo*.

Other examples: Say each word out loud and explain how both the *b* and *v* are pronounced:

vaca    _____

ave    _____

enviar    _____

bombón    _____

la bota    _____

# ALMA HISPÁNICA
# HISPANIC SOUL

## Benito Pérez Galdós

Benito Pérez Galdós is considered by many the greatest Spanish
writer after Miguel de Cervantes, a big claim that can only
be ascertained by the readers themselves. What can be said,
without any hesitation, is that he was Spain's greatest writer of
the nineteenth century, with a broad and profound vision of the
individual and the society of his time. He was born in Las Palmas,
Canary Islands, in 1843, and died in Madrid in 1920. His literary
production centers on *los Episodios Nacionales* (National
Episodes), the contemporary novel, and the theater; however,
he was above all a novelist. He was a very prolific writer, having
completed throughout his career 46 volumes of the *Episodios
Nacionales*, 34 novels, 24 plays, and another 24 volumes of
articles and other works, a phenomenal literary production rarely
equaled. He studied law without liking it, and soon abandoned it
to dedicate himself to his writing, especially after returning from
a trip to France in 1868. His realism and his vast and complex
creation of characters stand out as the basis for his work.

## The writings of Benito Pérez Galdós.

### *Episodios Nacionales (extract)*

...Así *atravesamos* la Mancha, triste y solitario país, donde el
sol está en *su reino* y el hombre parece obra exclusiva del sol y del
*polvo*; país entre todos famoso desde que el mundo entero *hase*
acostumbrado a suponer la inmensidad de sus *llanuras* recorrida
por el caballo de Don Quijote... Don Quijote no se comprende
sino en la grandeza de la Mancha... Don Quijote no hubiera
podido existir y habría muerto *en flor*, tras la primera salida, sin
asombrar al mundo con las grandes *hazañas* de la segunda. Don
Quijote necesitaba aquel horizonte, aquel *suelo* sin caminos, y
que, sin embargo, *todo él* es camino, aquella tierra sin direcciones,
pues por ella se va a todas partes, sin ir determinadamente a
ninguna.

To help you understand the passage, here is the meaning of some key words:

| | |
|---|---|
| *atravesamos* | crossed |
| *su reino* | its kingdom |
| *polvo* | dust |
| *hase>se ha* | *ha* (has), from the helping verb *haber* |
| *llanuras* | prairies |
| *en flor* | young/full of life |
| *hazañas* | deeds |
| *suelo* | soil |
| *todo él* | all of it |

### ¿Sabías que?

*La Mancha* (which literally means *the stain*, in English) is a vast region of Spain, northeast, west, and south of Madrid, composed of the provinces of Toledo, Cuenca, Ciudad Real, Guadalajara, and Albacete. The capital of the region is Toledo. It borders with other major regions: Aragón, Extremadura, Andalucía, Murcia, and Castilla y León.

# PLUMA EN MANO
# PEN IN HAND

### Sobre la amistad/About friendship

Difícil es en la vida encontrar (to find) un buen amigo. Todos tenemos muchos conocidos, gente que vemos de vez en cuando, aquí y allá (here and there), a la que saludamos (greet) y con las que charlamos casualmente. Si se me preguntase: ¿Cuánta gente conoces? Contestaría muchísimas, cientos de personas a lo largo de mi vida. De algunas (some of them) me acuerdo, de la mayoría ni idea tengo de quiénes fueron, dónde y cuándo las conocí. Pasaron por mi vida sin saber que pasaron, como dijo el poeta. Pero los amigos son algo muy distinto, y si se me preguntase: ¿Cuántos amigos tienes? Los podría quizás contar con los dedos de la mano, y aún quitando uno o dos. Éstos son los que no se olvidan, los que están muy cerca de nuestros corazones, los que han influenciado grandemente nuestro pensar y proceder (conduct). Un buen amigo nunca nos abandona y se mantiene firme a nuestro lado en las buenas y en las malas (in good and bad times), cuando necesitamos ayuda (help) y cuando no, cuando precisamos (need) un buen consejo (advice) que nos ayude a salir de un problema. A cambio (In exchange) de todo esto, de tanto cariño y comprensión (understanding), nada pide, nada exige (demands), sino saber que estando él en una situación similar, le paguemos con la misma moneda (we do likewise).

En mi caso, mi mejor amigo fue un muchacho cubano. No porque lo conocía desde hacía mucho tiempo, sino por la gran muestra de amistad (friendship) que me dio un día cuando yo menos lo esperaba (least expected it). Ocurrió así (It happened this way): Estando en la plaza del Capitolio en La Habana, allá por (around) 1955, escuchando un concierto (concert) de un pianista extranjero, tuve sin proponérmelo (unintentionally) un altercado (argument) con un grupo de muchachos revoltosos (rowdy) que se me habían acercado (that had approached me). Súbitamente, empezaron a volar puñetazos (punches). Yo en el suelo, y todos ellos encima (on top) de mí hasta que casi perdí el conocimiento (consciousness). En ese momento se les abalanzó alguien (someone leaped on them) y me los quitó de encima. Asustados (Frightened) y sorprendidos, salieron huyendo (they all fled) y desaparecieron (disappeared) en la muchedumbre (crowd). El muchacho cubano me tendió la mano (held out his hand) y me ayudó a levantarme. —¿Estás bien?—, me preguntó. Su nombre era Cecilio, y desde ese día nos hicimos (we became) amigos inseparables.

# BRAIN TICKLERS
### Set # 50

**Ejercicios**

A. Choose five words/idioms from the list below and write a Spanish sentence with each:

amistad
de vez en cuando
acordarse
nunca
altercado
tender la mano
perder el conocimiento
muchedumbre

B. Taken from the passage, give the infinitive forms of the following verbs:

1. vemos
2. saludamos
3. preguntase
4. empezaron
5. salieron

C. Write a brief composition in Spanish about your best friend. How you met him/her, where, and the reason why you consider him/her your best friend. Use no less than five sentences.

(Answers are on page 261.)

# ASÍ SOMOS
# THIS IS WHO WE ARE

## The Burial of the Count of Orgaz

In a small church, in the city of Toledo, Spain, there is one of the most famous paintings in the world: *El Entierro del Conde de Orgaz*, or The Burial of the Count of Orgaz, done by Domenicos Theotocopoulos, a Greek born in Candia, in the Island of Crete, called El Greco by the Spaniards. For a while, El Greco lived in Venice where he met Titian, his mentor. In 1570, he went to Rome, where he met Michelangelo. Around 1576 he went to Spain, where he was in the service of Philip II. He then moved to Toledo in 1580, where he lived until his death. In Toledo he rented the palace of the Marquis of Villena, which is now the Museum of El Greco. Here he had an affair with an aristocrat, Jerónima de las Cuevas, with whom he had an illegitimate son, Jorge Manuel, who later became an architect.

The painting of The Burial of the Count of Orgaz, an oil on canvas with a dimension of 16 × 11 feet 10 inches (487 × 350 cm), hangs in the vestibule of the church of Santo Tomé. The top of the painting, which is round, was meant to fit onto a wall of that shape. The painting depicts the burial of the count, a devout Catholic known for his piety. His soul, in the figure of a small child, is shown ascending to heaven, while his body is being placed into a coffin. The spirit of St. Augustine is on the right, and that of St. Stephen is on the left. Also in the painting is a small child, believed to be El Greco's son, and the painter himself looking out toward the viewer, immediately above St. Stephen. Depicted also in the painting is a group of elegantly dressed Spanish gentlemen showing great sorrow about the death of the Count. The church of Santo Tomé is located near the house of El Greco and the synagogue of el Tránsito. The church was built in the twelfth century and rebuilt in 1300.

# BRAIN TICKLERS—THE ANSWERS

## Set # 47, page 244

**A.**

1. necessity
2. to communicate
3. form
4. ceramic
5. sculpture
6. painting
7. characterized
8. abundance
9. aborigines
10. objects

**B.**

1. he sentido
2. el deseo y la esperanza
3. Desafortunadamente
4. obras maestras
5. tallados
6. oro y plata
7. Las pirámides y los templos
8. Las espadas
9. inolvidable
10. Por estar

**C.**

1. por poseer grandes artistas
2. México, Perú, Guatemala
3. Taxco
4. Bogotá
5. la América hispana

**D.**

1. F   2. F   3. V   4. V   5. F

**E.**

1. testimonio
2. poseer
3. puro/pura
4. el hierro
5. casi
6. la influencia
7. el carácter
8. allí
9. pre-Colombiano
10. mencionar

## Set # 48, page 248

**Piénsalo bien**

**A.**

1. y
2. o
3. Sin embargo
4. porque
5. Antes
6. con tal de que
7. a fin de que
8. sino
9. de modo que
10. No obstante

**B.**

Answers will vary.

## Set # 49, page 253

**A.**

1. <u>La casa de mis padres</u> – está en California.
2. <u>Los edificios de la ciudad</u> – son muy altos.
3. <u>El reloj de plata</u> – es un regalo de mi novia.
4. <u>Mi maestra de español</u> – es de Buenos Aires.

**B.**

1. La casa está en California.
2. Los edificios son muy altos.
3. El reloj es un regalo de mi novia.
4. Mi maestra es de Buenos Aires.

**C.**

Answers will vary.

## Set # 50, page 258

**Pluma en mano**

**A.**

Answers will vary.

**B.**

1. ver
2. saludar
3. preguntar
4. empezar
5. salir

**C.**

Answers will vary.

# El amor nos une a todos

# Love binds us together

Toda persona siente amor: amor por un ser querido, por el aire que se respira, por una flor silvestre, por los animales que le rodean.

*Sentir* amor es vivir, *sobre todo* al tratarse de otra persona. Con frecuencia *nos encontramos con alguien* que nos emociona y despierta en nosotros *sentimientos muy profundos* y que llegamos a querer *muchísimo*. Si es la persona ideal, la persona de nuestros *sueños*, formamos pareja como *novio* y *novia* y nos prometemos fidelidad *el uno al otro*. ¿Qué si he conocido yo a tal persona? *¡Desde luego que sí!* Su nombre es María Teresa y es mi compañera en la escuela. Nos vemos *todos los días*, y por la noche nos pasamos *largas horas* en el teléfono. No podemos estar sin vernos o hablar un sólo día. *Al conocernos*, al no más mirarnos, fue *amor a primera vista*, el corazón se nos salía del cuerpo. Realmente nos gustamos y estamos *muy enamorados*. ¡Qué bonito es el amor y qué necesario! Yo para ella soy el Príncipe Azul, y ella para mí la Princesa Encantada. Realmente nuestro romance es como un *cuento de hadas* y estoy seguro que tendrá *un buen fin*.

## ¡OJO!—WATCH OUT!

In Spanish, *to talk **on** the phone* is *hablar **por** teléfono.* Also, avoid the common mistake of writing *teléphono* instead of *teléfono*. Remember, there is no *ph* in Spanish.

## Vocabulario básico

| | |
|---|---|
| Sentir | To feel (irregular verb) |
| sobre todo | above all |
| nos encontramos con alguien | we meet someone |

| | |
|---|---|
| sentimientos muy profundos | very deep feelings |
| muchísimo | very much |
| sueños | dreams |
| novio | boyfriend (also fiancé) |
| novia | girlfriend (also fiancée) |
| el uno al otro | to each other |
| ¡Desde luego que sí! | Of course I have! |
| todos los días | every day |
| largas horas | a long time |
| Al conocernos | When we met |
| amor a primera vista | love at first sight |
| muy enamorados | very much in love |
| cuento de hadas | fairy tale |
| un buen fin | a happy ending |

## BRAIN TICKLERS
### Set # 51

*Ejercicios*

A. Answer these questions in complete sentences:
1. ¿Tienes tú novio/novia?
2. ¿Cómo se llama?
3. ¿Cómo lo/la conociste y dónde?
4. ¿Cuánto tiempo llevan juntos?
5. ¿Se quieren mucho?

B. Based on the previous story, say whether *verdadero o falso*:

1. Es humano sentir amor.                       V     F
2. María Teresa es la madre del que habla.   V     F
3. Los novios nunca hablan por teléfono.      V     F
4. Al no más conocerse se enamoraron.        V     F
5. Los dos se quieren entrañablemente:        V     F

C. Fill in the blanks with the correct Spanish word or words:

1. Me encanta _____ (to speak) por teléfono.
2. (I feel) _____ mucho (love) _____ por mis amigos.
3. (to fall in love) _____ es maravilloso.
4. Mi novio/novia y yo nos vemos (every day) _____.
5. (We are lucky) _____ de estudiar en un buen colegio.

D. Give the Spanish for the following words, and include the definite article for each noun:

1. prince _____
2. princess _____
3. romance _____
4. night _____
5. person _____

E. Unscramble these sentences, putting each word in the right order:

1. novia Luisa llama se mi.
2. teléfono su de número es _____.
3. suerte tengo mucha.
4. estudiar necesario es.
5. quieren mucho ellos se.

(Answers are on page 280.)

**267**

# PIÉNSALO BIEN
# THINK IT THROUGH

## The preposition. La preposición

### Some common prepositions in Spanish:

| | |
|---|---|
| *con* | with |
| *de* | of, from |
| *desde* | from, since, after |
| *durante* | during |
| *en* | in, on |
| *entre* | between, among |
| *hacia* | toward |
| *hasta* | until, up to |
| *según* | according to |
| *sobre* | on, upon, above, over |

There are others, but these are the ones you should know well.

In addition, there are many, hundreds, of prepositional phrases, both in Spanish and English, that very often present a problem in terms of translating them into English, especially when Spanish uses a preposition and English doesn't, as in: *alrededor de>* around, *antes de>* before, *acerca de>* about. If you leave the prepositions out in any of those phrases, they would be adverbs, not prepositions, as in:

Prepositional phrase:

| | |
|---|---|
| *La iglesia está alrededor de la esquina.* | The church is around the corner. |

Here, the prepositional phrase is *alrededor de* (around). Notice in Spanish the use of the preposition *de*.

Used as an adverb:

| | |
|---|---|
| *No hay nadie alrededor.* | There is nobody around. |

When not used in a prepositional phrase, the function of a preposition is simply to connect words and also to express the relationship between them, as in: *Manuel es de Barcelona* (Manuel is from Barcelona), *El reloj es de Pablo* (The watch is Paul's).

Prepositional phrases in English are also very difficult to translate into Spanish. Take, for example, the verb *to go*, and see how it changes meaning according to the various prepositions. In these cases, the use of the preposition results in a totally different word in Spanish.

*To go* in English generally is *ir* in Spanish. However, look at these prepositional phrases used with verbs:

| | |
|---|---|
| to go in | *entrar* (en) |
| to go out | *salir* (a, de) |
| to go up | *subir* (a) |
| to go down | *bajar* (a) |
| to go after | *perseguir* (a) |
| to go against | *oponerse* (a) |
| to go by | *pasar* (por) |
| to go off | *marcharse* (a, de) |
| to go on | *proseguir* (various ways of using it in Spanish) |
| to go under | *hundirse* (en) |

As you can see, none of those verbs in Spanish have anything to do with *ir* (to go), and the prepositions in Spanish generally do not correspond to English. In these cases, what you would most likely do is to translate the English phrase literally, thus saying, for example, for *to go up*: *ir arriba*, or in a sentence, *El niño va arriba al baño* (The child goes up to the bathroom), instead of *El niño sube al baño*, which is the common way of saying it in Spanish. Unfortunately, you have no other alternative but to memorize such phrases in Spanish, especially the common ones.

To help you out, we are giving you below some other common phrases using the prepositions *a* and *de*:

*a* followed by infinitives:

| | | |
|---|---|---|
| *ayudar a* | to help to | *La ayudo a estudiar.* (I help her study.) |
| *aprender a* | to learn to | *Queremos aprender a bailar.* (We want to learn how to dance.) |
| *decidirse a* | to decide to | *Se decidió a tomar el examen.* (He decided to take the exam.) |
| *contribuir a* | to contribute to | *Voy a contribuir a preparar la fiesta.* (I am going to contribute to preparing the party.) |

*de* followed by infinitives:

| | | |
|---|---|---|
| *acordarse de* | to remember to | *No me acordé de cerrar la puerta.* (I didn't remember to close the door.) |
| *cansarse de* | to get tired of | *Estamos cansados de estudiar.* (We are tired of studying.) |
| *acabar de* | to have just | *Juan acaba de regresar de un viaje.* (John has just returned from a trip.) |
| *olvidarse de* | to forget to | *Me olvidé de llamarla.* (I forgot to call her.) |

# MÁS ES MEJOR
# MORE IS BETTER

## Nouns

| | |
|---|---|
| el beso | kiss |
| la caricia | caress |
| el abrazo | hug |
| el deseo | desire |
| el cariño | affection |
| el amor platónico | platonic love |
| la chaperona | chaperone |
| el compromiso | engagement |
| el idilio | romance |
| la cita | date |
| enamorado | in love |
| la pasión | passion |
| celoso | jealous |

## Verbs

| | |
|---|---|
| amar/querer | to love |
| desear | to desire, want |
| gustar | to like |
| comprometerse | to get engaged |

| | |
|---|---|
| besar | to kiss |
| abrazar | to hug |
| tener celos | to be jealous |
| salir con un amigo/amiga | to date/go out on a date |
| enamorarse | to fall in love |

## Conjugation of gustar in the present:

gustar — *Gustar* is a special verb and is conjugated differently. Here, the subject of the verb is not the person, but the thing or things that are pleasing, and that are expressed by the use of the indirect object pronouns*. Let's look at this sentence:

**Me gusta la casa.**
(I like the house.)

In English, the thing that you like is the house, or the direct object, while in Spanish *la casa* is the subject. Also, in Spanish, the person who likes the thing is the indirect object, thus the indirect object pronouns must be used before the verb. *Gustar* is always used in the third person, either singular or plural, agreeing with the thing that is liked, as in:

**Me gusta la casa/me gustan las casas.**
(I like the house/I like the houses, or
The house is pleasing to me/The houses
are pleasing to me.)

Never say *me gusto*, or any of the other conjugated forms, but only the third person singular or third person plural. The **o** ending does not apply to *gustar*. This special conjugation of *gustar* applies equally to all verb tenses: past, future, imperfect, etc. Other verbs conjugated like *gustar* are *faltar* (to be missing), and *encantar* (to love/enjoy).

*The indirect subject pronouns are: *me, te, le, nos, os, les*, and, in the case of *gustar*, they always precede the conjugated verb form.

The other verbs above: *amar, desear, besar, abrazar* are all regular; *comprometerse* is both regular and reflexive, and *tener* and *salir* are irregular.

271

## Spanish love phrases

| | |
|---|---|
| Te amo./Te quiero. | I love you. |
| Me gustas. | I like you. |
| Te adoro/idolatro. | I adore you. |
| mi amor/mi cielo | |
| mi cariño/mi alma | |
| mi tesoro/ | |
| mi bombón/ | |
| mi encanto | my love/darling |
| papi/mami/ | |
| corazoncito/ | |
| azuquita/ | |
| caramelito | dear/honey |

Here is a very popular Spanish song you should learn by heart:

> *Bésame mucho*
>
> Bésame, bésame mucho
> como si fuera esta noche la última vez.
> Bésame, bésame mucho
> que tengo miedo a perderte
> perderte otra vez.

Do you know what it means? Try to figure it out by yourself. If you get stuck, listen to the song by the Beatles with the same title. Here is a translation:

> Kiss me, kiss me with all your heart
> as if this night would be the last
> Kiss me, kiss me with all your heart
> for I am afraid to lose you
> to lose you again.
> (However, translation may vary.)

## ¡OJO!—WATCH OUT!

One of the most important and common words in Spanish is the adjective *simpático - a*. It is the best compliment you can give to a Hispanic person, and it has several connotations. Basically, it means nice, pleasant, but also lovely, delightful, etc. Its opposite is *antipático*, which no one wants to be, much less to be called.

# HABLA POPULAR
# EVERYDAY SPEECH

## Idioms

| | |
|---|---|
| tener cuidado | to be careful |
| de vez en cuando | once in a while |
| está bien | okay/all right |
| a veces | sometimes |
| enseguida | at once/immediately |

## Common expressions

| | |
|---|---|
| quererse con locura | to love madly/to death |
| abrazarse como un oso | to hug like a bear |
| echar de menos | to miss (someone or something) |

# BIEN VALE LA PENA
# IT'S WELL WORTH IT

The neuter article *lo* (it) is mainly used to make an adjective a noun, to express an abstract idea, as explained earlier: *lo bello* (the beautiful*)*, *lo fantástico* (the fantastic). It should not be confused with the direct object *lo*, which we covered in Lesson 10, for example, as in: *lo hice* (I did it). This article *lo* is also used in many idiomatic phrases, such as: *lo dicho*/what has been said, or with an adjective or adverb, as in: *comprendo lo fácil que es*/I know how easy it is. Some common English expressions referring to persons, things, or events are totally left out in Spanish, as in *who is it* (¿quién es?), *what is it* (¿qué es?), *when is it* (¿cuándo es?), and in impersonal expressions, such as *it is nice to see you*/me alegro de verte, and when referring to the weather or time, as in *it is raining*/está lloviendo, *it is nine o'clock*/son las nueve en punto. It also expresses the relative pronoun in English, as in *no sé de lo que hablas*/I don't know what you're talking about.

**¿Te acuerdas?** These four articles in Spanish equal either *a*, *an*, or *some* in the plural:

| | |
|---|---|
| *un libro* | a book |
| *una casa* | a house |
| *unos libros* | some books |
| *unas casas* | some houses |

These four articles in Spanish equal "the":

| | |
|---|---|
| *el libro* | the book |
| *la casa* | the house |
| *los libros* | the books |
| *las casas* | the houses |

# DILO COMO YO
# SAY IT LIKE I DO

## The synalepha or linking of words.
## La sinalefa o enlace de palabras

This is a very common occurrence but only in spoken Spanish. The synalepha is the fusion into one syllable of vowels belonging to separate words, and resulting in the notion to the untrained ear that the speaker is speaking too fast, eating up letters. Let's see how the synalepha works.

Take this sentence as an example:

*Siempre te esperamos.*

Grammatically, this sentence, counting all three words, has a total of seven syllables:

*siem-pre-te-es-pe-ra-mos*

However, phonetically, it has only six because of the linking of *ee*:

*siempre-tees-pe-ra-mos*

Here is another example:

*dale agua>*      grammatically, four syllables: *da-le-a-gua;* phonetically, three syllables because of the linking of *ea*: *da-lea-gua*

There are cases, however, in which the synalepha does not occur because of the way certain vowels are pronounced—less open or more open—as in these examples: *aoa, aie, euo, oia,* and others. This, however, should not concern you at this time; we just want you to be aware of the synalepha, especially when you hear native speakers talk. It is not that they speak too fast, but because of the synalepha.

Following are some common examples of the synalepha:

| How is written | How is said |
|---|---|
| fiesta especial | fies(*ta es*)pecial |
| para mi hermano | para(*mi her*)mano |
| puede influir | pue(*de in*)fluir |
| sin tu esfuerzo | sin(*tu es*)fuerzo |
| si hubiera venido | (*si hu*)biera venido |
| uno a uno | u(*no a u*)no |
| entraba ahora | entra(*ba aho*)ra |

### ¡OJO!—WATCH OUT!

You must anticipate that when listening to a native speak Spanish it would not be the same as listening to your teacher in class. A teacher will always make the effort to speak slowly so you can understand him or her better, and may repeat a sentence more than once. In the real world, people just express themselves spontaneously, letting the language flow naturally, as it should.

# ALMA HISPÁNICA
# HISPANIC SOUL

## Ana María Matute

Her fiction is one of the most searing expressions of the turbulent time of the Spanish Civil War. Ana María Matute ignites every page in her books with memories of a youngster caught up in the midst of human passion and cruelty, of the struggle between two ideologies that tore apart an entire nation for three long years. She lived it, experienced it, and it crushed her heart, which she could only revive by expressing her most intimate feelings of suffering and anguish. She is widely hailed as one of Spain's greatest contemporary novelists, very well known and respected. Many of her works have been translated into several languages, including English. In 1966 and 1967, she was a visiting professor at Indiana University in Bloomington, where she taught advanced courses in Spanish literature.

Ana María Matute was born in Barcelona in 1926. Among her most famous novels are: *Los Abel* (1948), *Fiesta al noroeste* (1952), *Los hijos muertos* (1958), and *Los soldados lloran de noche* (1977). Two of her semiautobiographical novels are *La trampa* (1973), and *Luciérnagas* (1993).

## The writings of Ana María Matute

### Excerpt from Los soldados lloran de noche

*No te enfades*. Escucha, *sigo el hilo*: entré, y estaba él ahí, sobre la mesa, doblado. Parecía dormido, pero cuando le di un *empujoncito* en el hombro se derrumbó hacia la derecha, y cayó como un saco. Pobre señor, tenía el corazón *gastado*. Porque sabes, hijito, las vísceras, como las máquinas, se gastan, se estropean, se atrancan... El médico dijo que era una *angina de pecho*. Lloré mucho, te lo juro. Había rosas por todas partes, encarnadas, como a él le gustaban, y fui y traje todas las que pude, se las eché encima y me dije: es lo último que puedo hacer por ti, porque mi pobre guitarra no la oirás jamás.

To help you better understand this passage, here is the meaning of some key words:

| | |
|---|---|
| *no te enfades* | don't get upset |
| *sigo el hilo* | I continue with my train of thought |
| *empujoncito* | little push |
| *gastado* | wasted |
| *angina de pecho* | angina (heart attack) |

# PLUMA EN MANO
# PEN IN HAND

## La boda de mi hermano/
## My brother's wedding

Mi hermano Carlos se casa pronto, el 21 de noviembre de este año. La boda será en una iglesia muy bonita del pueblo donde vive, y la recepción en otro pueblo cercano. Piensan invitar a muchos familiares y amigos, casi doscientas personas en total, cada una de las cuales recibirá una invitación que están a punto de enviar. Hay muchos detalles que les preocupan, como, por ejemplo, la compra del traje de novia, los anillos de boda (ella ya tiene el anillo de compromiso), la decoración de la iglesia, la recepción, el fotógrafo y, claro está, el viaje de luna de miel que lo piensan hacer a Italia y España. La novia es preciosa y el novio, mi hermano, es guapísimo, así que ambos van a lucir de rechupete en ese día; son una pareja ideal. Las dos familias se llevan muy bien, y los suegros son ya muy buenos amigos. Como es costumbre, ambos tendrán sus fiestas de soltero antes de la boda, recordando los buenos y felices tiempos en que cada cual vivía a su manera. Me imagino lo emocionante que va a ser ese día, al llegar la novia con su padre del brazo, la Marcha Nupcial, cuando se pongan los anillos y juren quererse para siempre, cuando desfilen ambos unidos bajo una lluvia de pétalos de rosa. ¡Ay, hermano mío, cómo pasa el tiempo!

# ASÍ SOMOS
# THIS IS WHO WE ARE

## The legend of El Dorado/Eldorado

Gold, gold, gold—anything gold has been an obsession of humans since the beginning of time. In the sixteenth century, with the discoveries of Mexico and later of Peru, Europeans sought the precious metal for personal wealth and power, just as we do today. In terms of desiring it, of wishing to possess it, there is absolutely no difference between them and us— we live for it and die for it, fight wars, and go to the farthest confines of the earth to find it. It seems that the magic of gold is eternal.

The legend or myth of El Dorado is a logical consequence of the mentality of sixteenth-century Western Europe. Spain, England, France, Holland, among other nations, vied for power, and gold was the conduit to grab it and thus rule the world.

The legend of El Dorado originated in South America and may have been based on fact. In the region of New Granada (today's Colombia), there was an Indian tribe on the shores of Lake Guatavitá whose *cacique* or chief, during a ceremony, covered his body with gold dust stuck to his skin with some kind of glue. From a distance, he appeared to be made of solid gold. Then he boarded a boat with many pieces of gold and precious stones that were offered to the gods, jumped in the water, and washed away the gold dust. Following the conquest of Quito by Benalcázar, an Indian from the region informed captain Luis de Daza about the Indian chief and his custom, and the Spaniards went searching for the *Golden Man*, or *el Hombre Dorado*. Soon after, the man was forgotten but the myth took wings, being now not a man but an entire country where gold was plentiful. Although El Dorado, or Eldorado, was never found, it served a greater purpose, which was the discovery and exploration of vast South American lands, just as happened in North

America with Coronado and the Seven Cities of Cíbola and the city of Quivira.

The first expedition that specifically set out to look for El Dorado was one by Philip Hutten to the coast of Venezuela in 1541, which lasted five years. It was followed by one by Hernán Pérez de Quesada, also in 1541, along the shores of the Amazon River, and by Gonzalo Pizarro (1541–1543). Many years later, in 1560–1561, Pedro de Ursúa y Lope de Aguirre also set out from Peru to find it. The English explorer, Walter Raleigh, joined the group of El Dorado explorers in 1595 but was also unsuccessful.

The elusive El Dorado has remained hidden since the myth surfaced 500 years ago, although it may have resurfaced under a different disguise—the California Gold Rush? the Diamond Mines of South America or Brazil? the City of New York?

# BRAIN TICKLERS—THE ANSWERS

## Set # 51, page 266

**A.**
Answers will vary.

**B.**
1. V   2. F   3. F   4. V   5. V

**C.**
1. hablar
2. siento – amor –
3. enamorarse
4. todos los días
5. tenemos suerte

**D.**
1. el príncipe
2. la princesa
3. el romance
4. la noche
5. la persona

**E.**
1. Mi novia se llama Luisa.
2. Su número de teléfono es _____.
3. Tengo mucha suerte.
4. Es necesario estudiar.
5. Ellos se quieren mucho.

# La naturaleza es vida

# Nature is life

¿Puede haber algo más *placentero* que pasarse un día en el campo, fuera del *bullicio y ajetreo* de la ciudad, del *amontonamiento* de gentes, de sonidos estridentes e *inoportunos*. Allí, tirado *debajo de* un *árbol, dejando que* la brisa matinal *nos acaricie* la piel, respirando aire puro y sano, oyendo *el silbar* de los pájaros que *aceleran* el vuelo para *posarse* en alguna *rama* en la que *reposar*. El rumor de las tranquilas aguas de un *arroyuelo* o del *salpicar* de algún salto de agua, *el crujir* de las altas hierbas con *el azote* del viento.

Esto representa *a cabalidad* un día de campo que pasamos mi familia y yo en un pueblo de Castilla la Vieja, en la región llamada el Bierzo. Era un sábado en el mes de julio. Llegamos a las 10 de la mañana y nos situamos *a tiro de piedra* del río Burbia. A pesar de ser verano, hacía su poco de frío y más fría aún estaba el agua. Pero, *así y todo*, nos fuimos metiendo poco a poco en el río hasta que el agua *nos dio por el cuello*. Allí *retozamos*, jugamos, hicimos *maromas*, *nos zambullimos* varias veces. Aguas más cristalinas *no había visto* en mi vida, *ni siquiera* las de las bellas playas del Caribe, la de Varadero en Cuba, por ejemplo, o las de Viña del Mar en Chile, o la de Luquillo en San Juan Puerto Rico. *Debía haber sido* por la soledad de aquel *paraje* del Bierzo, no visitado por turistas ni aun por *los pueblerinos*.

Después del baño, *nos desplomamos* todos en la hierba, y mis primas prepararon la comida que se había llevado en dos grandes *cestas: salchichón*, chorizo, *tortilla española*, *queso manchego*, buenas *hogazas de pan*, y vino. Comimos con las dos manos y, acto seguido, medio adormecidos, nos *tomamos* una siesta olímpica. A eso de las 7 de la tarde, más contentos y satisfechos que un monarca, regresamos a casa. El campo, ¡oh el campo!, con su *embrujo*, con su serenidad, con su limpidez de cielo y tierra... Un día en el campo, haciéndole compañía a la naturaleza; *no hay nada igual*.

# Vocabulario básico

| | |
|---|---|
| placentero | enjoyable |
| bullicio y ajetreo | noise and hustle and bustle |
| amontonamiento | crowding |
| inoportunos | inopportune |
| debajo de | under |
| árbol | tree |
| dejando que | letting |
| nos acaricie | caresses us |
| el silbar | whistling |
| aceleran | speed up |
| posarse | to perch |
| rama | branch |
| reposar | rest |
| arroyuelo | brook |
| salpicar | to splash |
| el crujir | rustling |
| el azote | whipping |
| a cabalidad | faithfully |
| a tiro de piedra | next to/within a stone's throw |
| así y todo | even so |
| nos dio por el cuello | got up to our neck/was neck high |
| retozamos | frolicked |
| maromas | antics |
| nos zambullimos | we dived |
| no había visto | I had not seen |
| ni siquiera | not even |
| Debía haber sido | It could have been |
| paraje | place |
| los pueblerinos | townspeople |
| nos desplomamos | we collapsed |
| cestas | baskets |
| salchichón | sausage (similar to salami) |
| tortilla española | Spanish omelet |
| queso manchego | Manchego cheese |
| hogazas de pan | loaf of bread |
| tomamos una siesta | take a nap |
| embrujo | spell |
| no hay nada igual | there's nothing like it |

# BRAIN TICKLERS
## Set # 52

### Ejercicios

A. Traduce la palabra o las palabras que se dan en peréntesis:
1. No hay nada más (<u>enjoyable</u>) que un día en el campo.
2. Sueño con estar (<u>under</u>) un frondoso árbol.
3. Yo siempre cumplo (<u>faithfully</u>) con mi trabajo.
4. Si Carlos no salió bien en el examen, (<u>it could have been</u>) por estar enfermo.
5. Una vez probé la (<u>Spanish omelet</u>) y me gustó muchísimo.

B. Contesta estas preguntas en oraciones completas:
1. ¿Te gusta a ti el campo? ¿Por qué?
2. ¿Te has bañado alguna vez en un arroyuelo o río?
3. ¿Has probado alguna vez *chorizo español*? ¿Te gustó?
4. ¿Qué árbol te gusta más?
5. ¿Qué piensas tú de la naturaleza en general?

C. Basado en el pasaje anterior, dinos si cada una de estas afirmaciones es *verdadera o falsa*:
1. En el campo siempre hay bullicio y ajetreo.     V   F
2. A los pájaros les encanta posarse en una rama.   V   F
3. La playa de Varadero está en la costa de Perú.   V   F
4. La capital de los Estados Unidos es muy visitada por turistas.   V   F
5. Después de comer mucho, todos nos adormecemos un poco.   V   F

**¿Cuánto sabes?** ¿Puedes mencionar dos de las playas más famosas de México?

(Answers are on page 302.)

# PIÉNSALO BIEN
# THINK IT THROUGH

## The verb, Part 4. El verbo, Parte 4

Now you will learn about compound tenses of the indicative, conditional, and subjunctive, and how to form the past and present participles in Spanish, helping verbs, the active and passive voices, and transitive and intransitive verbs.

The past participle in Spanish, as in English, is used to form compounds of perfect tenses. Again, a compound tense simply means that you are using two verbs instead of one. The first verb is an auxiliary or helping verb, and the second a past participle. All past participles are invariable. In English, you form the past participle of regular verbs by adding *-ed* to the verb infinitive, as in: *walk>walk**ed**, work>work**ed***. That *-ed* in Spanish has two forms, as follows:

For the first conjugation (AR) you add *-ado*, as in: *caminar>camin**ado**, trabajar>trabaj**ado***. For the verbs of the second (ER) and third (IR) conjugations you add *-ido*, as in: *comer>com**ido**, vivir>viv**ido***. We repeat that these are the endings for all regular verbs, which happens to be the vast majority.

The helping verb in Spanish in the active voice is *haber*, which in English is *to have*. So you would form a compound or perfect tense thus:

| **Spanish** | **English** |
| --- | --- |
| *haber* + a verb ending in *-ado/-ido* | *to have* + a verb ending in *-ed* |

Here are some sentence examples:

*He trabajado mucho hoy.*
  I have worked a lot today.

*Hemos vivido aquí desde 1990.*
  We have lived here since 1990.

The helping verb *haber* is irregular in Spanish. Here is the conjugation in the present tense:

| haber | | | |
|---|---|---|---|
| he | I have | hemos | we have |
| has | you have | habéis | you have |
| ha | he/she/it has | han | they have |

### ¡OJO!—WATCH OUT!

Before we proceed, *haber* is not *tener*, which also means *to have*. So you don't get confused, use *haber* only as a helping verb in compound tenses and *tener* for all other cases.

Past participles can also be irregular both in English and Spanish. Following are some of the most common irregular past participles:

| | |
|---|---|
| *escribir>escrito* | to write>written |
| *hacer>hecho* | to do/make>made |
| *decir>dicho* | to say>said |
| *poner>puesto* | to put>put |
| *abrir>abierto* | to open>opened |
| *volver>vuelto* | to return>returned |
| *ver>visto* | to see>seen |

The three perfect tenses of the indicative:

| | |
|---|---|
| Present perfect: | uses the present tense of *to have* plus a past participle |
| Past perfect: | uses the past tense of *to have* plus a past participle |
| Future perfect: | uses the future tense of *to have* plus a past participle |

The three in Spanish are

| | |
|---|---|
| *Pretérito perfecto*: | uses the present tense of *haber* plus a past participle |
| *Pretérito pluscuamperfecto*: | uses the imperfect tense of *haber* plus a past participle |
| *Futuro perfecto*: | uses the future tense of *haber* plus a past participle |

Here are some sentence examples of the three:

*He hablado con el profesor.*
 I have spoken to the professor.
*Había hablado con el profesor.*
 I had spoken to the professor.
*Habré hablado con el profesor.*
 I will have spoken to the professor.

The conjugations of the helping verb *haber* in the three tenses:

| | |
|---|---|
| Present: | he, has, ha, hemos, habéis, han (irregular) |
| Imperfect: | había, habías, había, habíamos, habíais, habían (regular) |
| Future: | habré, habrás, habrá, habremos, habréis, habrán (irregular) |

The conditional has only one compound tense, which is formed with the conditional form of the helping verb plus a past participle, as in : *I would have studied. They would have called.* In Spanish, it is also formed by the conditional form of *haber* plus a past participle. Here is the conditional of *haber*:

| | |
|---|---|
| *habría* | I would have |
| *habrías* | you would have |
| *habría* | he/she/it would have |
| *habríamos* | we would have |
| *habríais* | you would have |
| *habrían* | they would have |

Here are the two sentence examples above in Spanish:

| | |
|---|---|
| *Habría estudiado.* | (I would have studied.) |
| *Habrían llamado.* | (They would have called.) |

For the subjunctive, we need only be concerned with two compound tenses: the present perfect and the past perfect. Here, you need the present and imperfect subjunctive of *haber*. Here are their conjugations:

Present subjunctive:

| | |
|---|---|
| *haya* | that I may have |
| *hayas* | that you may have |
| *haya* | that he/she/it may have |
| *hayamos* | that we may have |
| *hayáis* | that you may have |
| *hayan* | that they may have |

Imperfect subjunctive:

| | |
|---|---|
| *hubiera* | that I may have had |
| *hubieras* | that you may have had |
| *hubiera* | that he/she/it may have had |
| *hubiéramos* | that we may have had |
| *hubiérais* | that you may have had |
| *hubieran* | that they may have had |

Here are some sentence examples of both:

*Es posible que lo haya visto ayer.*
  (It is possible that I may have seen him yesterday.)
*Es posible que lo hubiera visto antes de que me llamara.*
  (It is possible that I may have seen him before he called me.)

## ¡OJO!—WATCH OUT!

Past participles can also function as adjectives, in which case they are generally used in English with *to be* and in Spanish with *estar*; as in: he is tired>*está cansado*. There is a major difference, however—as an adjective in Spanish, the past participle, now an adjective, must agree in gender and number with the subject, as in: *están cansados* (they are tired—masculine plural), *estamos cansadas* (we are tired—feminine plural).

The present participle is the verb ending in English in *-ing*, as in *singing, dancing*. This is the form used in the present progressive tense, which also takes a helping verb: *to be*, as in *I am singing; they are dancing*. In Spanish, that helping verb is always *estar*. To form the present participle in Spanish, you add to the stem or root the endings *-ando* (AR verbs), *-iendo* (ER/IR verbs). As with the past participle, the present participle is invariable. You conjugate *estar* (helping verb) and the present participle remains as is. Here are some sentence examples:

> *Estoy estudiando para el examen de español.*
> (I am studying for the Spanish exam.)
> *Estamos escribiendo en la clase.*
> (We are writing in class.)

Of course, *estar* can be conjugated in any tense, for I may be doing something now, was doing something yesterday, or may be doing something tomorrow. It can also be conjugated in any compound tense, as in: *He estado estudiando toda la noche* (I have been studying all night). Why is it called present progressive? Simply because it denotes an action that is in progress, that is happening at the time we say it. If I say, *leo en la clase* (I read in class), it is not the same as saying, *estoy escribiendo en la clase* (I am writing in class). The *leo en la clase* can be at any moment, any day, while *estoy escribiendo en la clase* denotes that I am doing it right now, as I speak. As we said, I could also refer to an action in progress in the past, as in: *estaba mirando televisión cuando mi madre entró* (I was watching television when my mother came in). Here, the watching of television is an action that was in progress when the other action (my mother came in) took place. It is an action in the imperfect but in progress, using *estar* in the imperfect plus the present participle of *mirar* (to watch).

# MÁS ES MEJOR
# MORE IS BETTER

## Nouns

| | |
|---|---|
| la hoja | leaf |
| el tronco de árbol | tree trunk |
| el lago | lake |
| la montaña | mountain |
| la colina | hill |
| la roca | rock |
| el paisaje | landscape |
| la hoguera | campfire |
| el campesino | country person |
| la tienda de campaña | tent |
| el bicho | bug |
| el bosque | woods |
| la raíz | root |
| la paja | straw |
| el terremoto | earthquake |
| el arco iris | rainbow |
| el derrumbamiento | landslide |
| la marea | tide |
| el desfiladero | ravine/gorge |
| el barranco | gully/ravine |
| el pantano/la ciénaga | swamp |
| la bruma | mist |
| la semilla | seed |
| la cuerda | rope |
| la sabia | sap |
| la leña | firewood |
| el fuego | fire |
| el valle | valley |
| la piedra | stone |
| el arroyo | creek |
| la planta | plant |

## Verbs

| | |
|---|---|
| acampar | to camp |
| florecer | to flower/bloom |
| despejar | to clear up |

| | |
|---|---|
| trepar | to climb |
| deslizarse | to glide |
| remar | to row/paddle |
| encender | to light up/turn on |
| apagar | to put out/turn off |
| sembrar | to plant |
| cortar | to cut |
| clavar | to hammer |
| ir de caminata | to hike |
| quemar | to burn |

### ¿Sabías que?

The first Catholic church in North America was built by Friar Francisco de Pareja in St. Augustine, Florida, in 1560.

And the Smith Chair, specifically meant for the study of Spanish, was established at Harvard University in 1815. Abel Smith, a graduate of the institution, donated $20,000 for this purpose.

# HABLA POPULAR
# EVERYDAY SPEECH

Here are more common Spanish verb idioms/expressions:

| | |
|---|---|
| pasar por alto | to overlook |
| estar emberrenchinado | to be mad/upset |
| dar el gato por liebre | to trick somebody |
| arrancar los motores/ ponerse las pilas | to get going |
| pasar las de Caín | to go through a tough situation |
| enredar la pita | to get entangled/complicated |
| dárselas de sabio | to pretend to know it all |
| quedarse en babia | to not understand something |
| dormir a pierna suelta | to sleep well |
| fruncir el ceño | to frown |
| ser testarudo | to be stubborn |
| ser un simplón | to be empty-headed |
| tener algo en la punta de la lengua | to have something on the tip of your tongue |
| ser un bocón | to have a big mouth |

# BIEN VALE LA PENA
# IT'S WELL WORTH IT

## Augmentatives and diminutives.
## Aumentativos y diminutivos

The difference between *pequeño* and *pequeñito* is the size.
*Pequeño* means small, and *pequeñito* means very small. Those
are adjective examples, and, as adjectives, they agree in gender
and number with the noun. Regarding nouns:

| | | |
|---|---|---|
| hombre> | man | |
| hombrón/hombrote> | big man | endings: -ón and -ote |
| hombrecito> | small man | ending: -ito |

Besides indicating size, at times the augmentative and
diminutive suffixes denote certain disdain or mockery. For
example, if I say, *hombracho*, or *mujerzuela*, using the suffixes
*-acho* and *-uela*, I am talking disdainfully about a man and a
woman. In other words, there are various kinds of suffixes
applied to both nouns and adjectives, and they can denote
either size or disdain. They can also denote certain affection or
esteem. Look at these examples:

| | |
|---|---|
| Carlos | means Charles |
| Carlitos | means little Charles |
| Carliños | means something like loving little Charles |
| | |
| chico | means small |
| chiquito | means very small |
| chiquilín | means something lovably small |

In short, augmentative and diminutive suffixes can denote
size, affection, or disdain.

The most common augmentative suffixes in Spanish are

| masculine | feminine | examples | |
|---|---|---|---|
| -ón | -ona | caserón | big house |
| -azo | -aza | perrazo | big dog |
| -acho | -acha | hombracho | big man |
| -ote | -ota | grandote | very big |

The most common diminutive suffixes in Spanish are:

| -ito | -ita | muñequita | little doll |
| -illo | -illa | nubecilla | little cloud |
| -ico | -ica | gatico | little cat |

Here are a few other examples of augmentatives and diminutives:

| Noun | Augmentative | Diminutive |
|---|---|---|
| niño | niñote | niñito |
| animal | animalazo | animalito |
| mujer | mujerona | mujercita |
| amigo | amigazo | amiguito |
| carro | carrote | carrito |
| paquete (package) | paquetón | paquetico |
| comida | comelona | comidita |
| fiesta | fiestón | fiestecilla |
| árbol | arbolazo | arbolito |
| bicho (bug) | bichote | bichito |
| lata (can) | latona | latica |
| carretera (highway) | carreteraza | carreterilla |

## BRAIN TICKLERS
### Set # 53

### Ejercicio

Give the augmentative and diminutive
for the following nouns, using -ote and
-ito or the feminine form if required:

| Noun | Augmentative | Diminutive |
|------|-------------|------------|
| 1. hermano | _____ | _____ |
| 2. cama | _____ | _____ |
| 3. mata | _____ | _____ |
| 4. luna | _____ | _____ |
| 5. rato | _____ | _____ |

(Answers are on page 302.)

# DILO COMO YO
# SAY IT LIKE I DO

## Footnote to Spanish pronunciation

As said earlier, Spanish is basically one language, both in the
way that it is spoken and written. However, the Hispanic world
is very vast and complex, having been profoundly influenced
by many cultures and races, just as Spain was through its early
history up to the fifteenth century. Logically, all of those influences
have impacted the language through the acquisition of new words,
intonation, and rhythm of the spoken language. What this means
is that you can't expect every single Hispanic person to express
himself/herself exactly the same, which may present a bit of a
challenge to you when you're talking to a native speaker, watching
Spanish-language television, or listening to Spanish radio. Your
ear has to get used to/adapted to various language nuances, just

as happens here in the United States between speakers from Boston and Mississippi, or with speakers from England, Australia, or India. They all speak basically the same language, but it just sounds different. Besides that, Spanish pronunciation presents numerous phonetic barriers or challenges that can add to your uneasiness and frustration. But you shouldn't get discouraged! You have the interest and willingness to learn, and that's what really counts. Just be aware of the differences and be prepared. Remember that eventually you will overcome them, as well as some other roadblocks that you may find along the way.

Key Spanish letter sounds to watch out for:

| | | | |
|---|---|---|---|
| b-v | d-t | h | j |
| ñ | q | rr | z |

> ¿Te acuerdas? Spanish uses two words for congratulations! One is *¡felicidades!* and the other one is *¡enhorabuena!*

# ALMA HISPÁNICA
# HISPANIC SOUL

## José Hernández

José Hernández (1834–1886) is all about the gaucho, the legendary man of the *pampas*, the forgotten and underestimated man who lived a life of his own, always asserting his own personality and roots. This was the gaucho until José Hernández took it upon himself to bring him out from obscurity and hail his unique human traits through his work *Martín Fierro*. The long poem is divided into two parts: *La Ida* (1872)

and *La Vuelta* (1879), and is directed both to the intellectual and to the gaucho himself. There are two distinct messages for each: to proclaim justice for the gaucho, and to awaken in the gaucho a sense of self-worth in order to better his condition. It has been called an epic poem by some critics, while for others it is more of a popular poem, deeply rooted in the oral tradition of the *pampas* and the gaucho. Hernández was active in politics and stood up against several of the regimes of the time, including the government of Alsina, and participated in the battles of Cepeda and Pavón. In 1880, he was elected president of the Argentinian Congress and provincial senator in 1881, reelected in 1885. While president of the Congress, he campaigned for the project of federalization, which resulted in establishing Buenos Aires as the capital of the country.

## The writings of José Hernández

From *Martín Fierro*.
First Part: La Ida.

### 1

Aquí me pongo a cantar
al compás de la vigüela,
que el hombre que lo desvela
una pena extraordinaria
como la ave solitaria
con el cantar se consuela.

### 2

Pido a los santos del Cielo
que ayuden mi pensamiento;
les pido en este momento
que voy a cantar mi historia
que refresquen la memoria
y aclaren mi entendimiento.

### 3

Vengan santos milagrosos,
vengan todos en mi ayuda,
que la lengua se me añuda
y se me turba la vista;
pido a mi Dios que me asista
en una ocasión tan ruda.

### 6

Cantando me he de morir,
cantando me han de enterrar,
y cantando he de llegar
al pie del Eterno Padre:
desde el vientre de mi madre
vine a este mundo a cantar.

To help you better understand this poem, here is the meaning of some key words:

| | |
|---|---|
| *vigüela> vihuela* | early guitar |
| *desvela* | doesn't let one sleep |
| *ave* | bird |
| *consuela* | consoles, comforts |
| *refresquen* | refresh |
| *aclaren* | clear up |
| *entendimiento* | mind |
| *que la lengua se me añuda* | I get tongue-tied |
| *se me turba la vista* | my sight gets blurry |
| *ruda* | tough |
| *desde* | from |
| *vientre* | womb |

## Review

Answer these questions in English:

1. Why is the man asking for help?

2. What is he saying about his singing?

# PLUMA EN MANO
# PEN IN HAND

### El Boquerón/The Boquerón

En San Salvador, la capital de El Salvador, muy cerca de la ciudad, se encuentra un volcán, ya extinguido, que es una de las vistas naturales más impresionantes del país, aunque no tanto, claro está, como el volcán Izalco, el más conocido y que aún sigue echando humo y bramando (spewing smoke and roaring). Aunque el nombre propio del volcán es San Salvador, se le conoce (it is

known) generalmente por el nombre del Boquerón, realmente una gigantesca boca que espanta (frightens) sólo de verla.

Lo visitamos por primera vez hace muchos años con un grupo de amigos, todos avecindados (residing) en El Salvador. No sé la causa, pero al llegar allí quisimos pretender ser osados aventureros y descender al fondo (bottom) del cráter, a una distancia de la cima (top) de unos cinco kilómetros. Dispuestos a hacer alarde (show off) de valentía y arrojo, comenzamos el descenso abriéndonos paso (making way) entre matorrales y pisando ceniza movediza (ash like quicksand). De pronto, a mitad del camino, y resollando (breathing heavily) como bueyes, mi hermana resbaló (slipped) y se asió (grabbed/held onto) del tronco de un pequeño árbol que a su lado estaba, quedándose con él en la mano con raíz y todo. Si no hubiera sido por la pronta ayuda que sin vacilar (without hesitation) le dimos, mi hermana se hubiera caído dando vueltas (tumbling) al fondo del cráter. Superado el susto, proseguimos nuestra marcha y llegamos al fondo. Allí nos quedamos pasmados (shocked) con los ojos abiertos observando aquella maravilla de la naturaleza. Después de un merecido reposo, y como ya se hacía tarde y empezaba a obscurecer, emprendimos el viaje de regreso subiendo la cuesta (uphill) con mucho más trabajo que al bajar, y nos encontramos en el camino a un señor llevando sobre sus hombros una pesada carga de leña (firewood). – ¿Y usted, cómo lo hace? – Lo hago, señor, para vender la leña en el mercado del pueblo y así poder alimentar a mi familia. Asombroso, realmente asombroso. Aquel hombre, que tenía sobre sesenta años de edad, subía y bajaba el volcán tres veces al día para al final recibir unos cuantos colones por su esfuerzo.

En los días siguientes visitamos también el Izalco, los Chorros, los Planes de Renderos, desde donde se nos presentaba en toda su amplitud la ciudad de San Salvador. Este país es, sin duda alguna, uno de los más pintorescos y atractivos de Centroamérica y, si le sumamos la gente y sus costumbres, difícil es encontrarle igual.

# BRAIN TICKLERS
### *Set # 54*

*Ejercicios*

A. Choose five words from the list below and write a Spanish sentence with each:

nombre propio      pasmados

avecindados         reposo

osados               carga

ceniza               pintoresco

B. Taken from the passage above, give the infinitive forms of the following verbs:

1. espanta
2. quisimos
3. resollando
4. caído
5. subiendo

C. Write a composition in Spanish about a trip you made to the countryside. Use no less than five sentences.

**¿Cuánto sabes?** Here is a little project for you: Do you know what the words *pampa* and *gaucho* mean? Look them up on the web and give your answer.

(Answers are on page 302.)

# ASÍ SOMOS
# THIS IS WHO WE ARE

## The City of Buenos Aires

It is called the *Paris of the Americas* and in many aspects it well deserves the name. Buenos Aires is indeed one of the greatest cities, not only in the Americas, but in the world with magnificent buildings, spacious avenues and boulevards, well-manicured and well-kept public parks and squares. The city is tidy, exceedingly clean, and inviting, while also well-known for its restaurants, shopping, and, of course, its nightlife. Like most major Hispanic cities, it comes alive after midnight with thousands of people strolling through the streets, filling the movie theaters, eateries, nightclubs, the many museums and art galleries, or just sitting out at a sidewalk café, chatting about the news of the day. The city was made for walking since most sites to see are within easy reach. The Plaza de Mayo, where mothers gather every Thursday to pray for relatives missing during the 1980 military rule, has been the heart of the city since 1580. It is surrounded by the Catedral Metropolitana, finished in 1862, where General José de San Martín is buried, the Banco de la Nación, the Casa Rosada (Government House), and El Cabildo (Town Hall.) Other interesting sites are the Museo Nacional de Bellas Artes, with art relics dating back to the 12th century, the Teatro Colón, for the finest opera and ballet, the Obelisco, rising over 70 meters high, the Parque de la Costa, for shows and dancing, and the Barrio de San Telmo, especially on Sundays from 10 to 6, where tango comes alive by Argentina's finest performers. Calle Florida is the place for shoppers, packed with trendy and very chic stores sure to please the most demanding tastes.

Buenos Aires is a city built mostly by immigrants, just like New York. Spanish, Italian, Portuguese, German, and British immigrants left their native countries in search of opportunity, of a new way of life, fell in love with the city and settled there. Each one of these cultures contributed in large measure to the development of Buenos Aires and of Argentina in general.

When and by whom was Buenos Aires founded? The city was founded in 1536 by Pedro de Mendoza who named it *Nuestra Señora del Buen Aire*, or Our Lady of the Good Air. It was later abandoned in 1541 and replaced by La Asunción, but eventually, due to the strategic location of its harbor, was re-settled by Juan Torres de Vera in 1580. The people from Buenos Aires are called *porteños* because of Buenos Aires' port or harbor.

# BRAIN TICKLERS — THE ANSWERS

## Set # 52, page 285

**A.**

1. placentero
2. debajo de
3. a cabalidad

4. pudo haber sido
5. tortilla española

**B.**

Answers will vary.

**C.**

1. F    2. V    3. F    4. V    5. V

**¿Cuánto sabes?**

Answers will vary. Sample answer is: Acapulco y Cancún.

## Set # 53, page 295

**Bien vale la pena**
**A.**

1. hermanote – hermanito
2. camota – camita
3. matota – matita

4. lunota – lunita
5. ratote – ratito

## Set # 54, page 300

**Pluma en mano**
**A.**

Answers will vary.

**B.**

1. espantar
2. querer
3. resollar

4. caer
5. subir

**C.**

Answers will vary.

**¿Cuánto sabes?**

Answers will vary.

# APPENDIX A

## Spanish online reference sources

Recommended online reference sources for Spanish language and Hispanic culture.

### Real Academia de la Lengua Española

*www.rae.es*
By far the best online reference sources for all matters pertaining to the Spanish language. All explanations are given in Spanish; often includes examples.

*www.yourdictionary.com*
Good reference source for Spanish grammar. All explanations are given in English.

*www.wikipedia.org*
One of the best reference sources for all matters pertaining to the Spanish language and Hispanic culture.

*www.donquijote.org*
Good reference sources for Spanish games.

*www.wordreference.com*
Good reference source for English/Spanish words, sayings, idioms, etc.

*www.babylon.com*
Very good reference source for Spanish to English, English to Spanish translations.

*www.thefreedictionary.com*
Very good reference source for English to Spanish translations.

*www.yahoo.es*
Very good reference source for Spanish grammar in general, and in particular for spelling of Spanish words.

*www.urbandictionary.com*
Very good reference source for American idioms; often includes Spanish equivalents or translation of terms and phrases.

*www.etymonline.com*
Very good source for English/Spanish etymologies.

# APPENDIX B

## Spanish Model Verb Conjugation

Included are the full conjugations of regular verbs ending in
*-AR*, *-ER*, and *-IR*. Note that the imperfect subjunctive has two
forms, and that the future indicative and the conditional simple
are formed by keeping the whole infinitive to which the endings
are added. The "pretérito anterior" is not included as it is
seldom used. Same applies to the "future perfect" of the
subjunctive as it is only used in literary language.

## Names of tenses/moods in English and Spanish

| English | Spanish |
|---|---|
| infinitive | infinitivo |
| gerund | gerundio |
| past participle | participio pasado |
| indicative | indicativo |
| conditional | potencial/condicional |
| subjunctive | subjuntivo |
| command/imperative | imperativo |
| present | presente |
| preterite/past | pretérito/pasado |
| imperfect | imperfecto |
| future | futuro |
| present perfect | pretérito perfecto |
| past perfect | pretérito pluscuamperfecto |
| future perfect | futuro perfecto |
| conditional perfect | potencial/condicional perfecto |

## Other verb-related words:

| | |
|---|---|
| mood | el modo |
| verb | el verbo |
| verb tense | el tiempo verbal |
| verb root | la raíz verbal |
| verb ending | la terminación verbal |
| simple tense | el tiempo simple |
| compound tense | el tiempo compuesto |

# –AR

| | |
|---|---|
| Infinitive | cantar |
| Gerund | cantando |
| Past participle | cantado |

## Indicative

*Past*

| Present | Preterite | Imperfect | Future |
|---|---|---|---|
| canto | canté | cantaba | cantaré |
| cantas | cantaste | cantabas | cantarás |
| canta | cantó | cantaba | cantará |
| cantamos | cantamos | cantábamos | cantaremos |
| cantáis | cantasteis | cantabais | cantaréis |
| cantan | cantaron | cantaban | cantarán |

| Present Perfect | Past Perfect | Future Perfect |
|---|---|---|
| he cantado | había cantado | habré cantado |
| has cantado | habías cantado | habrás cantado |
| ha cantado | había cantado | habrá cantado |
| hemos cantado | habíamos cantado | habremos cantado |
| habéis cantado | habíais cantado | habréis cantado |
| han cantado | habían cantado | habrán cantado |

| Conditional | Conditional Perfect |
|---|---|
| cantaría | habría cantado |
| cantarías | habrías cantado |
| cantaría | habría cantado |
| cantaríamos | habríamos cantado |
| cantaríais | habríais cantado |
| cantarían | habrían cantado |

## Command

canta
cante
cantemos
cantad
canten

## Subjunctive

| Present | Imperfect | Present Perfect |
|---------|-----------|-----------------|
| cante | cantara/cantase | haya cantado |
| cantes | cantaras/cantases | hayas cantado |
| cante | cantara/cantase | haya cantado |
| cantemos | cantáramos/cantásemos | hayamos cantado |
| cantéis | cantarais/cantaseis | hayáis cantado |
| canten | cantaran/cantasen | hayan cantado |

**Past Perfect**
hubiera/hubiese cantado
hubieras/hubieses cantado
hubiera/hubiese cantado
hubiéramos/hubiésemos cantado
hubierais/hubieseis cantado
hubieran/hubiesen cantado

## –ER

| Infinitive | comer |
|------------|-------|
| Gerund | comiendo |
| Past participle | comido |

## Indicative

| Present | Preterite | Imperfect | Future |
|---------|-----------|-----------|--------|
| como | comí | comía | comeré |
| comes | comiste | comías | comerás |
| come | comió | comía | comerá |
| comemos | comimos | comíamos | comeremos |
| coméis | comisteis | comíais | comeréis |
| comen | comieron | comían | comerán |

| Present Perfect | Past Perfect | Future Perfect |
|-----------------|--------------|----------------|
| he comido | había comido | habré comido |
| has comido | habías comido | habrás comido |
| ha comido | había comido | habrá comido |
| hemos comido | habíamos comido | habremos comido |
| habéis comido | habíais comido | habréis comido |
| han comido | habían comido | habrán comido |

### Conditional

comería
comerías
comería
comeríamos
comeríais
comerían

### Conditional Perfect

habría comido
habrías comido
habría comido
habríamos comido
habríais comido
habrían comido

## Command

come
coma
comamos
comed
coman

## Subjunctive

| Present | Imperfect | Present Perfect |
|---------|-----------|-----------------|
| coma | comiera/comiese | haya comido |
| comas | comieras/comieses | hayas comido |
| coma | comiera/comiese | haya comido |
| comamos | comiéramos/comiésemos | hayamos comido |
| comáis | comierais/comieseis | hayáis comido |
| coman | comieran/comiesen | hayan comido |

### Past Perfect

hubiera/hubiese comido
hubieras/hubieses comido
hubiera/hubiese comido
hubiéramos/hubiésemos comido
hubierais/hubieseis comido
hubieran/hubiesen comido

## -IR

| Infinitive | vivir |
|------------|-------|
| Gerund | viviendo |
| Past Participle | vivido |

## Indicative

| Present | Preterite | Imperfect | Future |
|---------|-----------|-----------|--------|
| vivo | viví | vivía | viviré |
| vives | viviste | vivías | vivirás |
| vive | vivió | vivía | vivirá |
| vivimos | vivimos | vivíamos | viviremos |
| vivís | vivisteis | vivíais | viviréis |
| viven | vivieron | vivían | vivirán |

| Present Perfect | Past Perfect | Future Perfect |
|-----------------|--------------|----------------|
| he vivido | había vivido | habré vivido |
| has vivido | habías vivido | habrás vivido |
| ha vivido | había vivido | habrá vivido |
| hemos vivido | habíamos vivido | habremos vivido |
| habéis vivido | habíais vivido | habréis vivido |
| han vivido | habían vivido | habrán vivido |

| Conditional | Conditional Perfect |
|-------------|---------------------|
| viviría | habría vivido |
| vivirías | habrías vivido |
| viviría | habría vivido |
| viviríamos | habríamos vivido |
| viviríais | habríais vivido |
| vivirían | habrían vivido |

## Command

vive
viva
vivamos
vivid
vivan

## Subjunctive

| Present | Imperfect | Present Perfect |
|---------|-----------|-----------------|
| viva | viviera/viviese | haya vivido |
| vivas | vivieras/vivieses | hayas vivido |
| viva | viviera/viviese | haya vivido |
| vivamos | viviéramos/viviésemos | hayamos vivido |
| viváis | vivierais/vivieseis | hayáis vivido |
| vivan | vivieran/viviesen | hayan vivido |

**Past Perfect**
hubiera/hubiese vivido
hubieras/hubieses vivido
hubiera/hubiese vivido
hubiéramos/hubiésemos vivido
hubierais/hubieseis vivido
hubieran/hubiesen vivido

# APPENDIX C

Some Irregular gerunds and/or past participles in Spanish.
Regular forms are excluded and marked "–."

| Infinitive | Gerund | Past participle |
|---|---|---|
| abrir (to open) | – | abierto |
| caer (to fall) | cayendo | – |
| competir (to compete) | compitiendo | – |
| componer (to compose/ repair) | – | compuesto |
| creer (to believe) | creyendo | – |
| cubrir (to cover) | – | cubierto |
| decir (to say/tell) | diciendo | dicho |
| descubrir (to discover) | – | descubierto |
| devolver (to give back) | – | devuelto |
| digerir (to digest) | digiriendo | – |
| dormir (to sleep) | durmiendo | – |
| escribir (to write) | – | escrito |
| freír (to fry) | friendo | frito |
| hacer (to do/make) | – | hecho |
| huir (to flee/escape) | huyendo | – |
| imprimir (to print) | – | impreso |
| ir (to go) | yendo | ido |
| leer (to read) | leyendo | – |
| mentir (to lie) | mintiendo | – |
| morir (to die) | muriendo | muerto |
| oír (to hear) | oyendo | – |
| pedir (to ask for) | pidiendo | – |
| poder (to be able to/can) | pudiendo | – |
| poner (to put) | – | puesto |

| | | |
|---|---|---|
| preferir (to prefer) | prefiriendo | – |
| reír (to laugh) | riendo | – |
| resolver (to solve) | – | resuelto |
| romper (to break) | – | roto |
| satisfacer (to pay/settle) | – | satisfecho |
| seguir (to follow) | siguiendo | – |
| sentir (to feel) | sintiendo | – |
| sugerir (to suggest) | sugiriendo | – |
| traer (to bring) | trayendo | – |
| venir (to come) | viniendo | – |
| ver (to see) | viendo | visto |
| vestir (to dress) | vistiendo | – |
| volver (to return) | – | vuelto |

# APPENDIX D

## Spanish word order exercise

Put the following ten sentences in the right word order following the basic Spanish sentence structure:

Subject + Predicate + complement of the Predicate

Keep in mind that the subject can also have a complement. The first word has a capital letter and the last has a period.

visita niña La abuelos en a Buenos Aires. sus

_____

Right order: La niña visita a sus abuelos en Buenos Aires.

juegan amigos Los parque. a baloncesto el en

_____

Right order: Los amigos juegan a baloncesto en el parque.

comida la perro en cocina. El come la

_____

Right order: El perro come la comida en la cocina.

al ayuda maestra La estudiante la con tarea.

_____

Right order: La maestra ayuda al estudiante con la tarea.


dimos lo Se ella su a casa. en

_____

Right order: Se lo dimos a ella en su casa.


Juan muy novia La es bonita de inteligente. e

_____

Right order: La novia de Juan es muy bonita e inteligente.


gusta No me puerco el ni pescado. el ni

_____

Right order: No me gusta ni el pescado ni el puerco.


fiesta en mi hermana. bailando la Estamos mucho de

_____

Right order: Estamos bailando mucho en la fiesta de mi hermana.


hecho tarea todavía. han la No

_____

Right order: No han hecho la tarea todavía.


reunión. mañana venga la a que Ojalá

_____

Right order: Ojalá que venga mañana a la reunión.

# APPENDIX E

## Matching exercise

Match each item in column A with the corresponding item in Column B.

### Column A

1. the author of "Don Quijote"
2. the capital of Spain
3. the meaning of the verb "soñar"
4. the direct object pronoun "it"
5. the indirect object pronoun "them"
6. the meaning of "se" added to the end of a Spanish infinitive
7. the main auxiliary verb in Spanish
8. the ending of a regular past participle for "AR" verbs in Spanish
9. the possessive pronoun "my" singular
10. the demonstrative adjective "this" masculine singular
11. pronunciation of the "h" in Spanish
12. fourth letter of the Spanish alphabet
13. famous Chilean writer
14. main square in Mexico City
15. an adverb of time in Spanish
16. an adjective in Spanish
17. "I have" in Spanish
18. "they have opened the door" in Spanish
19. The gerund of "leer"
20. a huge mountain range in South America
21. the number "26" in Spanish
22. ancient Mexican civilization
23. a diphthong in Spanish
24. the only nasal sound in Spanish
25. "I am hungry" in Spanish

### Column B

a. silent, mute
b. han abierto la puerta
c. veintiséis
d. Los Andes
e. Miguel de Cervantes
f. haber
g. temprano
h. Gabriela Mistral
i. Aztecs
j. ai
k. ado
l. tengo hambre
m. to form a reflexive verb
n. ñ
o. El Zócalo
p. tengo
q. leyendo
r. Madrid
s. lo/la
t. mi
u. contento
v. les
w. to dream
x. este
y. ch

| | | | | | |
|---|---|---|---|---|---|
| 1. e | 6. m | 11. a | 16. u | 21. c | |
| 2. r | 7. f | 12. y | 17. p | 22. i | |
| 3. w | 8. k | 13. h | 18. b | 23. j | |
| 4. s | 9. t | 14. o | 19. q | 24. n | |
| 5. v | 10. x | 15. g | 20. d | 25. l | |

# APPENDIX F

## Vocabulary exercise—Juego "El Ahorcado" (Hangman)

Write in the blanks each of the letters in the right order corresponding to each Spanish word. Use accent marks where needed. Don't forget that double consonants (*ll*, *rr*) count as one letter in Spanish as well as *ch*.

___ ___ ___ ___ ___ ___ ___ ___        elephant

___ ___ ___ ___ ___ ___ ___ ___ ___        railroad

___ ___ ___ ___ ___ ___ ___ ___ ___        airport

___ ___ ___ ___ ___ ___ ___ ___ ___        Christmas Eve

___ ___ ___ ___ ___ ___ ___ ___        highway

___ ___ ___ ___ ___ ___ ___        rainy

___ ___ ___ ___ ___ ___ ___ ___ ___ ___        university

___ ___ ___ ___ ___ ___ ___ ___ ___ ___ ___ ___        catastrophic

___ ___ ___ ___ ___ ___ ___        chemistry

___ ___ ___ ___ ___ ___ ___ ___        scarf

___ ___ ___ ___ ___ ___ ___ ___ ___        nice/pleasant

**Answers in order of appearance:** elefante, ferrocarril, aeropuerto, nochebuena, carretera, lluvioso, universidad, catastrófico, química, bufanda, simpático

313

# APPENDIX G

## Dividing words into syllables/ The orthographical accent

Following is a list of 18 Spanish words. Some need accent marks, others don't. Listen to your teacher as he/she reads each word twice and 1) divide the word into syllables; 2) place the accent mark, if needed, on the correct syllable.

español

es-pa-ñol

contemporaneo

con-tem-po-rá-ne-o

clase

cla-se

estudiante

es-tu-dian-te

dandoselo

dán-do-se-lo

refrigerador

re-fri-ge-ra-dor

Mexico

Mé-xi-co

costumbre

cos-tum-bre

repleto

re-ple-to

Camagüey

Ca-ma-güey

cafeteria

ca-fe-te-rí-a

caballero

ca-ba-lle-ro

trabalenguas

tra-ba-len-guas

fisiologico

fi-sio-ló-gi-co

sombrero

som-bre-ro

suramericano

sur-a-me-ri-ca-no

guantes

guan-tes

camara

cá-ma-ra

# INDEX

**A**

Accents, xiv
Active voice, 226–227
Adjectives, 11, 49, 148–150
Adverbs, 176–177
Alcazar of Segovia, 165
Alhambra of Granada, 165
Alphabet, xiii, 17–18
Americas
  early education in, 80
  Hispanic heritage of the,
    107–108
  history of, 63
  women in, 138
Anatomy, 96
Aqueduct of Segovia, 164
Articles, 4, 6, 274
Augmentative, 293–294
Azorín, 104–105
Aztecs, 34, 63, 189–190, 234

**B**

Body, 96
Buenos Aires, 300–301
Bullfighting, 40
*Burial of the Count of Orgaz, The*
  (Theotocopoulos), 259

**C**

*Camino de Perfección* (de Jesús),
  60
Capitals, 42–43
Cardinal numbers, xi–xiii, 55
*Castilla* (Ruiz), 105
Chibcha, 63
Cognate, 3
Colon, Diego, 138
Colors, 49–50
Columbus, Christopher, 13, 138

Commands, 91, 116, 117, 120–123
Common expressions. *See*
  Idioms
Comparatives, 149
Compound tenses, 91–92, 286–290
Conjunction, 246–247
Constants, double, 103
Coordinated sentences, 246
Countries, 42–43
Currency, 184
Curriculum vitae, 155–157

**D**

Date, 51
Days, 50
de Ávila, Santa Teresa, 59–60
de Bobadilla, Isabel, 138
de Cervantes, Miguel, 19–20
de Jesús, Santa Teresa, 59–60
de Soto, Hernando, 138
de Toledo, María, 138
de Vega, Lope, 39
de Vivar, Rodrigo Diaz, 23
Definite articles, 4, 6
Demonstrative pronouns, 216,
  219–220
Dentales, 57–58
Diminutives, 293–294
Diphthongs, 227–228
*Don Quijote de la Mancha* (de
  Cervantes), 19–20
*Doña Bárbara* (Gallegos), 160

**E**

El Dorado, 279–280
El Escorial, 167
Exclamation marks, 5
Exclamatory phrases, 221
Expressions. *See* Idioms

315

## F

Family, vocabulary, 9
First name, 14, 16
Formal affirmative commands, 123
Future tenses, 287–288

## G

Galdós, Benito Pérez, 255–256
Gallegos, Rómulo, 159
Gender, 4
Gómez, Esteban, 30
Government, 214–215

## H

Helping verb, 287–289
Hernández, José, 296–298
Hispanics, 234–235
Holidays, 201
Human body, 96

## I

Idioms, 13, 33, 54, 73, 97, 126,
    180–181, 225–226, 251, 273, 292
Imperfect subjunctive, 119–120,
    288–289, 304
Imperfect tense, 93
Incas, 34, 63, 234
Indefinite articles, 6
Indefinite pronouns, 216, 219, 221
Indicative, description of, 91–92
Informal affirmative commands,
    123
*Interior Castle* (de Jesús), 59
Interjection, 70
Interrogative phrases, 221
Intransitive verbs, 125, 286

## J

Jiménez, Juan Ramón, 134
Job interview, 181–182

## L

Last name, 14, 16
Lorca, Federico García, 229–231
Love phrases, 272

## M

Machado, Antonio, 185–186
Martí, José, 77–78
Matute, Ana María, 276–277
Mayas, 34, 63, 234
Mexico, treasures of, 189–190
Missionaries, 31, 80, 149, 251
Months, 50–51
Moods, 91, 304

## N

Nationalities, 42
Names, 14–17
Negative commands, 120–122
Neuter articles, 147, 219, 274
Nicknames, 14, 304–309
No accents, xv
Noun(s)
    adjectives, 11
    articles, 4
    and business, 151
    and clothing, 95
    colors as, 49
    and education, 125
    food-related, 71–72
    gender, 4, 11
    house-related, 53–54
    order and agreement, 11
    plural, 11–12
    Spanish, 4
    sports, 32–33
    and travel, 199
    and vehicles, 178–179
Nouns, articles, 6
Numbers
    cardinal, xi, 55–56
    ordinals, 73–74

## O

Ordinal numbers, 73–74

## P

Palma, Ricardo, 203–205
Passive voice, 226–227
Past participle, 286–288

Past tense, 92–94, 153–154, 287

Perfect tense of indicative, 287–288

*Peribáñez y el comendador de Ocaña* (de Vega), 39

Personal object pronouns, 217

Peru, treasures of, 208–209

Prado Museum, 166

Predicate, 87, 252–253, 310

Prepositions, 268–270

Present indicative, 100

Present participle, 98, 117, 217, 286, 290

Present subjunctive, 100, 119–121, 289

Present tense, 90–92

Professions, 127

Pronoun(s)
  demonstrative, 219–220
  indefinite, 221
  personal, 216
  placement, 215–216
  possessive, 216–217
  relative, 220–221

Pronunciation(s)
  accents, xiv
  b and v, 254
  b-v, 132
  c and q, 75–76
  d, 133
  dentales, 57–58
  double consonants, 103
  g and j, 102
  h, 158–159
  key letters, 295–296
  multiple syllables, xiv
  ñ, 131
  no accents, xv
  of vowels, xiii, 202
  rules, xiv
  x, y, z, 184–185

Punctuation, 5

**Q**

Question marks, 5

**R**

Reference pages, xi–xv

Reflexive pronouns, 117, 215

Reflexive verbs, 116

*Relations* (de Jesús), 59

Resume, 155–157

Ruiz, José Martínez, 104–105

**S**

Sayings, 13

Sentence
  compound, 245–246
  Spanish structure, 252–253

Spain
  history of, 23, 80
  language in America, 31
  treasures of, 164–167

Spanish language
  in America, 31
  history of, 198
  pronunciation in, xiv–xv, 295
  romance language, 198

Subject, 252, 310

Subjunctive verbs, 288–289

Subordinated sentences, 246

Superlative, 148–149

Syllable, xiv, 37–38

Synalepha, 275–276

**T**

Theotocopoulos, Domenicos, 259

Time, 128–130

Transitive verbs, 125, 286

**U**

United States, hispanic heritage of, 107

**V**

Verbs
  common, 33–34
  compound tenses of, 286–288
  conjugation of, 87–90, 304–309
  future tenses, 116
  helping, 287–289

intransitive, 125
mood of, 91–94
past participle, 286–288
present participle, 290
reflexive, 116–117
subjunctive, 118–123, 288–289
transitive, 125
troublesome, 152–154
Vocabulary
adjectives, 10
art-related, 242–243, 249–250
basic, 3, 29, 47
courtesy phrases, 35–36
economy-related, 144, 151–152
education-related, 113, 125–126
everyday speech, 54, 73
family, 9
family parties, 21
food-related, 67–68, 71–72
government, 214–215, 223–225
greetings and introductions, 10

holidays, 201
house-related, 53–54
human body, 96
for love, 265–266, 270–271, 272
of nature, 284
nature, 291
nouns, 32–33
professions, 127
relate to mail, 161–162
related to dress, 85–86, 95
time, 128–130
traveling, 195–196, 199–200
vehicles, 174–175, 178–179
verbs, 33
weather, 99–100
Voice, 226–227
Vowels, xiii, 202

# W

Weather, 97–100

# BARRON'S takes learning to the next level — FUN!

**Just visit *barronsbooks.com/painless/***

Learning has never been this fun, easy…or painless!